Adult Social Care Law in England

Reshaping Social Work Series

Series Editors: **Robert Adams, Lena Dominelli and Malcolm Payne**

The **Reshaping Social Work** series aims to develop the knowledge base for critical, reflective practitioners. Each book is designed to support students on qualifying social work programmes and update practitioners on crucial issues in today's social work, strengthening research knowledge, critical analysis and skilled practice to shape social work to meet future challenges.

Published titles

Anti-Racist Practice in Social Work Kish Bhatti-Sinclair
Spirituality and Social Work Margaret Holloway and Bernard Moss
Social Work Research for Social Justice Beth Humphries
Social Work and Social Policy under Austerity Bill Jordan and Mark Drakeford
Social Care Practice in Context Malcolm Payne
Critical Issues in Social Work with Older People Mo Ray, Miriam Bernard and Judith Phillips
Social Work and Power Roger Smith
Doing Residential Social Work Colin Turbett
Adult Social Work Law in England John Williams, Gwyneth Roberts and Aled Griffiths

Forthcoming titles

Globally Minded Social Work Practice Janet Anand and Chaitali Das
Social Work Communication Andrew Beck and Roger Smith
Rejuvenating Family Support Karen Broadhurst
Cultural Diversity in Social Work Practice Helen Charnley
Social Work and Community Development Catherine Forde and Debby Lynch

Invitation to authors

The Series Editors welcome proposals for new books within the *Reshaping Social Work* series. Please contact one of the series editors for an initial discussion:

- Robert Adams at rvadams@rvadams.karoo.co.uk
- Lena Dominelli at lena.dominelli@durham.ac.uk
- Malcolm Payne at macolmpayne5@gmail.com

Reshaping Social Work
Series Editors: **Robert Adams, Lena Dominelli and Malcolm Payne**
Series Standing Order ISBN 978–1–4039–4878–6
(outside North America only)

You can receive future titles in this series as they are published by placing a standing order. Please contact your bookseller or, in the case of difficulty, write to us at the address below with your name and address, the title of the series and the ISBN quoted above: Customer Services Department, Macmillan Distribution Ltd, Houndmills, Basingstoke, Hampshire, RG21 6XS, UK

Adult Social Care Law in England

John Williams
Gwyneth Roberts
and
Aled Griffiths

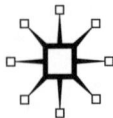

© John Williams, Gwyneth Roberts and Aled Griffiths 2014

All rights reserved. No reproduction, copy or transmission of this publication may be made without written permission.

No portion of this publication may be reproduced, copied or transmitted save with written permission or in accordance with the provisions of the Copyright, Designs and Patents Act 1988, or under the terms of any licence permitting limited copying issued by the Copyright Licensing Agency, Saffron House, 6–10 Kirby Street, London EC1N 8TS.

Any person who does any unauthorized act in relation to this publication may be liable to criminal prosecution and civil claims for damages.

The authors have asserted their rights to be identified as the authors of this work in accordance with the Copyright, Designs and Patents Act 1988.

First published 2014 by
PALGRAVE MACMILLAN

Palgrave Macmillan in the UK is an imprint of Macmillan Publishers Limited, registered in England, company number 785998, of Houndmills, Basingstoke, Hampshire RG21 6XS.

Palgrave Macmillan in the US is a division of St Martin's Press LLC, 175 Fifth Avenue, New York, NY 10010.

Palgrave Macmillan is the global academic imprint of the above companies and has companies and representatives throughout the world.

Palgrave® and Macmillan® are registered trademarks in the United States, the United Kingdom, Europe and other countries

ISBN 978–0–230–28010–6

This book is printed on paper suitable for recycling and made from fully managed and sustained forest sources. Logging, pulping and manufacturing processes are expected to conform to the environmental regulations of the country of origin.

A catalogue record for this book is available from the British Library.

A catalog record for this book is available from the Library of Congress.

Typeset by Cambrian Typesetters, Camberley, Surrey, England, UK

Printed and bound in the UK by The Lavenham Press Ltd, Suffolk

Contents

List of Tables and Figures	ix
List of Case Examples and Boxes	xi
List of Abbreviations	xii
The Legal Toolbox	xiii
Preface	xxi

1 Social Work Practice and the Law — 1

Introduction	1
The organizational and administrative framework	3
Community care services	5
Directions and guidance	5
Powers and duties	6
Human Rights Act 1998	7
Anti-discrimination	13
Director of Adult Social Services	16
Social work practice and the law	17
Delegated and designated functions	19
Registration of social workers	19
Standards of proficiency	23
Partnership and coordination	24
Accountability	25
Conclusion	26

2 Legal Capacity — 27

Introduction	27
Assessing capacity	28
Mental Capacity Act 2005	28
Code of practice	31
How does the Mental Capacity Act 2005 define capacity?	31
Unable to make a decision	34
Retaining information	37
Inability to communicate	37

	Fluctuating capacity	38
	Decision-making for people who lack capacity	38
	Other forms of decision-making	43
	Lasting Powers of Attorney	45
	Court of Protection	46
	The implications of the *Bournewood* case	47
	Deprivation of Liberty Safeguards	48
	Conclusion	52
3	**Referral and Assessment**	53
	Referrals	53
	The duty to assess	55
	The assessment process	57
	Assessment following discharge from hospital	62
	The single assessment process for older people	65
	Mental health services users	67
	People with learning disability	68
	Conclusion	68
4	**Community Care Services**	69
	Determining the need for community care services	69
	Eligibility criteria	72
	The provision of community care services	76
	The legal definition of community care services	77
	The nature of community care services	77
	The delivery of community care services	80
	The role of the voluntary sector	81
	The role of the private sector	82
	Direct payments	82
	Changes since the Community Care (Direct Payments) Act 1996	82
	Direct payments, capacity and mental disorder	83
	Making use of direct payments	84
	Person-centred planning	84
	Personal budgets	85
	Registration and regulation	86
	Care Quality Commission	88
	Paying for domiciliary care	91
	Paying for residential care	92
	Self-funders	93
	Issues of choice	93
	Proposals for reform	94
	Conclusion	95

5	**Carers**	96
	The contribution of carers	96
	Carers and human rights	97
	Who is a carer?	97
	The legal definition of a carer	98
	Carers and community care	100
	Assessment of carers	101
	Disabled Persons (Services and Consultation and Representation) Act 1986	101
	Carer (Recognition of Services) Act 1995	102
	Carers and Disabled Children Act 2000	103
	Carers (Equal Opportunity) Act 2004	104
	Provision of services	104
	The legal consequences of caring	106
	Young people as carers	108
	Young carers and services	109
	The law and young carers	110
	Conclusion	111
6	**Mental Health Law**	112
	Introduction	113
	Admission to hospital under the Mental Health Act 1983	113
	The Mental Health Act Code of Practice	116
	Key definitions	117
	Learning disability	118
	Treatability	119
	Appropriate medical treatment	120
	The practitioners involved in the admission process	120
	The nearest relative	121
	Informal admission under the Mental Health Act 1983	123
	Formal admission for assessment under s.2 Mental Health Act 1983	124
	Formal admission for treatment under s.3 Mental Health Act 1983	124
	Formal admission for assessment in cases of emergency under s.4 Mental Health Act 1983	125
	The application process	125
	Admission of patients already in hospital under s.5 Mental Health Act 1983	126
	The medical treatment of detained patients	127
	Removal to a place of safety	128
	Guardianship: s.7 Mental Health Act 1983	128
	Community provision	130
	Community Treatment Orders	130

	Leave of absence	131
	Hospital Managers and Mental Health Review Tribunals	132
	Conclusion	133

7 Adult Safeguarding and Protection — **134**
- Introduction — 134
- Vulnerable adults — 135
- What amounts to abuse and neglect? — 137
- National statistics — 138
- What is safeguarding? — 139
- Existing law and procedure — 141
- What does 'No Secrets' require of practitioners? — 143
- The criminal law — 145
- Prosecution — 147
- The criminal justice system — 150
- Civil law — 152
- Adult safeguarding boards — 154
- Serious Case Reviews — 154
- Functions of a Serious Case Review — 155
- The Law Commission's report and the Scottish legislation — 156
- Conclusion — 158

8 Seeking Redress — **159**
- Introduction — 159
- Informal mechanisms — 161
- Councils with Social Services Responsibilities complaints procedures — 162
- The local government ombudsman — 163
- Judicial review — 166
- Legal action — 168
- Whistle-blowing — 169
- Other avenues of complaint or redress — 171
- Conclusion — 172

Appendix 1: Cases — 173
Appendix 2: Statutes and Statutory Instruments — 176
Bibliography — 178
Index — 187

List of Tables and Figures

Tables

1.1	Number of clients receiving community-based services by type	2
1.2	Number of people in residential and nursing care by type of accommodation	2
1.3	Selected Articles from the European Convention on Human Rights	9
1.4	Standards of Proficiency required of social workers	20
4.1	Criteria used for the allocation of resources for the vulnerable elderly	74
4.2	The types of community care service available under the current law	78
6.1	Patient safeguards under the Mental Health Act 1983	127
7.1	Analysis of referrals, repeat referrals and completed referrals by age group	138
7.2	Range of offences that may arise out of cases of abuse	146
8.1	Prescribed bodies that may be relevant for social care practitioners	171

Figures

1.1	Contact hours in millions for home care provided during the year, by sector, 2006–07 to 2011–12	4
3.1	Origins of referral for social care services	54
3.2	The individual context of an assessed person	58
3.3	The broader context of making an assessment	59
4.1	An outline of the process for deciding on personal budgets	86
5.1	Assessing carers' needs	101

6.1	Detentions under the Mental Health Act 1983 in NHS facilities and independent hospitals by legal status, 2008–09 to 2012–13	115
7.1	Number of referrals by relationship of alleged perpetrator	138
7.2	Type of abuse by age group	139
8.1	Procedures for seeking redress	161
8.2	Outline of CSSR complaints procedures	163

List of Case Examples and Boxes

Case examples

1.1	*R v North Yorkshire CC ex parte Hargreaves*	7
1.2	*R (on the application of H) v Mental Health Review Tribunal, North and East London Region and Another*	11
1.3	*R (on the application of Heather) v Leonard Cheshire Foundation*	12
2.1	*DL v A Local Authority*	33
2.2	*Re Y (adult patient (transplant: bone marrow))*	40
2.3	*HE v A Hospital NHS Trust*	44
2.4	*R v Bournewood Community and Health NHS Trust ex parte L*	47
3.1	*R v Bristol City Council ex parte Penfold*	57
4.1	*R v Gloucestershire County Council and another ex parte Barry*	70
4.2	*R (K) v Camden and Islington Health Authority*	79
4.3	*Clunis v Camden and Islington Health Authority*	79
4.4	*YL v Birmingham City Council*	90
5.1	*Instan* and *R v Stone*	107
6.1	*JT v UK*	122
6.2	*GJ v The Foundation Trust*	123
7.1	The exercise of autonomy	140
7.2	Based on a Serious Case Review relating to A1: Worcestershire Safeguarding Adults Board, 2010	155

Boxes

1.1	*R v London Borough of Islington ex parte Rixon*	6
1.2	Example: 'No Secrets'	6
1.3	Example: Eligibility criteria guidance	6
5.1	Impacts experienced by carers	98
8.1	*Kent County Council (11 009 473)*, 11 October 2012	165
8.2	*Suffolk County Council (11 017 875 & 6 others)*, 11 October 2012	165

List of Abbreviations

ADSS   Association of Directors of Social Services
AMHP   Approved Mental Health Professional
ASW   Approved social worker
CPA   care programme approach
CPS   Crown Prosecution Service
CQC   Care Quality Commission
CSSR   Council with Social Services Responsibilities
CTO   Community Treatment Order
DOLS   Deprivation of Liberty Safeguards
DSPD   dangerous severe personality disorders
ECHR   European Convention on Human Rights
HCPC   Health and Care Professions Council
ILF   Independent Living Fund
IMCA   Independent Mental Capacity Advocate
LPA   Lasting Power of Attorney
MHRT   Mental Health Review Tribunal
SAP   single assessment process
SCT   supervised community treatment
SOAD   second opinion appointed doctor

The Legal Toolbox

The hierarchy of the courts

SUPREME COURT
APPEALS ON A POINT OF LAW
JUSTICES OF THE SUPREME COURT

COURT OF APPEAL
APPEAL ON POINTS OF LAW TO EITHER THE CRIMINAL OR CIVIL DIVISION
LORD CHIEF JUSTICE AND COURT
OF APPEAL JUDGES

HIGH COURT
CHANCERY, QUEEN'S BENCH AND FAMILY DIVISIONS.
APPEALS FROM LOWER COURTS, AS WELL AS HEARING CASES FOR THE FIRST TIME –
E.G. JUDICIAL REVIEW. (SEE CHAPTER 8, p. 166)
HIGH COURT AND DEPUTY HIGH COURT JUDGES

CROWN COURT
JURY TRIAL FOR SERIOUS CRIMINAL
CASES. APPEALS AGAINST CONVICTION
AND SENTENCE FROM THE MAGISTRATES.
CIRCUIT JUDGES, RECORDERS AND JURIES

COUNTY COURT
HEARING FOR MOST CIVIL LAW CASES
CIRCUIT JUDGES, RECORDERS, DISTRICT
JUDGES, DEPUTY DISTRICT JUDGES

MAGISTRATES COURTS
TRIAL OF MOST CRIMINAL OFFENCES.
SOME CIVIL AND FAMILY MATTERS.
MAGISTRATES, DISTRICT JUDGES (MC),
DEPUTY DJ (MC)

The courts

What do courts do? Courts have two roles to perform:

1. To decide questions of fact. For example, in a criminal case involving alleged abuse of an adult at risk, the court will decide whether the evidence is sufficient to convict the accused person.
2. To decide questions of law. This is a tricky area. Most of the lower courts (e.g. the magistrates) simply apply the law as it exists. Their primary role is to apply the law to the facts of the case. However, the higher courts will also:
   (a) interpret relevant legislation – see, for example, the *Gloucestershire* case (Chapter 4: p. 70);
   (b) see if there is a judicial precedent (see p. xv) that can be applied to the case before the court; or
   (c) in some situations, fill in any gaps left by the legislation, or the lack of a precedent. When doing this, they are creating a precedent.

Evidence: the burden and standard of proof

Courts decide cases based on the evidence presented by the parties at the trial or hearing. That evidence is subject to the law of evidence that lays down the rules as to when a piece of evidence is admissible. Courts may exclude some types of evidence that you might rely on outside of the courtroom setting. Hearsay evidence is a good example – other than in exceptional cases, it will be excluded. Therefore, the statement by Jane that 'John told me that he saw Sally take the money' will not usually be admissible because the key witness to the alleged theft is John, rather than Jane. Jane is simply passing on what John told her. As Jane was not there, she is unable to verify whether Sally took the money.

The rules of evidence also identify who has to prove the case before the court – or, who has the burden of proof. The general rule is that the person who asserts has the burden of proving. Therefore, in criminal cases the prosecution (usually the Crown Prosecution Service) has the burden of proving that the defendant is guilty. The defendant does not have to prove his or her innocence. In civil cases, the burden is on the plaintiff or the applicant – the person who is making the claim.

The party who has the burden of proof must satisfy the standard or proof required. For criminal proceedings, the standard of proof is 'beyond all reasonable doubt'. This is a demanding standard and underlines the need to ensure that the collection of evidence (including interviewing suspected victims of abuse) is done properly. In non-criminal cases (e.g. Mental Capacity Act 2005 applications), the standard is on a balance of probabilities – it is more likely than not that the case is proven.

Case law

Why are so many cases referred to in the book? What is their significance?

Cases, or case law, play an important part in the working of the law. Cases are heard by judges (and sometimes, in criminal cases, with a jury) in one of the courts referred to above. When a case is before the court, a number of things may be going on.

1. The court may be weighing up the evidence and then making a decision on the facts of the case. Did Jack say this to Jill? Or, was Chris in the High Street at 10.00 pm on Friday night. In some criminal cases (in the Crown Court), these findings of fact might be made by a jury. In other cases (e.g. the magistrates' courts), the judge (or magistrate) hearing the case will decide on the facts.
2. The court applies the law to the facts of the case once they are established under point 1 above. In some cases – indeed, in many cases – the law is clear. In others, it is less clear and the judge has to apply what he or she thinks is the law. If one of the parties disagrees with the judge's decision on the law, it may be possible to appeal to a higher court. However, there are limits imposed on the right of parties to appeal and clear grounds have to be established. Frivolous appeals are not allowed.
3. In the higher courts (the High Court, the Court of Appeal and the Supreme Court) the judges may be required to fill in any gaps in the law (look, for example, at the development of the law on mental capacity prior to the Mental Capacity Act 2005). It may involve the interpretation of a word in a statute that is unclear or ambiguous. It may also involve an area where there is no established law. In this situation, the judges might be able to develop the law, unless they think that it is inappropriate and that Parliament should make the law. If the judges do develop the law in this way, the body of rules is known as judicial precedent or the 'common law'. The basic rule is that the higher court decision will bind all lower courts – decisions of the Supreme Court bind all lower courts; decisions of the Court of Appeal will bind all lower courts, but not the Supreme Court.
4. A case may either be a 'first instance' decision, or it may be an 'appeal'. A first instance case is one that has not been heard previously by any court. The courts from the High Court downwards can hear first instance cases. Special rules apply as to what cases can be initiated in what court. An appeal case (note the courts that can hear appeals in the diagram on p. xiii) involves an appeal from a

The Legal Toolbox

lower court, most commonly on the basis that one of the parties thinks the lower court got the law wrong. Permission (or leave) to appeal is usually required – either from the first instance court, or the court where the appeal would be heard.

Therefore, cases tell us what the law is – either through the interpretation of the words in a statute, or through the development of the common law.

What are the strange references to cases in Appendix 1?

As one might expect, lawyers have their own way of referring to or citing cases. The code is relatively easy to crack. In the chapter on mental capacity, we come across the case of *St George's Healthcare NHS Trust v S (No.1)*. If you look at Appendix 1, you will find the name of the case and see that it is followed by '[1998] 3 All ER 673'. This is known as the 'citation'. What does this mean? The citation enables lawyers and others to find the full report of the case and the judgements of the judges in the higher courts.

St George's Healthcare NHS Trust v S (No.1)	[1998] or (1998)	3 All ER 673
This refers to the parties to the case. The case involves legal action between the St Georges Healthcare NHS Trust and S. The reason why S is used rather than the person's name is to preserve their anonymity – in very sensitive issues (e.g. involving vulnerable adults or children the person's identity is not usually disclosed). The 'v' indicates that one party is bringing an action against the other. The reference to 'No.1' indicates that a number of applications had to be made to the court in respect of the subject matter of the case.	This indicates the year in which the decision of the court was reported in the law reports. Not all cases are reported. Only those in the High Court and above will reach the law reports. Lawyers attach special significance to the use of [ ] brackets or ( ) brackets when referring to the year. If square brackets are used it means that the year is the way in which the appropriate volume is identified. If round brackets are used, they will be followed by a volume number; this enables us to identify the appropriate volume. But do not worry about that!	This is the reference to the law report where the decision of the court is recorded. In this example, it is Volume 3 of the All England Law Reports, page 673. There are many different types of law reports and digests. Some case reports may be freely accessible online: type the case name into a search engine and you may well find a copy of the court's opinion. Decisions of the European Court of Human Rights are also available online. Cases decided by the Supreme Court are also available on its website.

To simplify online searching, a new system of 'neutral citation' was introduced in 2001. It is structured as follows:

[YEAR] COURT CASE NUMBER

So, if you enter [2010] EWHC 978 into a search engine, you will find the report on the case of *A Local Authority v A and another*. 'EWCH' refers to the fact that it was a case in England and Wales that was heard by the High Court.

In some of the cases referred to in the book, there are odd case names. For example, in the chapter on Adult Safeguarding and Protection the case of *R v Smellie* is mentioned. The '*R*' indicates that this is a case where the state is involved – the '*R*' stands for Regina (Queen). This will be the typical reference for criminal cases, of which *R v Smellie* is an example.

You will also encounter cases such as *Re F (Mental Health Act guardianship)* [2000] 1 FLR 192, referred to in Chapter 6. 'Re' is a Latin term for 'in the matter of'. It is used when there are no parties to the case as such, but something of importance in relation to the matter has to be resolved by the courts. In this case, it was whether F could be subject to guardianship.

Legislation

There are many references to legislation in the book. What do I need to know about legislation?

Legislation is also referred to as statutes or Acts of Parliament. Many pieces of legislation are discussed in this book. Legislation is passed by Parliament. It is referred to by NAME and DATE. For example, you will encounter the following:

Mental Capacity Act 2005
Mental Health Act 1983
National Health Service and Community Care Act 1990

Some Acts of Parliament have rather complex names; for example, the Health and Social Services and Social Security Adjudications Act 1983 or the Disabled Persons (Services and Consultation and Representation) Act 1986. This reflects the desire by Parliament to ensure that the name reflects the content.

Much of the legislation is now online and can be accessed at http://www.legislation.gov.uk. One word of caution, make sure that what you are reading is the most up-to-date version of the legislation. It may have been amended (changed by later legislation), repealed (i.e. no longer in force), or consolidated (where a number of pieces of legislation on one topic are combined in one consolidating piece of legislation). So, for example, if you read the Mental Health Act 1983 as it was passed by Parliament in 1983, you would be reading out-of-date law as this Act was heavily amended by the Mental Health Act 2007.

Each piece of legislation is broken down into smaller components: Sections, Subsections and Schedules.

Term	Example	Explanation
Sections	s.25	The main components of a statute
Subsections	s.25(1)	The parts of a section; they can be further broken down into sub-subsections –e.g. s.25(1)(b)
Schedule	Schedule1	At the back of most pieces of legislation are Schedules. Typically, these contain a great deal of the details about how the legislation will work, or they will outline the pieces of earlier legislation that may be have been amended or repealed. Schedules may divided into different Parts and then into paragraphs –e.g. Schedule 1, Part 1, para 3, Mental Capacity Act 2005 contains details of what happens if a Lasting Power of Attorney is not made in the prescribed form (see Chapter 2, p. 45).

Sometimes mention is made of regulations, statutory instruments or delegated legislation. What are they?

Not everything can be included in the primary legislation (the Act of Parliament). A great deal of detail needs to be worked out and to include that in the main Act would make it cumbersome. To overcome this, legislation often gives the power to make regulations – sometimes referred to as 'secondary legislation'. This is achieved through delegated legislation or statutory instruments (abbreviated as SI). For example, in Chapter 4 the following regulations will be encountered.

Care Quality Commission (Registration) Regulations	2009	(SI 2009 No 3112)
Title of the regulation	Year of approval	Reference – SI (Statutory Instrument) and it was number 3112 of that year.

Regulations are broken down into paragraphs and sub-paragraphs in the same way as Acts of Parliament. In most circumstances, secondary legislation is as binding as primary legislation.

Background material

Very often there is considerable background material to legislation. This may be in the form of government Green Papers or White Papers; the former are ways in which the government tests the water with ideas and the latter (often following a Green Paper) present the government's settled view of the basis of proposed legislation. Other ideas may come from the Law Commission. The Law Commission is a body set up to keep under review the reform of the law. As seen in Chapter 4, it has completed a review of Adult Social Care Law. It adopts a two-stage process: a consultation paper is published asking for views on possible approaches to reform; this is then followed with a final report, which often contains a draft Bill. Other background material includes specific reports commissioned by government; the best example in adult social care is the Griffiths Report on community care which laid the foundations for the National Health Service and Community Care Act 1990 (see Chapter 3). Political parties, professional bodies, third-sector organisations and regulatory bodies also publish reports on the state of adult social care and provide a valuable insight into the workings of the law.

Devolution

This book explains the law as it exists in England. Since devolution, Wales has responsibility for most aspects of adult social care. The Scottish Parliament and the Northern Ireland Assembly also have adult social care responsibilities. This may raise issues when a service user moves from one of the four nations to another. The legal basis of adult social care may differ and, in the future, is highly likely to differ substantially.

Language

No legal toolkit would be complete without reference to the use of language. For the lawyer, precision in the use of language is important, as it should be for social care practitioners. This is important when writing reports, especially those that may be used in court proceedings. However, the use of plain English by practitioners in communications of any kind is to be encouraged. There is no need to resort to legal jargon. In addition, practitioners should not assume that service users will understand the jargon and the abbreviations that litter social care.

The above is an overview of the legal framework and material within which practitioners operate in the field of social care. It is included here to help you understand the legal terms and references which are used throughout the book. It should prove sufficient to meet a social care practitioner's needs. There will be circumstances, however, where a practitioner will need to seek more detailed and expert legal advice. No one expects social care practitioners to be expert lawyers. The important thing is to be aware of circumstances where further advice is required.

Preface

The purpose of this book is to provide social work students and practitioners with a guide to adult social care law in England, an area of law subject to constant revision and change. The law, as set out here, relates specifically to England since, as a result of devolution, a distinctive social care sector has emerged, and will continue, to emerge in Wales. Consequently, there is increasing divergence between social care provisions in the two countries. Students and practitioners in Wales are referred to the Care Council Wales's publication *Gofal 2*, which is specifically concerned with social care in Wales.

The book aims to explain, in the first place, the meaning of social work law before placing statutory social work practice within its organizational context. It also refers to the relevance to social work practice of legislation such as the Human Rights Act 1998 and the Equality Act 2010. Since social work is now a regulated profession, it is also necessary for social workers to be aware of the Standards of Proficiency with which they must comply as registered social work practitioners.

Another important basis for social work practice in the field of adult social care is an understanding of the rules concerning incapacity and the importance of ensuring that the concepts of liberty and autonomy are understood and followed, but that it is also recognized that mentally incapacitated individuals have a right to a safe and, where necessary, protective environment. Such concerns are also raised in Chapter 7, where the rules concerning the protection of vulnerable adults are discussed. The law relating to mentally disordered service users, as set out in the Mental Health Act 1983, is also relevant in social work practice, as is the assessment of service users and the rules relating to the delivery of social care. The unpaid carers of vulnerable adults are a particular group whose contribution, although recognized in legislation, remains relatively unacknowledged. The book concludes with a discussion of the procedures, both informal and formal, for obtaining redress if and when individuals become dissatisfied with the way they are treated, or have been, treated.

The text contains a number of exercises that enable readers to reinforce their knowledge, not only of the specific area under discussion, but of other provisions which may be of relevance to a proper resolution of a problem. This emphasizes the importance of recognizing that social work practice is multidimensional in nature, and that a particular case may require the application of several sources of knowledge, if practice is to be other than narrow, limited and unprofessional.

The reader will also find the Legal Toolbox, set out on p xiii, useful in explaining the legal terms, processes and procedures referred to in various parts of the book.

JOHN WILLIAMS
GWYNETH ROBERTS
ALED GRIFFITHS

chapter 1
Social Work Practice and the Law

In this chapter, you will learn about:
- The organizational and administrative framework
- Community care services
- Directions and guidance
- Powers and duties
- Human Rights Act 1998
- Anti-discrimination
- Director of Social Services
- Social work practice and the law
- Delegated and designated functions
- Registration of social workers
- Standards of proficiency
- Partnership and coordination
- Accountability
- Conclusion

Remember to consult The Legal Toolbox on pp. xiii–xx. This will help you to understand processes and procedures referred to in this chapter.

Introduction

Social work law is the basis of social work practice. It determines the organizational setting in which social work takes place; it defines what social workers are employed to do; and, by setting out what redress is available when things go wrong, it determines the boundaries of social work action and the nature and extent of social work accountability. It is the law that defines the individuals towards whom social workers have responsibilities, such as, vulnerable adults and their carers, and which determines, often in broad terms, the nature and extent of social work intervention (such as prevention, protection and rehabilitation). The law also sets out the conditions under which compulsory intervention is permissible, as well as the safeguards that should ensure that such intervention takes place in accordance with due process and in adherence to human rights. An important aspect of the social work task is to determine appropriate levels of support, care, protection and control, taking into account the inevitable constraints imposed by the availability of

Table 1.1 Number of clients receiving community-based services by type

	18–64	65 and over
Day care	77,000	83,000
Direct payments	78,000	61,000
Equipment and adaptations	100,000	330,000
Home care	103,000	415,000
Meals	4,000	56,000
Other	45,000	62,000
Professional support	166,000	102,000
Short-term residential (not respite)	13,000	57,000

Source: Health and Social Care Information Centre (2013a).

Table 1.2 Number of people in residential and nursing care by type of accommodation

Year	Council-staffed homes	Independent residential care	Independent nursing care
2001	42,300	138,600	73,900
2002	37,100	149,500	72,600
2003	34,100	166,300	78,400
2004	31,800	164,700	75,800
2005	27,800	160,500	73,900
2006	25,200	157,100	73,500
2007	23,500	152,400	70,100
2008	21,500	149,100	65,500
2009	19,700	149,400	60,800
2010	18,000	148,800	58,800
2011	16,100	146,300	57,200
2012	13,275	149,300	57,150

Source: Health and Social Care Information Centre (2013a).

resources. It is the law, too, that identifies the strategic aims and objectives that underpin the delivery of services, both nationally and locally. In essence, social work law consists of three elements: a set of organizational and administrative processes and procedures; a specific body of statutes and judicial decisions; and a body of professional ethics and values. The law provides 'the essential bone structure of social work practice' (Roberts and Preston-Shoot 2000) and so helps to determine its nature and character.

Significant numbers of people rely on social services, either partially or completely. For example, Tables 1.1 and 1.2 present the number of people receiving domiciliary and residential/nursing care.

Given these numbers, it is crucial that social workers understand the nature and extent of their legal mandate, and how it affects the lives of those who need their help or support.

The organizational and administrative framework

The administrative and organizational framework for the delivery of social services is to be found mainly in the Local Authority Social Services Act 2000 (LASSA 1970), as amended, and the Local Government Act 2000 (LGA 2000).

The law recognizes the concept of an artificial legal person created by an Act of Parliament. Legal persons of this kind are collectively known as 'corporations', of which local authorities are an important example. As such, local authorities are capable of assuming legal powers and responsibilities to enable them to provide or arrange a range of services in their locality. The structure of local government in England is complex and varied. However, s.1 LASSA 1970, identifies the units of local government with legal responsibility for providing or arranging social services in their area. These consist currently of the metropolitan districts (such as Sheffield and Wolverhampton) and the London boroughs (such as Wandsworth and Brent, and the City of London Council); the county councils (such as, Lancashire and Kent); and the unitary authorities (such as Cornwall and Shropshire) (s.1 LASSA 1970, as amended). For ease of reference, these will be referred to as Councils with Social Services Responsibilities (CSSR). The LGA 2000 requires such authorities to set up an executive structure with decision-making powers and responsibilities, including the provision of social services that are required to undertaken under s.1A LASSA 1970. The Secretary of State may designate other social services functions to be performed by these local authorities.

A significant feature of the development of social services over the past few years has been the increased involvement of the independent sector in the provision of services; that is, profit-making organizations, as well

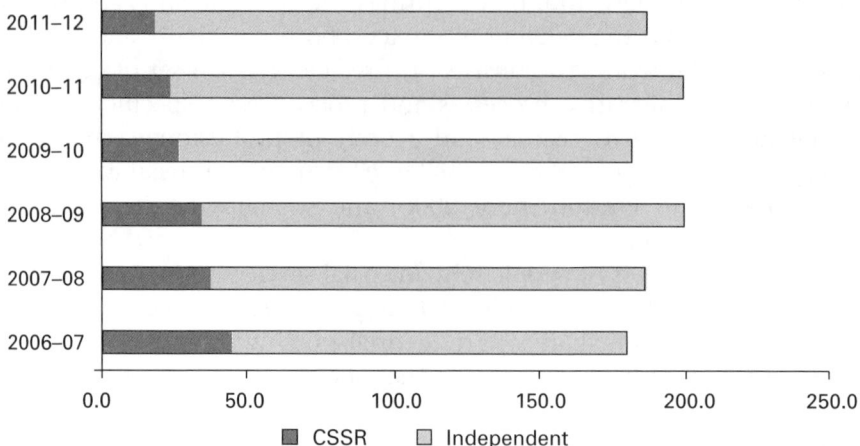

Figure 1.1 Contact hours in millions for home care provided during the year, by sector, 2006–07 to 2011–12
Source: Health and Social Care Information Centre (2013a).

as voluntary organizations. The Griffiths Report and the subsequent National Health Service and Community Care Act 1990 (NHSCCA 1990) developed a more open market for the provision of community care and residential care for adults (Griffiths 1988). Table 1.2 shows that residential care provided directly by local authorities represents a small proportion of the total provision. As Figure 1.1 shows, for domiciliary care the major provider is the independent sector.

> **Exercise 1.1**
>
> Choose a local authority with social services responsibility and identify the following characteristics:
>
> - The demography of the local authority area (structure of population: age, disability, gender, ethnicity, etc.) and its economic profile (e.g. unemployment levels, social housing, and indicators of deprivation).
> - The level of expenditure on social services for the area and how it is distributed between various groups (e.g. children, older people, mental health, learning disability).
>
> Much of this data should be available on the authority's website.
>
> 1. Do you consider this information is easily accessible to members of the public?
> 2. Are there any gaps in the information provided by the authority?

Community care services

As defined in s.46(3) NHSCCA 1990, 'community care services' for adults are services that a local authority may provide or arrange to be provided in its area under:

- ss.21–29, Part III, National Assistance Act 1948.
- s.45 Health Services and Public Health Act 1968.
- s.254 and Schedule 20 National Health Service Act 2006.
- s.117 Mental Health Act 1983.

Since the NHSCCA 1990, further legislation has come into force (such as the Equality Act 2010 (EA 2010) plus no fewer than three separate enactments relating to carers). These are discussed in the chapters that follow.

Directions and guidance

Much of the legislation concerning services for adults is set out in very general terms. More detailed provisions have been issued by the Department of Health in the form of Directions and Regulations and, exceptionally, in the form of Circulars. As long as they are properly made and issued, such documents often have, in practice, the same legal effect as the original legislation. They are open to challenge only if their contents are inconsistent with the terms of the original legislation, or the Human Rights Act 1998 (HRA 1998).

Another means by which gaps in the legislation are filled is through guidance issued by the Department of Health. Section 7 LASSA 1970, states that:

> Local authorities shall, in the exercise of their social services functions, including the exercise of any discretion conferred by any relevant enactment, act under the general guidance of the Secretary of State.

As will become apparent later in the book, a substantial amount of s.7 guidance has been issued. What is its legal significance? (See Box 1.1.)

The consequence of not following s.7 guidance is that the action may be rendered unlawful. The guidance in s.7 is authoritative and valuable, and local authorities and courts should make clear that they have had regard to it when making decisions.

There are many examples of guidance issued by the Secretary of State. Boxes 1.2 and 1.3 illustrate how guidance can provide a framework that supports social work.

Box 1.1 *R v London Borough of Islington ex parte Rixon*

According to Sedley J., Parliament did not intend local authorities to be free to take it or leave it.

> Such a construction would put this kind of statutory guidance on a par with the many forms of non-statutory guidance issued by departments of state. While guidance and direction are semantically and legally different things, and while 'guidance does not compel any particular decision' …, especially when prefaced by the word 'general', in my view Parliament by s.7(1) has required local authorities to follow the path charted by the Secretary of State's guidance, with liberty to deviate from it where the local authority judges on admissible grounds that there is good reason to do so, but without freedom to take a substantially different course.

Box 1.2 Example: 'No Secrets'

There is no equivalent in England to the Scottish law on safeguarding adults at risk. However, the Department of Health and the Home Office published guidance on developing and implementing multi-agency policies and procedures to protect vulnerable adults from abuse.

Source: Department of Health and Home Office (2000).

Box 1.3 Example: Eligibility criteria guidance

> This guidance seeks to 'to assist councils with adult social services responsibilities to determine eligibility for adult social care, in a way that is fair, transparent and consistent, accounting for the needs of their local community as a whole as well as individuals' need for support'.

Source: Department of Health (2010a).

Powers and duties

In some cases, legislation, directions and guidance will create a *duty* to act. For example, s.47 NHSCCA 1990 imposes a duty on a CSSR to assess a person who appears to be in need of community care services, subject to certain conditions being met (see Chapter 3, p. 55). In other cases, the legislation may grant *powers* to act. This provides a CSSR with discretion whether to exercise the power or not. However, CSSRs cannot 'fetter' the use of a discretionary power by adopting blanket policies the effect of which is that they will never use the power. It must decide each case on its merits. So, for example, a blanket policy that it will never provide a particular type of service that it has the power to provide is unlawful and subject to challenge.

> **case example**
>
> **1.1 *R v North Yorkshire CC ex parte Hargreaves***
>
> In this case, the CSSR's policy of only funding a particular kind of service to the exclusion of others was held by the court to be an unlawful fettering of their discretion. The CSSR therefore had to reconsider their policy and its application in relation to the claimant.

> **Exercise 1.2**
>
> Read s.47(1) NHSCCA 1990
>
> 1. What does this duty mean?
> 2. Can a CSSR refuse to assess someone on the grounds that it lacks the resources to do so?
>
> (See also Chapter 3, p. 55.)
>
> **Scenario**
>
> Mrs Jones has moved to live nearer her family in another CSSR area. In the former area, she was receiving day centre provision twice a week, which she valued. In the new area, the CSSR informs her that her package of care will not include day centre provision.
>
> 3. If there is a duty to provide day care facilities, would this refusal be lawful?
> 4. If there is simply a power to provide, on what grounds could the CSSR claim that this was a lawful exercise of their discretion?

Human Rights Act 1998

A piece of legislation with particular relevance to social work is the HRA 1998. This imposes a duty on 'public authorities' not to act in a way that is incompatible with the European Convention on Human Rights (ECHR) (s.6 HRA 1998) and enables 'victims' of a violation to use the ECHR in national courts and tribunals. The ECHR was ratified by the UK in 1951; however, unlike most other signatories, the UK did not incorporate its provisions into domestic law until the HRA 1998. The only redress available prior to the HRA 1998 was for the victim to take their case to the European Court of Human Rights in Strasbourg. There were some notable changes to our law as a result of findings against the UK by the European Court. However, this process was expensive and slow, and did not create the impression that the UK took human rights seriously. Since the HRA 1998, it is still possible to take a case to the European Court, but most human rights cases are now resolved by our domestic courts.

Social workers need to be aware of the overarching effect of the HRA 1998 and its importance in ensuring that the rights contained in the ECHR are respected. Recognition of the human rights of service users and carers is an integral part of good social work practice. The implications of the HRA 1998 are discussed throughout the book.

Proportionality is a concept that derives from European Law and which is having a significant impact on the law of the United Kingdom. In discussing human rights, you will encounter the principle of proportionality. This principle is recognized by the European Union by Article 5 of the Treaty on European Union. It states that European Community law should go no further than is necessary to achieve its objectives. Any action taken must be appropriate, necessary and not excessively burdensome. The principle is now applied to public law generally, so that decisions taken by a CSSR could be challenged on the grounds that it is disproportionate.

Rights under the ECHR are referred to as *first generation rights*, all of which are of direct relevance to social work practice. First generation rights cover civil and political rights; second generation rights cover economic, social and cultural rights. Table 1.3 identifies the main first generation rights and related social work values, with a number of examples of how they can affect practice.

Some of these rights are absolute. The state cannot interfere with these. For example, the right to have life protected, and the right not to be subjected to inhuman and degrading treatment impose absolute duties on the state. Some rights are specifically limited by the ECHR. For example, Article 5 may be infringed if it is in accordance with a procedure set out in the law, and is for one of a specified number of reasons; the Deprivation of Liberty Safeguards ('DOLS') (see Chapter 2, p. 48) are a good example of this. The safeguards in the Mental Capacity Act 2005 (MCA 2005) lay down the procedure outlined by the law, and Article 5(2) states that a person may be deprived of their liberty if they are of 'unsound mind'. Other rights are qualified. For example, the right in Article 8 to private life, family life, home and correspondence may be qualified if it is lawful to do so, is for a legitimate purpose specified in Article 8(2) and is proportionate. Article 8(2) refers to the interference being 'in the interest of national security, public safety or the economic

Table 1.3 Selected Articles from the European Convention on Human Rights

Values	Examples
Article 2: Everyone's right to life shall be protected by law	
- Dignity - Equality - Protecting life	- The use of 'do not resuscitate' policies based solely on age - Failure to intervene in cases of the abuse of adults at risk - The effect of moving an older person from one residential setting to another – this is known to have an impact on their wellbeing and life expectancy
Article 3: No one shall be subjected to torture, or to inhuman or degrading treatment or punishment	
- Autonomy - Dignity - Equality - Protection	- Abuse - Neglect - Failure to investigate abuse or neglect - Inappropriate sedation
Article 5: Everyone has the right to liberty and security of person	
- Dignity - Equality - Freedom - Liberty	- Falsely imprisoning somebody in their own home, or in a hospital, or care home - The ongoing use of sedation to prevent a person wandering
Article 6: The right to a fair hearing	
- Dignity - Equality	- Lack of representation at tribunal hearings - Lack of advocacy services - Failure to provide an appropriate remedy in cases of abuse
Article 8: Right to private and family life, home and correspondence	
- Autonomy - Choice - Dignity - Equality - Individualism - Privacy	- Failure to consult and involve service users - Preventing contact between a person in a care home and their family - Placing somebody in a care home without their consent – or without using the deprivation of liberty authorization procedure (see Chapter 2, p. 48)
Article 9: The right to freedom of thought, conscience and religion	
- Choice - Dignity - Diversity - Equality - Non-judgemental	- Imposing the festivals of one religion on all residents in a care home - Failure to take account of religious beliefs in deciding what is in the best interests of a person who lacks capacity

(continued overleaf)

Table 1.3 *continued*

Values	Examples
Article 10: The right to freedom of expression, including holding any ideas, without interference by public authority	
– Autonomy – Choice – Diversity – Equality – Non-judgemental – Participation	– Unjustified assumptions about a person's capacity based on whether they make 'acceptable' or 'rational' decisions
Article 11: The right to freedom of peaceful assembly and to freedom of association with others	
– Choice – Dignity – Equality – Participation	– Preventing people in care homes or hospitals from participating in the democratic process
Article 12: Men and women of marriageable age have the right to marry and to found a family	
– Choice – Equality	– Preventing people with learning disability from marrying

well-being of the country, for the prevention of disorder or crime, for the protection of health or morals, or for the protection of the rights and freedoms of others'. If the state can justify interference under one of these headings, then the right will be qualified to achieve that purpose. However, the intervention must be proportionate; it must be the minimum intervention necessary to achieve the stated aim. For example, one resident in a care home may need 24-hour observation. Placing CCTV in the resident's room *may* be justifiable for reason of protection of health. Placing CCTV in all the other residents' rooms would be disproportionate.

First generation rights are in contrast to what are termed *second generation rights*, which concentrate on economic, social and cultural rights. The latter includes such rights as employment, housing, adequate food and clothing, adequate health care and social security. Many argue that, for disadvantaged members of society, second generation rights are of more immediate benefit. Ife (2001: 28) concludes that the concentration on first generation human rights encourages the view that human rights are the domain of 'only a minority of social workers, whereas the inclusion of second and third generation rights would effectively define all social workers as doing human rights work'. This is not the case. Most social workers will encounter situations where the first generation rights of the

ECHR apply. Although the introduction of protection for second generation rights would greatly improve the position of many social work service users, the importance of the first generation rights in the ECHR should not be underestimated. Decisions under the 1983 Mental Health Act (MHA 1983), community care assessments, assessments of carers, decisions on residential care, the use of medication, issues surrounding dignity, and the withdrawal of services, all engage ECHR rights.

The HRA 1998 ensures that the rights contained in the ECHR can be argued before any court or tribunal in the United Kingdom. By virtue of s.3(1) HRA 1998, all courts and tribunals must interpret legislation 'so far as is possible ... in a way that is compatible with the Convention rights'. Courts and tribunals now have a primary duty, over and above the use of the traditional methods of interpretation, to ensure that legislation complies with the ECHR. The duty under s.3 HRA 1998 applies to all legislation and is not confined to post-1998 Acts. In this context, it is important to note that it applies to the National Assistance Act 1948 (NAA 1948), the MHA 1983 and the NHSCCA 1990.

Section 3(1) uses the words 'so far as is possible'. This covers those cases where no amount of legal creativity will allow the words used in a particular piece of legislation to be interpreted consistently with the ECHR rights. An example of such legislation is found in ss.72 and 73 MHA 1983.

1.2 *R (on the application of H) v Mental Health Review Tribunal, North and East London Region and Another*

case example

This case involved a patient who was detained in a secure hospital under the Mental Health Act 1983 and was applying to a Mental Health Review Tribunal for discharge. The burden of proof, in such cases, was on the applicant to show that they no longer satisfied the conditions for continued detention under the Act. The Court of Appeal found that since the section imposed the burden of proof on the applicant, it violated the right to liberty as guaranteed by Articles 5(1) and 5(4) of the ECHR. The lawfulness of continued detention should be proved by the state rather than its unlawfulness proved by the defendant. In the light of this argument, the court felt that the case for what is known as a 'declaration of incompatibility' had been made out. Following this decision, the legislation was amended.

There may be occasions when social workers are required to use legislation that is in violation of the ECHR. In such circumstances, there is no choice other than to follow the letter of the incompatible legislation.

Those who work in the independent sector, that is in either a voluntary or for-profit organization which provides a significant amount of residential and domiciliary care (previously provided by a CSSR) come under a different classification. As such do they perform a 'function of a public nature'?

1.3 R (on the application of Heather) v Leonard Cheshire Foundation

case example

The issue in this case was discussed by the Court of Appeal. The Foundation, under a contract with a CSSR and health authority, provided a number of long-term residential places. In making the arrangements, the CSSR was acting under its duty to provide residential accommodation under ss21 and 26 NAA 1948. The Foundation decided it would close one of its homes and open a number of small community-based units in its place. The residents sought judicial review of the decision, claiming that their right under Article 8 of the ECHR (the right to private life, family life, home and correspondence) was being violated. Since the Foundation was providing accommodation funded by the CSSR, the residents argued that it was a public authority and bound to act in accordance with the ECHR. The Court of Appeal rejected this argument, saying that there was no evidence of a 'public flavour' in what the Foundation was doing – it was not 'standing in the shoes' of the authority. The best that the Court could offer the residents was that the CSSR or the health authority could, in arrangements made after the coming into force of the HRA 1998, include a provision in the contract protecting the residents' rights under Article 8.

The House of Lords in the case of *YL v Birmingham City Council [2008] 1 AC 95* followed this line of reasoning. It held that a private care home providing accommodation for a fully public-funded resident was not performing a public function. The result of these decisions was that care home residents, even those funded with public money, were denied the direct protection of the HRA (1998).

This is a highly unsatisfactory situation. It means that whether a resident is directly entitled to the protection of s.6 HRA 1998 will depend on whether they are placed in CSSR-owned accommodation or in independent sector accommodation, albeit paid for in whole or part by the CSSR. Such inconsistencies are unacceptable and undermine the protection given by the HRA 1998. As far as residential care is concerned, the decision was partially reversed by the Health and Social Care Act (HSCA 2008). This provides that a private or voluntary sector care home provider, providing accommodation under arrangements made with a CSSR, is exercising a function of a public nature under s.6 HRA 1998. The effect of this is that funded residents are directly protected by the HRA 1998; self-funders are not protected in this way.

> **Exercise 1.3**
>
> The word 'dignity' often appears in the account of human rights given here. It might be argued that 'dignity' is the foundation of human rights.
> 1. What is 'dignity'?
> 2. In what ways do you think that 'dignity' can be denied to social services users?

Anti-discrimination

Other legislation that has particular significance for social work practice relates to anti-discriminatory practice. The EA 2010 consolidates much of the law relating to discrimination. It replaces the previous equality law, including the Sex Discrimination Act 1975 (SDA 1975), the Race Relations Act 1976 (RRA 1976) and the Disability Discrimination Act 1995 (DDA 1995). Much of the new law is based on the previous legislation, but there are some important differences (Hepple 2010). The principle behind the EA 2010 is that everyone has the right to be treated fairly at work and in the provision of services. This resonates with the inclusiveness of the ECHR and other international instruments (such as the Universal Declaration of Human Rights). The EA 2010 protects people from discrimination on the basis of certain characteristics that they possess. These are known as 'protected characteristics'. The protected characteristics are:

- Disability
- Sex
- Gender reassignment
- Pregnancy and maternity
- Race
- Religion or belief
- Sexual orientation
- Age – that is, those aged 18 years or above. (It is not age discrimination if it can be shown that the treatment of a person is a proportionate way of achieving a legitimate aim – e.g. the provision of sheltered accommodation for older people.)
- Marriage and civil partnership. This characteristic is only protected in the employment context and not in relation to the provision of services (ss.4–12 EA 2010).

Employers and service providers have a duty under the law to treat employees and service users fairly. A service provider is a person or organization that provides goods, facilities or services to the public, or a section of it, whether or not it is paid for or free of charge.

Social Work Practice and the Law

Direct discrimination occurs when a person is treated *worse than somebody else* because of their protected characteristic (s.13(1) EA 2010). So, for example, to restrict access to a service on the basis of a person's sexual orientation is 'direct discrimination'. In the case of pregnancy and maternity, direct discrimination can occur without the need to compare the person to somebody else.

Indirect discrimination is more subtle, but equally unacceptable. This involves putting in place criteria or policies that will have a disproportionate impact on an individual with a protected characteristic than cannot be objectively justified (*London Underground Ltd v Edwards*). A claim based on indirect discrimination could arise if the hours of work specified make it difficult for a woman to apply for or to continue in employment (*Debique v Ministry of Defence*). A claim for indirect discrimination would succeed if it could be shown that the work could be undertaken at a more convenient time of day. An example of indirect discrimination in social care would be if a residential care home had a strict rule that evening meals are served between 5.30 and 6.30 so that catering staff do not have to be paid overtime. Whereas that may be acceptable for most residents, it may indirectly affect the ability of a Muslim to celebrate Ramadan.

People are also protected from discrimination where there is a mistaken belief that they possess one of the protected characteristics. Thus, if a person were discriminated against because the discriminator wrongly believes they have a mental illness, it would still be unlawful. Similarly, a person may be discriminated against because they are associated with someone who has a protected characteristic. A parent of an adult with learning disability, or the carer of an older person will fall into this category.

Other forms of conduct are unlawful under the EA 2010. Harassment is unwanted conduct that violates a person's dignity; or is hostile, degrading or humiliating; or offensive to somebody with a protected characteristic; or in a way that is sexual in nature. So, for example, where a client who has undergone male to female gender reassignment is referred to as 'sir' or 'mate' by the practitioner, this is probably unlawful harassment. It is also unlawful to victimize a person because they have taken action, or are thinking about taking action, under the EA 2010, or where they assist somebody to do so.

The EA 2010 does not allow positive *discrimination* in the provision of services; however, it does allow for positive *action*. This is not a legal duty but, rather, a discretionary power. Under s.158 EA 2010, positive action may be taken in favour of certain groups where the provider reasonably thinks that:

- persons who share a protected characteristic suffer a disadvantage connected to the characteristic;

- persons who share a protected characteristic have needs that are different from the needs of persons who do not share it; or
- participation in an activity by persons who share a protected characteristic is disproportionately low.

Positive action *may* be taken in these circumstances provided it is a proportionate means of achieving the aim of:

- enabling or encouraging people who share the protected characteristic to overcome or minimize the disadvantage;
- meeting those needs; or
- enabling or encouraging people sharing the protected characteristic to participate in the activity.

A CSSR may take positive action in favour of a group if its members' participation in a service is disproportionately low. For example, if the use of day centres by men is lower than that of women, positive action may be taken to encourage more men to use the service. Two notes of caution must be emphasized: first, this is discretionary and not mandatory; second, the action taken must be proportionate.

One exception to the ban on positive discrimination is in relation to the duty to make 'reasonable adjustments' for people with disabilities. A reasonable adjustment involves making changes to practices or to the physical environment, or providing additional equipment for a person with a disability. If an obstacle exists to a person with a disability accessing a service, then the provider should first consider whether that obstacle can be removed. This may include a physical obstacle, schedule or facility. If that cannot be done, can it be altered so that the barrier is removed? Is it possible to avoid the particular barrier? If this fails, what alternative provision can be made to ensure that people with disabilities can benefit from the service? (s.20 and Schedule 2 EA 2010). The adjustment must be a 'reasonable' adjustment. The EA 2010 does not impose an open-ended duty on service providers or employers to remove the barrier.

A very important duty in the EA 2010 is that imposed on public authorities to have 'due regard' to the need to:

- eliminate discrimination, harassment, victimization and any other conduct that is prohibited by the EA 2010;
- advance equality of opportunity between persons who share a protected characteristic and those who do not;
- foster good relations between persons who share a relevant protected characteristic and those who do not (s.149 EA 2010).

This requires public authorities to consider the needs of all people in the way in which they provide their services and in relation to their employees. The important words are 'due regard'; this does not impose a very onerous duty on public authorities. Challenges have been made claiming a breach of this duty when, for example, local authorities seek to cut services because of financial restraints. All the public authority has to do is show that it had the equality duty 'in mind' when making its decision. It appears that there is no statutory *duty* to carry out a formal equality impact assessment (*R (on the application of D and another) v Manchester City Council*).

The impact of legislation on discriminatory attitudes is debatable. The Equal Opportunities Commission concluded that, 25 years after the introduction of anti-discrimination legislation:

> assumptions are still made about the roles, behaviour, abilities and needs of women and men. This is sex stereotyping and it can be found throughout society, influencing attitudes, expectations, choices and decisions which are made in all spheres of our lives. (Equal Opportunities Commission 2011)

This situation still prevails. Nevertheless, legislation can play its part and is an important feature of the legal framework within which social workers practice.

Director of Adult Social Services

Under the provisions of the LASSA 1970, an authority with social service functions must appoint a Director of Adult Social Services to be responsible for the strategic and day-to-day delivery of the services. Two or more authorities may jointly appoint one person as Director of Adult Social Services for their areas. A director for children's services must be appointed under the Children Act 2004 (CA 2004). An authority must also appoint an adequate number of staff to assist the director (s.6(6) LASSA 1970), as well as ensuring the appointment, under Schedule 1 LASSA 1970 of Approved Mental Health Professionals (AMHPs) (formerly known as Approved Social Workers).

It is difficult to assess what, in this context, can be regarded as adequate staff. This was considered in *R v Hereford and Worcester CC (ex parte Chandler and ex parte Bevan)*. The case involved successful applications for leave to bring judicial review proceedings, with lack of adequate staffing being one of the issues. (Judicial review is discussed more fully in Chapter 8.) The court made it clear that it regarded the duty as more than mere aspiration. Clements and Thompson (2011), commenting on the need for adequate staffing, suggest that an aggrieved individual could challenge the level of staffing and base their case on the minutes of the social services committee, or relevant minutes under the executive model of local government. Whereas the courts may generally appear tolerant over the issue of staffing levels, *R v Hereford and Worcester CC* (*ex parte Chandler and ex parte Bevan*) emphasizes that there are limits to such tolerance and that woefully inadequate levels may well form the basis for a successful challenge. There is also evidence of a high turnover of staff and a failure to fill vacancies, although a recent survey found a decrease in this trend in some settings for 2013 (National Carers Forum 2013).

Social work practice and the law

What is the relationship between law and professional social work practice? Does the law challenge or support social work values? Decision-making in social work should take account of social work values (such as respect for the individual) and reflect that people must be treated equally and with dignity. In truth, the law embodies many values (such as partnership; and the rights of individuals to receive care, treatment and control in the context of the least restrictive alternative).

However, social work is often practised in highly complex situations. A practitioner may be required to undertake assessments (see Chapter 3, p. 55) and to make professional judgements that are, of necessity, likely to involve very personal matters for the service user, and which may involve the use of legal powers that restrain personal liberty (see Chapter 2, p. 48, and Chapter 6). It should be recognized that the law may work against the interests of an individual service user, particularly in relation to the allocation of resources (see Chapter 4, p. 72). There is also the requirement to consider the needs of a range of service users who may have competing interests (e.g. in responding to the needs of a service user as against those of an unpaid carer). There will be occasions where recognizing and observing the responsibilities, rights and needs of one individual need to be balanced against the responsibilities, rights and needs of others and, in certain circumstances, those of the community at large.

Although the law tells social workers what they can do, since 'most decisions in social work involve a complex interaction of ethical, political, technical and legal issues which are all inter-connected', it does not necessarily tell them what they ought to do in any given situation' (Banks 2012). In addition, whilst social work law partly defines social work, 'it is itself also defined by social work objectives ... Practitioners must [therefore] develop the ability to engage in critical analysis of the legal framework, reflecting on the nature of the duties and powers available and using them to support ethical practice' (Braye *et al.* 2003). Law and values should not be divorced one from the other as, together, they form the basis of good practice.

The MCA 2005 provides an example of how the current legislative principles have developed. As will be seen in Chapter 2, the MCA 2005, s.1, lays down a number of statutory principles that are relevant to all those to whom the MCA 2005 applies. These principles include the right of an individual to make unwise or eccentric decisions, a presumption of capacity, and that an act undertaken on behalf of a person without capacity is undertaken in their 'best interests'. Similarly, in deciding whether a particular course of action is in the best interests of a person who lacks capacity, the decision-maker must have regard to a number of principles found in s.4 MCA 2005. These include not making an assessment based on a person's age, appearance or behaviour, which might lead others to make unjustified assumptions about what might be in that person's best interests.

There may be situations, however, where a particular piece of legislation is out-of-date and no longer reflects values currently regarded as acceptable social work norms. Section 29 NAA 1948 defines as 'disabled' people who are:

> blind, deaf or dumb [or who suffer from mental disorder of any description], and other persons [aged eighteen or over] who are substantially and permanently handicapped by illness, injury, or congenital deformity or such other disabilities as may be prescribed by the Minister.

It is inevitable that legislative provisions are likely to become dated over time. When values are embodied in such provisions, the law should be revised by government in order to accommodate both changing attitudes and, where possible, developments in social work values and practice. Unfortunately, governments do not always respond to the need for change in a timely manner.

As mentioned, social workers are expected to work in a professional manner. Although it is not easy to provide a definitive description of a profession, it will have certain characteristics, one of which is that a professional practitioner must apply knowledge, skill and values in making an assessment and in reaching a decision and judgement. The courts are generally reluctant to unpick a professional decision and impose their own assessment or judgement. In the case of *Carty (by his Litigation Friend) v Croydon London Borough*, it was said that the courts would only find negligence on the part of an employee, if it were shown that the person had failed to act in accordance with a practice accepted at the time as proper by a responsible body of persons of the same profession or skill. It does not follow that every practitioner will arrive at the same professional assessment. Where there is disagreement, practitioners should discuss this and attempt to reach an agreement. However, the law accepts that there may be legitimate differences of opinion between individual practitioners.

On occasion, social workers may feel it necessary to report concerns that they have about particular situations that have not been resolved within the CSSR. In such cases, they may have to report the matter outside of the CSSR. This is often referred to as 'whistle-blowing'. There are statutory procedures to be followed in such cases and these are discussed in Chapter 8 (pp. 169–71).

> **Exercise 1.4**
>
> Draw up a balance sheet of aspects of the law and social work that may help you to work effectively for services users, and aspects of the law that may not.
>
> (Braye and Preston-Shoot 2009)

Delegated and designated functions

Although it is on the local authority as a corporate body that the law places direct responsibility for delivering social services in the community, the day-to-day task of implementing them is delegated to individual social workers. The nature and extent of a social worker's responsibilities will be determined by the terms of their contract of employment, and delegated through the management structure of the department in which they work, or exceptionally by being designated to act, as in the case of AMHPs, under the MHA 1983 (see Chapter 6, p. 120). Employment within a Department of Adult Social Services is thus a key factor in shaping a local authority social worker's practice. Practitioners should resist accepting a delegation that is beyond their contractual and/or statutory obligations, or their professional competence. (See also Table 1.4 for the Standards of Proficiency.) Wider issues of accountability are discussed in Chapter 8.

Registration of social workers

Since 2005, social work has become a regulated profession. Only those whose name is entered on the relevant register (now maintained and administered in England by the Health and Care Professions Council (HCPC)) are allowed, by law, to describe themselves as 'social workers' under s.61 Care Standards Act 2000 (CSA 2000). The HCPC is the independent regulator of health and care professionals. Previously, regulatory functions in relation to social work were the responsibility of the General Social Care Council, which was abolished in July 2012.

The register is a public document that is accessible by any member of the public. Social workers must maintain their registration with the HCPC in order to continue to practise, and must declare on each occasion that they continue to meet the standards of proficiency that apply to their 'scope of practice'.

Table 1.4 Standards of proficiency required of social workers

Social workers must be able to:
Practise safely and effectively within their scope of practice – Know the limits of their practice and when to seek advice or refer to another professional – Recognize the need to manage their own workload and resources and be able to practise accordingly – Be able to undertake assessments of risk, need and capacity and respond appropriately – Be able to recognize and respond appropriately to unexpected situations and manage uncertainty – Be able to recognize signs of harm, abuse and neglect and know how to respond appropriately
Practise within the legal and ethical boundaries of their profession – Understand current legislation applicable to the work of their profession – Understand the need to promote the best interests of service users and carers at all times – Understand the need to protect, safeguard and promote the wellbeing of children, young people and vulnerable adults – Understand the need to address practices which present a risk to or from service users and carers, or others – Be able to manage competing or conflicting interests – Be able to exercise authority as a social worker within the appropriate legal and ethical frameworks – Understand the need to respect and uphold the rights, dignity, values and autonomy of every service user and carer – Recognize that relationships with service users and carers should be based on respect and honesty – Recognize the power dynamics in relationships with service users and carers and be able to manage those dynamics – Appropriately understand what is required of them by the Health and Care Professions Council.
Maintain fitness to practise – Understand the need to maintain high standards of personal and professional conduct – Understand the importance of maintaining their health and wellbeing – Understand both the need to keep skills and knowledge up to date and the importance of career-long learning – Be able to establish and maintain personal and professional boundaries – Be able to manage the physical and emotional impact of their practice
Practise as an autonomous professional, exercising their own professional judgement – Be able to assess a situation, determine its nature and severity and call upon the required knowledge and experience to deal with it – Be able to initiate resolution of issues and be able to exercise personal initiative – Recognize that they are personally responsible for, and must be able to justify, their decisions and recommendations – Be able to make informed judgements on complex issues using the information available – Be able to make and receive referrals appropriately

Table 1.4 *continued*

Social workers must be able to:
Be aware of the impact of culture, equality and diversity on practice – Be able to reflect on and take account of the impact of inequality, disadvantage and discrimination on those who use social work services and their communities – Understand the need to adapt practice to respond appropriately to different groups and individuals – Be aware of the impact of their own values on practice with different groups of service users and carers – Understand the impact of different cultures and communities and how this affects the role of the social worker in supporting service users and carers.
Practise in a non-discriminatory manner – Be able to work with others to promote social justice, equality and inclusion – Be able to use practice to challenge and address the impact of discrimination, disadvantage and oppression
Maintain confidentiality – Be able to understand and explain the limits of confidentiality – Be able to recognize and respond appropriately to situations where it is necessary to share information to safeguard service users and carers or others
Communicate effectively – Be able to use interpersonal skills and appropriate forms of verbal and non-verbal communication with service users, carers and others – Be able to demonstrate effective and appropriate skills in communicating advice, instruction, information and professional opinion to colleagues, service users and carers – Understand the need to provide service users and carers with the information necessary to enable them to make informed decisions or to understand the decisions made – Understand how communication skills affect the assessment of and engagement with service users and carers – Understand how the means of communication should be modified to address and take account of a range of factors including age, capacity, learning ability and physical ability – Be aware of the characteristics and consequences of verbal and non-verbal communication and how this can be affected by a range of factors including age, culture, disability, ethnicity, gender, religious beliefs and socio-economic status – Understand the need to draw upon available resources and services to support service users' and carers' communication, wherever possible – Be able to communicate in English to the standard equivalent to level 7 of the International English Language Testing System, with no element below 6.5 – Be able to engage in inter-professional and inter-agency communication – Be able to listen actively to service users and carers and others – Be able to prepare and present formal reports in line with applicable protocols and guidelines.   *(continued overleaf)*

Table 1.4 *continued*

Social workers must be able to:
Work appropriately with others
– Understand the need to build and sustain professional relationships with service users, carers and colleagues as both autonomous practitioner and collaboratively with others
– Be able to work with service users and carers to enable them to assess and make informed decisions about their needs circumstances, risks, preferred options and resources
– Be able to work with service users and carers to promote individual growth, development and independence and to assist them to understand and exercise their rights
– Be able to support service users' and carers' rights to control their lives and make informed choices about the services they receive
– Be able to support the development of networks, groups and communities to meet needs and outcomes
– Be able to work in partnership with others, including those working in other agencies and roles
– Be able to contribute effectively to work undertaken as part of a multi-disciplinary team
– Recognize the contribution that service users' and carers' own resources and strengths can bring to social work
– Be able to work with resistance and conflict
– Be able to understand the emotional dynamics of interactions with service users and carers
Maintain records appropriately
– Be able to keep accurate, comprehensive and comprehensible records in accordance with applicable legislation, protocols and guidelines
– Recognize the need to manage records and all other information in accordance with applicable legislation, protocols and guidelines
Reflect on and review practice
– Understand the value of critical reflection on practice and the need to record the outcome of such reflection appropriately
– Recognize the value of supervision, case reviews and other methods of reflection and review
Assure the quality of their practice
– Be able to use supervision to support and enhance the quality of their social work practice
– Be able to contribute to processes designed to evaluate service and individual outcomes
– Be able to engage in evidence-informed practice, evaluate practice systematically and participate in audit procedures
Understand the key concepts of the knowledge base relevant to their profession
– Recognize the roles of other professions, practitioners and organizations
– Be aware of the different social and organizational contexts and settings within which social work operates

Table 1.4 *continued*

Social workers must be able to:

- Be aware of changes in demography and culture and their impact on social work
- Understand in relation to social work practice:
  • social work theory
  • social work models and interventions
  • the development and application of relevant law and social policy
  • the development and application of social work and social work values
  • human growth and development across the lifespan and the impact of key developmental stages and transitions
  • the impact of injustice, social inequalities, policies and other issues which affect the demand for social work services
  • the relevance of psychological, environmental, sociological and physiological perspectives to understanding personal and social development and functioning
  • concepts of participation, advocacy and empowerment
  • the relevance of sociological perspectives to understanding societal and structural influences on human behaviour

Draw on appropriate knowledge and skills to inform practice - Be able to gather, analyse, critically evaluate and use information and knowledge to make recommendations or modify their practice - Be able to select and use appropriate assessment tools - Be able to prepare, implement, review, evaluate, revise and conclude plans to meet needs and circumstances in conjunction with service users and carers - Be able to use social work methods, theories and models to achieve change and development and improve life opportunities - Be aware of a range of research methodologies - Recognize the value of research and analysis and be able to evaluate such evidence to inform their own practice - Be able to demonstrate a level of skill in the use of information technology appropriate to their practice - Be able to change their practice as needed to take account of new developments or changing contexts
Establish and maintain a safe practice environment - Understand the need to maintain the safety of service users carers and colleagues - Be aware of applicable health and safety legislation and any relevant safety policies and procedures in force at the workplace, such as incident reporting, and be able to act in accordance with these - Be able to work safely in challenging environments, including being able to take appropriate actions to manage environmental risk

Standards of proficiency

A social worker's scope of practice is the area or areas of their profession in which they have the knowledge, skills and experience to practise lawfully, safely and effectively in a way that meets the HCPC's standards and does not pose any danger to the public or themselves. As autonomous professionals, social workers must make informed and reasoned decisions about their practice to ensure they meet the standards that apply to them. This includes seeking advice and support from education providers, employers, colleagues, professional bodies, trades unions and others to ensure that the wellbeing of service users is safeguarded at all times. If social workers do so and can justify their decision if asked to, it is unlikely that they will not meet the required standards, as set out in the relevant Standards of Proficiency (Health and Care Professions Council 2012).

> **Exercise 1.5**
>
> 1. As a social care practitioner, what would you do if asked by your line manager to undertake a task, (e.g. to deliver a particular service to a service user) that you felt you were not qualified or competent to undertake?
> 2. The Proficiency Standards set out in Table 1.4, make only one direct reference to law and legislation. From what you have so far learnt in this chapter, to what extent do the other standards imply that knowledge of the law is required in order to be a competent practitioner?

Partnership and coordination

Although social services departments are primarily responsible for ensuring appropriate social welfare provision is available in the community, service users' needs rarely fit neatly into one category. The broader social context includes other agencies with specific remits, funding levels, cultures and vocabulary, including the police, in relation, for example, to vulnerable adult protection procedures, as envisaged in 'No Secrets' (Department of Health and Home Office 2000). Working cooperatively with these bodies is a challenge for all concerned. 'Welfare' is a wide term, including not only social services, but also education, housing and the environment. Much of social work practice is undertaken in a multi-or inter-disciplinary environment. One critical example of inter-disciplinary working is that between health and social services, especially in relation to vulnerable adults leaving hospital and needing community or residential care. Health and social services are different public bodies; they have different funding streams and requirements on charging service users. Under the National Health Service Act 2006 (s.82 NHSA 2006), a duty is placed on health authorities and local authorities to collaborate 'to secure and advance the health and welfare of the people of England and Wales'. This provision recognizes the importance of partnership in commissioning and delivering care, as well as at a strategic planning level.

Exercise 1.6

1. Using what you discussed in the earlier exercises, consider and discuss the following scenario from the point of view of the HRA 1998, the Code of Practice for Social Workers, and the EA 2010.

Scenario

Some 30 years ago, the appellant was a prima ballerina. At the age of 56 years, she suffered a stroke, leaving her with severely limited mobility. She has recently fallen and broken her hip, and was in hospital for four months. She then suffered two further falls, each leading to further hospitalization. She suffers from a condition that makes her have to use the toilet some two to three times a night. Previously, she used a commode with the help of a night-time carer provided by the CSSR. Recently, the CSSR have proposed that she should use incontinence pads or special sheeting, which would avoid the need for the carer. The CSSR say that this would provide her with greater safety (avoiding the risk of injury whilst using the commode). It would also enhance her independence and privacy, and reduce the cost to the CSSR by some £22,000 per year, which the authority states would be spent on providing services for other users. She is appalled at the thought of being treated as incontinent (which she is not) and having to use pads. She considers this an intolerable affront to her dignity.

Now read the case of *R (on the application of McDonald) v Royal Borough of Kensington and Chelsea* on which this scenario is based.

2. Do you agree with the decision of the Supreme Court?

Accountability

CSSRs, as public bodies, are subject to accountability in the courts through the use of procedures (such as judicial review and declarations), or through actions for breach of statutory duty and negligence. In addition, they are accountable through the use of non-judicial procedures (such as complaint procedures). These are discussed more fully in Chapter 8, where the circumstances in which individual responsibility, as well as the concept of vicarious liability, are discussed.

Conclusion

This introductory chapter has outlined the significance of the law in social work practice. It illustrates how the law provides social work with its administrative and organizational framework, how it sets out functions and objectives of social work, and how it influences social work's professional values and standards of proficiency. In effect, knowledge of the law is an essential component of effective and competent practice.

In the following chapters, the law's application is discussed in relation to the delivery, in specific circumstances, of community social care to adults. Chapter 2 considers legal capacity. It is discussed at this early stage as it is an area of which social workers must be aware in all aspects of their work. Given that personal autonomy and the right to decide are threads that run through the whole of social work practice, possessing the capacity to exercise them is crucial. How we assess capacity and what happens if a person lacks capacity will now be discussed.

chapter 2
Legal Capacity

In this chapter, you will learn about:

- Assessing capacity
- Mental Capacity Act 2005
- Code of practice
- How the Mental Capacity Act 2005 defines capacity
  - Unable to make a decision
  - Retaining information
  - Fluctuating capacity
- Decision-making for people who lack capacity
- Other forms of decision-making
  - Lasting Powers of Attorney
  - Court of Protection
- The implications of the *Bournewood* case
- Deprivation of Liberty Safeguards (DOLS)

Remember to consult The Legal Toolbox on pp. xiii–xx. This will help you to understand processes and procedures referred to in this chapter.

Introduction

The rights to self-determination and choice are two of the key principles of social work practice. Such an approach is underpinned by the basic legal presumption that adults have the necessary mental capacity to exercise self-determination and choice. However, social work may involve working with service users who lack legal capacity, or have fluctuating capacity, or whose legal capacity is uncertain. It is therefore important for social workers to be aware of the legal rules that help to define mental incapacity and the possible effects that incapacity may have on the rights of a service user.

Assessing capacity

Capacity is usually taken for granted; we are rarely asked whether we have the capacity to make a decision. Yet, having capacity is essential if a decision is to be respected by professionals and, ultimately, by the law. Incapacity presents many challenges for social work practitioners. Assessing someone as lacking capacity has significant implications for that person. Imagine a situation where you are unable to make decisions for yourself – for example, a decision on medical treatment, where you live, your relationships, what you buy, or legal agreements. Others would make these decisions for you – in your 'best interests'. Obviously, such decisions directly engage human rights: the right to a private life, to a family life, to a home and the freedom to decide may all be affected by decisions on incapacity. The Mental Capacity Act 2005 (MCA 2005) reflects such values and represents a landmark in the development of legislation relating to vulnerable adults.

Very often, capacity is discussed only in the context of consent; for example, agreeing to receiving medical treatment. However, it is also essential when considering the ability to refuse to agree to something. Both are equally important. To treat acquiescence as valid consent may disguise the fact that the person lacks legal capacity. The fact that they appear to 'consent' may result in something being done to them without legal authority. This may incur criminal and/or civil liability. Similarly, refusal by a person to accept what is arguably a reasonable and sensible course of action may (wrongly) lead a professional to question that person's capacity. The decision not to follow professional advice may be considered irrational and lead to an assumption that the person lacks capacity. As will be seen, this does not represent the law.

Mental Capacity Act 2005

Until the MCA 2005, the law on legal capacity was largely based on a hotchpotch of uncoordinated new and old statute law, regulations and guidance, the decisions of judges, and the principles of human rights (MacDonald 2010). It was clear that the law was too complex to be developed further on this piecemeal basis. The courts had expressed concern that only Parliament could provide the necessary certainty (*Re F (adult: court's jurisdiction) 2000*). In addition, the judges were unable to ensure that appropriate legal safeguards existed to protect those at risk of being assessed as lacking capacity. The MCA 2005 codifies the law and provides the framework within which decisions on capacity and best interests are made. It provides a means by which decisions are recorded, checked and, if necessary, challenged.

The provisions of the MCA 2005 can be broadly divided into two parts:

- the rules used *to decide whether a person has sufficient mental capacity to make a particular decision* at a particular time; and
- the rules that apply when an individual is *assessed as lacking the necessary capacity to make the particular decision* in question.

It is important to note the *five statutory principles* set out in s.1 MCA 2005. Incorporating principles into legislation is unusual; it is more common for general principles to be in codes or general guidance, rather than in legislation. Incorporation into the MCA 2005 means they are legally binding and enforceable. Failure to follow them would need to be legally justified and could be open to legal challenge. As has been stated:

> Actions or decisions that clearly conflict with the principles are unlikely to be lawful, although there may be occasions on which the principles are in tension with each other, and some balancing may be required. (British Medical Association and Law Society 2010)

The five principles are:

1. A person must be *assumed* to have capacity unless it is established that they lack capacity – the so-called *presumption of capacity*.
2. A person is not to be treated as unable to make a decision *unless all practical steps to help them to do so have been taken without success*.
3. A person is not to be treated as unable to make a decision *merely because they make an eccentric or unwise decision*.
4. Acts undertaken, or decisions made under the MCA (2005) for or on behalf of a person who lacks capacity must be undertaken *in their best interests*.
5. Before any act is undertaken or decision made, regard must be given as to whether the purpose for which it is needed can be more effectively achieved *in a less restrictive way*.

A number of points arise out of these principles. Under *Principle 1*, practitioners cannot argue that certain groups, such as those with a learning disability, automatically lack capacity, or that someone must prove that they have it. Such a misunderstanding also finds expression in claims that people detained under the Mental Health Act 1983 (MHA 1983) (e.g. in *Re C (Adult, refusal of treatment)*), or anybody over the age of 85 years, must lack capacity. Any practice or decision based on these misguided ideas must be challenged, as must the assumption that, once lost, capacity is irretrievable. Although a person who is, for example, in the later stages of dementia is unlikely to regain any of the capacity they may have had, a person who lacks capacity temporarily, because they are unconscious as the result of an accident, or through sedation, will regain it. Medication might also lead to a temporary loss of capacity.

The burden of establishing incapacity is on the person seeking to establish it, rather than on the individual to prove that they have capacity (*Scamell v Farmer*). The MCA 2005 makes it clear that lack of capacity cannot be established merely based on age, appearance or condition, or an aspect of behaviour that might lead others to make unjustified assumptions about a person's capacity (s.2(3) MCA 2005). This is sometimes referred to as the principle of *equal consideration*. The standard of proof required for making a decision under s.2 MCA 2005, is *the balance of probability* (s.2(4) MCA 2005); *Re F* [2009]. This means that the practitioner must be satisfied that it is more likely than not that the person satisfies the test set out in the MCA 2005.

Principle 2 makes it clear that practitioners must do all they can to help somebody decide for themselves. This has implications for the way in which practitioners provide information. In making a decision relating to social care, the person is entitled to information on such matters as the financial implications of their decisions. The Mental Capacity Act Code of Practice states:

> It is important to do everything practical ... to help a person make a decision for themselves before concluding that they lack capacity to do so. People with an illness or disability affecting their ability to make a decision should receive support to help them make as many decisions as they can. This principle aims to stop people being automatically labelled as lacking capacity to make particular decisions. Because it encourages individuals to play as big a role as possible in decision-making, it also helps prevent unnecessary interventions in their lives. (Department of Constitutional Affairs 2005)

According to the Code, the type of support a person could be given might include:

- using a different form of communication (e.g. non-verbal);
- providing information in more accessible form (e.g. photos, drawings);
- treating a medical condition that may be affecting the person's capacity;
- having a structured programme to improve a person's capacity to make particular decisions (e.g. helping a person with learning disabilities to learn new skills).

(Department of Constitutional Affairs 2005, para. 2.7)

Principle 3 refutes another misconception; namely, that an irrational decision suggests a lack of capacity. Making good or bad decisions is a basic right; no inference of incapacity can be drawn from the fact that others may disagree with a decision (*St George's Healthcare NHS Trust v S (No.1)*; *Re JT (Adult: Refusal of Medical Treatment*; *Re B v An NHS Hospital Trust*). In addition, no one is obliged to give reasons for rejecting the advice of practitioners. However, the Code recognizes that there may be cause for concern should a person repeatedly make unwise decisions. This does not necessarily mean they lack capacity, but it might justify further investigation that would address such questions as whether the person needs more information in order to help them understand the consequences of their action (Department of Constitutional Affairs 2005, para. 2.11).

Principle 4 introduces the *best interests* test. This is discussed on p. 39.

Principle 5 reminds us that, even though there may be a power to do something in relation to a person who lacks capacity, this does not mean that the most extreme and restrictive action is justified. Practitioners must always consider whether the purpose of the intervention can be achieved through a less restrictive intervention that maximizes the person's rights and freedoms of action. In short, the action must be proportionate.

> **Exercise 2.1**
>
> Relate the five Principles to the rights set out in the European Convention on Human Rights as incorporated into our law by the Human Rights Act 1998 (see Chapter 1, p. 7).

Code of practice

As noted (see p. 30), a code of practice has been issued under the MCA 2005. Although not legally binding as such, anyone who departs from it will need to give good reasons for doing so. Social workers and care managers are specifically referred to in the Code and are required to 'have regard' to its contents when acting, or making decisions, under s.42 MCA 2005. They should be able to provide evidence on how the Code was used.

How does the Mental Capacity Act 2005 define capacity?

The MCA 2005 introduced a *single test of capacity*, although s.27 MCA 2005 excludes the following decisions from the scope of the legislation:

- decisions relating to marriage or civil partnership;
- sexual relations;
- divorce or dissolution of civil partnership (two-year separation with consent to dissolution);
- being placed for adoption;
- the making of an adoption order.

For the test of capacity to marry, see *Park v Park*.

In such situations, a court uses its *inherent jurisdiction* to protect people who lack capacity. Inherent jurisdiction is a residual power vested in the courts to protect vulnerable people not otherwise protected by the law.

Exercise 2.2

Scenario

H, aged 29 years, had been diagnosed with mild learning difficulties and atypical autism with a full scale IQ of 64. Her history showed a very deep degree of sexualization. At least one man was convicted of a sexual offence against her. Other men were engaging in sexual behaviour which, whilst she consented to it, was probably exploitative. The authorities were alerted to H's sexual activities, vulnerability and disinhibition. She gave her psychiatrist 'an extensive, if confused, history of the willingness to have sex with anyone including strangers'. Enquiries revealed that she considered herself as obligated to submit to what, in fact, was rape. She was detained under the Mental Health Act 1983. She was eventually discharged. She lacked capacity to decide where she lived, her care and support arrangements, contact and her finances. At the time of the court hearing, she lived in accommodation provided by a private agency under a contract with the CSSR. She was supervized on a one-to-one basis at all times and was not free to leave the accommodation unaccompanied. People entering the property were also carefully regulated. The purpose of those restrictions was to prevent H from having sexual relations that would be potentially exploitative and damaging. The court was asked to consider whether H had the capacity to consent to sexual relations.

1. What problems arose in managing this case and what human rights might be engaged?
2. What social work values are also involved?

The facts in Exercise 2.2 are based on the Court of Protection case of *A Local Authority v H*. The Court said that a person must have a basic understanding of the mechanics of the physical act and an understanding that intercourse might lead to pregnancy. It also required some understanding of sexual health issues at a rudimentary level; for example, that risks could be reduced by use of a condom. The moral aspect was important, but it could have no specific role in a test of capacity. As to the emotional component, the question was whether the person understood that they had a choice and could refuse.

Note that the power under inherent jurisdiction could be used in circumstances where an individual has mental capacity, but is vulnerable and deemed in need of protection.

2.1 *DL v A Local Authority*

> case example

In this case, the victims of abuse had legal capacity, but the abuser was exercising undue influence over them and preventing them from exercising a free choice. As they had capacity, the MCA 2005 did not apply. However, the Court held that it had power to intervene to protect them under its inherent jurisdiction and in support of their right under Article 8 of the ECHR to respect for their private and family life.

Inherent jurisdiction is broad in its application. It includes not only intervening when there is a necessity to do so, or the lawfulness of an act is in issue, but can extend to making a declaration as to what is in the best interests of the individual (*St Helens BC v PE*).

Under the previous law, the judges developed a *functional test* of capacity; this is now enshrined in s.2 MCA 2005. The test is not based on establishing capacity by reference to a person's status, or the rationality of the decision. Section 2(1) states:

> a person lacks capacity *in relation to a matter if at the material time he is unable to make a decision* for himself in relation to the matter because of an impairment of, or a disturbance in the functioning of, the mind or brain [emphasis added].

Four key points need to be emphasized:

- *in relation to a matter*: these words make it clear that capacity is subject sensitive. It does not follow that once a person is found to lack capacity to make a particular decision (e.g. agreeing to the sale of a house) they lack capacity to do anything else (e.g. the capacity to open a savings account). Incapacity to do one thing does not necessarily mean incapacity to do other things; care should be taken when applying the blanket label of 'incapacity'.

Legal Capacity

The s.2 MCA 2005 test is linked to the decision or decisions to be made, rather than capacity in general.
- *at the material time*: again, this places the decision in a context; namely, the time at which the assessment is undertaken. People can fluctuate in and out of capacity. It is important to recognize that incapacity is rarely a blanket state of mind. An assessment of incapacity should be reviewed, at which point the person may be assessed as having full capacity.
- *unable to make a decision*: this is discussed in more detail below.
- *because of*: note that there is a causal link between the inability to decide and the impairment/disturbance of the mind or brain. An inability to decide does not itself establish incapacity; neither does the impairment/disturbance do so on its own.

Unable to make a decision

Being *unable to make a decision* is defined in s.3 MCA 2005. It states that a person is unable to decide if they are unable:

- to understand the information relevant to the decision;
- to retain that information;
- to use or weigh that information as part of the process of making the decision.

Only if a person cannot satisfy one or more of these three elements, do they lack capacity (*Re MB (Caesarean Section)*). The more serious the consequences of the decision, the greater the level of capacity required to take it (*Re T*).

Exercise 2.3

Scenario

Mr Smith, an elderly man with early signs of dementia, has recently entered a contract to pay £250 a month to a gardening firm for routine maintenance. He has a small garden, which he has always maintained to a high standard. Before the onset of dementia, he was very careful with his money. His only daughter, an assertive woman, has made a number of inquiries and has found out that her father had overpaid the cleaner on a number of occasions. She claims that, in the past, he would never have done such a thing. Mr Smith has also made payments from his savings about which he cannot give an account. His daughter has taken control of his cheque book, assuring him that she will make quite sure that he has enough money for his daily needs. A neighbour contacts the local CSSR, claiming that Mr Smith is very unhappy with this

> situation, but reluctant to say anything to his daughter for fear of upsetting his only child.
>
> Applying the above criteria, discuss what factors are relevant in assessing Mr Smiths' mental capacity.

Understanding the information presupposes that information is provided. In making a decision relating to matters of social care, a person is entitled to information that will assist in that process. For example, in deciding whether to enter a care home following an assessment under s.47 National Health Service and Community Care Act 1990 (NHSCCA 1990) (see Chapter 3, p. 57, and Chapter 4, p. 76), the person is entitled to information on the financial implications of the decision. Such information is particularly significant if they own their house or have substantial capital assets. It would be unreasonable for them have to make the decision without being aware of the effect that it will have on the ownership of their property.

How extensive is the duty on the practitioner to provide information in such cases? The law is not precise on this matter, but the following can be distilled from the cases of *Sidaway v Bethlem Royal Hospital Governors and others* and *Pearce and another v United Bristol Healthcare NHS Trust*. Both cases are from medical law, although the principles apply equally to social care decisions.

- The decision on how much information to provide is a matter of professional judgement. The decision on whether a professional judgement was negligent is decided by the test applied in *Carty*; namely, would the practitioner's decision gain the approval of a responsible body of professional opinion (see Chapter 1, p. 18);
- Any decision not to disclose information must be reasonable and responsible. As Lord Woolf put it in the *Pearce* case:

> If there is a significant risk which would affect the judgment of the reasonable patient, then in the normal course it is the responsibility of the doctor to inform the patient of that significant risk, if the information is needed so that the patient can determine for him or herself as to what course he or she should adopt.

Thus, if the risk is significant in relation to the decision to be made, practitioners should inform the person. More generally, s.3(4) MCA 2005 states that information relevant to a decision includes information about the reasonably foreseeable consequences of:

- deciding one way or another; or
- failing to make the decision.

The Mental Capacity Act Code of Practice states that, in providing information, the following apply:

- Take time to explain anything that might help the person make a decision. It is important that they have access to all the information they need to make an informed decision.
- Try not to give more detail than the person needs – this might confuse them. In some cases, a simple, broad explanation will be enough. But it must not miss out important information.
- What are the risks and benefits? Describe any foreseeable consequences of making the decision, and of not making any decision at all.
- Explain the effects that the decision might have on the person and those close to them – including the people involved in their care.
- If there is a choice, give the person the same information in a balanced way for all the options.
- For some types of decisions, it may be important to provide access to advice from elsewhere. This may be independent or specialist advice (for example, from a medical practitioner or a financial or legal adviser). But it might simply be advice from trusted friends or relatives. (Department of Constitutional Affairs 2005, para. 3.9)

Practitioners must be aware of information overload as this can lead to bad decision-making.

It is also important to note that a person is not unable to make a decision unless all practical steps to help them to do so have been taken without success. This requires practitioners to give information in a way that is accessible and appropriate to the abilities of the person making the decision. The statutory principle is reinforced by s.3(2) MCA 2005. This emphasizes that a person is not to be regarded as unable to understand the information relevant to a decision if they are able to understand an explanation of it given in a way that is appropriate to their circumstances. For example, this might mean using simple language, visual aids or any other means.

The use of appropriate language and methods of communication is important and a part of the legal requirement under this principle. Providing information in a technical or inaccessible form may reduce the ability of the person to understand it and to use it effectively to make the decision, particularly if the person may have borderline capacity. Similarly, the choice of time and venue may have an effect on the ability of the person to make a decision. Practitioners must make sure that they can demonstrate that they made every effort to help the person decide for themselves.

Retaining information

The second requirement of s. 3 MCA 2005 is that the person must be able to retain the information. For how long must the information be retained? A seemingly glib answer is 'for as long as it takes'. This response may have some merit, although it does ignore the fact that a decision may be required within a relatively short time. The answer must also recognize that some people have fluctuating capacity; their competence to decide is time-limited. In normal circumstances, the person may have a reasonable amount of time to make a decision. For somebody with fluctuating capacity, it may be necessary to condense the time for reflection into a shorter period. Doing this enables the person to make the decision, rather than another person having to resort to the best interests approach. Under s.3(3) MCA 2005 the fact that a person is able to retain the information relevant to a decision for a short period only does not prevent them from being regarded as able to make the decision. The person must then be able to use the information in order to come to a decision. Remember that under Principle 3, the person has the right to make an unwise decision.

Inability to communicate

The functional test outlined (p. 33) is the one that a social work practitioner will encounter most often. There is, however, an additional element of the test for being 'unable to decide' under s.3 MCA 2005. This is where the person is unable to decide because they are *unable to communicate* the decision, whether by talking, using sign language or any other means. Great care must be taken not to use this test inappropriately. It is a residual component of the test that it be used rarely. It assumes that the person is able to satisfy the functional test (or, as far as can be ascertained, they would be able to do so), but something prevents them from communicating the decision. This does not cover cases where the person has communication difficulties that can be overcome. Rather, it requires a complete inability to communicate which cannot be overcome. The example usually given of such a condition is locked-in syndrome (Department of Constitutional Affairs 2005, para. 4.23). The courts recognize that, in some instances, alternative forms of communications such as muscle movements are sufficient (*Re AK* (*Adult Patient*) (*Medical Treatment: Consent*)). This residual category of people who are unable to decide does not reduce the responsibility of practitioners to assist people to communicate their decision.

> **Exercise 2.4**
>
> In order to assist a person to make a decision for themselves, all possible and appropriate means of communication should be tried. (See Department of Constitutional Affairs 2005 at paras 2.7 and 3.10.)
>
> 1. How would you ensure compliance with this requirement?
> 2. What options are available and how would you explore their possibilities?

Fluctuating capacity

Section 2(2) MCA 2005 states that it does not matter whether the impairment or disturbance is permanent or temporary. As noted above, fluctuating capacity may mean that the period for which a person is able to retain the information in order to arrive at a decision is condensed. However, a decision made during capacity will survive subsequent incapacity and can be revoked only when the person regains capacity. The statutory principles, in particular Principle 2, apply. Can the decision be delayed until the person regains capacity, or must it be taken immediately? What help is available for the person to make the decision? If a decision must be taken immediately, then it needs to be the least restrictive in the circumstances. It is also necessary to review assessments of capacity on a regular basis (Department of Constitutional Affairs 2005, para. 2.9).

Particular difficulties arise where the fluctuations are rapid with relatively short periods of capacity followed by relatively short periods of incapacity. It may be difficult in such cases to conclude that the person is able to retain the information long enough to make the decision, particularly in relation to a complex decision. However, each case depends on its own circumstances and assumptions must not be made.

Decision-making for people who lack capacity

Who decides whether a person lacks capacity? Usually, it is the individual concerned with person's care when the decision is required. Social work practitioners may be required to assess a person's capacity to make a decision, such as the decision to live in a care home. The practitioner may also be involved in deciding what is in the best interests of a person lacking capacity. It is often a matter of balancing the rights of adults against the need to protect them (John 2007). If professionals, family and carers are ultimately unable to agree on the question of capacity, it then becomes a matter for the Court of Protection to decide.

As noted, decisions made for or on behalf of a person who lacks capacity must be in their *best interests* in accordance with Principle 4 of the statutory principles set out in s.1 MCA 2005 (p. 29). Nowhere is this term defined in the MCA (2005), although it is a concept known to the judges for many years as in the 1989 case of *Re F (Mental Patient: Sterilisation)* [1990] where the court had to consider whether the sterilization of a woman lacking capacity was lawful.

The test was criticized by the European Court of Human Rights in the case of *HL v UK*. The MCA 2005 seeks to address the human rights deficit identified by the Court. Nobody can deny the complexity and implications of making decisions on what may be in another's best interests. The simple answer is that probably we can never know. If the person was able to decide, they may consider refusal of life-saving treatment, or continuing to live in what others may consider squalid conditions, to be in their best interests. The person's family and the practitioners may come to different conclusions. All that can be done is to maximize the involvement of the person (as required under the statutory principles) and to try to get to know the person as much as possible in the circumstances. The decision-maker must try to identify all of the matters that the person would take into consideration if they were making the decision. To assist in this, and to meet the concerns of the European Court of Human Rights, the MCA 2005 contains a *best interest checklist*.

Before considering the checklist, the following general points should be considered. First, it is a misconception that a person's best interests are always what professionals, family members or others suppose it to be. Second, the MCA 2005 encourages people to think ahead about the possible future loss of capacity and to make provision; this may include putting their thoughts into a prior statement. It would be wrong not to include them in the decision, although at times the evidence of what was or was not said may be unclear or contradictory. This often presents very difficult evidential problems for decision-makers.

The Code of Practice emphasizes that the application of the best interest test and the checklist must be flexible. Without flexibility, it would be impossible to prioritize factors in different cases – and it would be difficult to ensure that the outcome is the best possible for the person who lacks capacity to take the particular decision (Department of Constitutional Affairs 2005, para. 5.62). The courts have taken a broad view of what are a person's best interests.

> **case example**
>
> **2.2 *Re Y (adult patient (transplant: bone marrow))***
>
> In this case, the decision for the court was whether a woman who lacked capacity could act as a bone marrow donor for her sister. Was this in the best interest of the sister without capacity? The court held that the risks from the invasive procedure were low and did not outweigh the emotional, psychological and social benefit of her contact with her family.

'Best interests', as the overriding principle, is set out in s.4 MCA 2005 and discussed, for example, in *Re P*. The case identifies a number of relevant factors; these are not in any order of importance and the weight given to each depends on the individual circumstances of the case. The person's wishes will always be significant, but there is no overriding importance given to them (*Re M; ITW v Z*). What factors should be considered as part of the checklist?

- *Age and appearance.* As with determining capacity, a person's age or appearance, condition, or any aspect of their behaviour that may cause people to make unjustified assumptions about them, also apply to the use of the best interests test. For example, general assumptions such as that anybody over 80 years of age is 'better off' in residential care are wrong.
- *Will the person regain capacity?* If it is likely that the loss of capacity is temporary (e.g. the result of medication), then it will usually not be in their best interests to make serious but non-urgent decisions if it is likely that they will regain capacity in sufficient time to decide for themselves.
- *Participation.* The participation of the person is important and, as required by statutory Principle 2, every effort must be made to allow them to participate fully in the process.
- *Life-sustaining treatment.* During the Parliamentary debates on the MCA 2005, concern was expressed that the legislation would provide a legal basis for the compulsory euthanasia of some groups of people lacking capacity. Although this is not the case (the deliberate killing of another person remains a criminal offence, as does assisted suicide), specific safeguards are found in the MCA 2005 in relation to end-of-life decision-making. As far as the best interest test is concerned, any decision to initiate, continue or discontinue life-sustaining treatment, must not be motivated by a desire to bring about the person's death. At first reading, this is confusing: surely, the withdrawal of the treatment will inevitably lead to death. However, the question is whether it is in the person's best interests to remain alive, rather than whether they are better dead. This is a subtle, but meaningful and critical decision (*Airedale NHS Trust v Bland*).

- *Past and present wishes and feelings.* Insofar as they are reasonably ascertainable, account must be taken of the following:
  - any statements made by the person when they had capacity (in particular, any written statements);
  - beliefs and values that would have influenced the person if they had capacity;
  - other factors the person would have considered if they had been able to do so;
  - significant weight must be attached to the person's wishes and feelings, although they are not necessarily decisive (*Re P*).
- *The views of others.* If it is practicable and appropriate, the following people should be consulted:
  - anybody named by the person to be consulted on this matter;
  - anyone engaged in caring for the person, or interested in their welfare;
  - any person acting as a Lasting Power of Attorney (LPA) (see p. 45);
  - any deputy appointed by the Court (see p. 46).

It is important to note that the people listed here have a right to be consulted *on what is in the person's best interest* and *not* on what they personally wish to see happen.

Exercise 2.5

Scenario 1

Mrs P, who is 90 years of age, has been living for the past three years in a nursing home with specialist provision for the mentally infirm. She was transferred there after an assessment of her medical condition. This confirmed that Mrs P was suffering from the early stages of dementia, in that she was unable to retain certain information and showed a tendency to wander when she was a hospital in-patient. The assessment team's recommendation was an immediate secure placement. Mrs P was therefore transferred directly and abruptly from the hospital to the nursing home.

Prior to her assessment, Mrs P had been living with her daughter and son-in-law. She had been widowed early in life and moved to live with her daughter some 40 years previously, ostensibly to help at the time of the birth of her first granddaughter. A second granddaughter was born a few years later and Mrs P settled into the role of housekeeper extraordinaire. She lived for 'the family' and she regularly expressed the wish to die at home. Her only other social contact was with her sisters, who lived some 40 miles away. Mrs P had no outside interests and rarely left the house except in the company of her daughter. She remained physically strong and contributed a great deal to the domestic organization of the home.

The hospital assessment had been arranged by her GP as a result of increasing tension between Mrs P and her daughter. Their relationship had always been close, but Mrs P had recently become aggressive towards her with outbursts of bad temper of increasing regularity. This was affecting her daughter's health and causing family concern.

Mrs P's placement at the nursing home proved misconceived from the outset. Her appearance and demeanour were in sharp contrast to that of most of the other residents, in that she epitomized the 'picture book' grandmother and was very compliant. She told her relatives that the behaviour of some of the other residents frightened her, and she wondered why she was there. What had she done wrong? Why was she being punished? Why could she not go home? Throughout her stay, Mrs P appealed to her family to take her home. Direct answers were side-stepped by suggesting that the doctors were still assessing her.

Some members of staff showed concern and attempted to facilitate her integration by taking her out to a local cafe. Such trips were arranged regularly during the first few weeks but became less frequent and eventually stopped. Her mental faculties deteriorated progressively, to the extent that it is doubtful whether she recognized members of her family. They, in turn, had become increasingly concerned about the standard of care being provided. New clothes were bought for her but she was rarely found to be wearing them. Such issues had been raised with staff, but without any changes in practice.

1. Do you consider the interventions in Mrs P's life to have been appropriate and proportionate? If so, why? If not, why not?
2. Was earlier and better intervention possible in this case?
3. Given her current circumstances, what action might now be appropriate?

Scenario 2

Susan is an adult in her thirties. She is assessed as having 'moderate to severe learning disability'; she also suffers from autism and epilepsy. She is cared for by her widowed father who, allegedly, has a drink problem. This means that he is not always able to provide Susan with the care she needs. A com-

> munity nurse, who visits the home regularly, claims to have witnessed the father punching his daughter in the face on several occasions. Following a case conference, the CSSR is of the opinion that Susan lacks the mental capacity to make a decision on where she should live, as well as on what would be the best care for her. The CSSR also concluded that it would be better for Susan to be in residential care and that any future contact with her father should be supervized. On the other hand, her father claims that he is able to care for her and that this would be the better solution in Susan's best interests (*S v London Borough of Newham*).
>
> Discuss the legal issues and options available to the CSSR. (In order to fully do so, you also need to refer to the discussion on mental health issues, set out in Chapter 6, and the discussion on safeguarding adults, set out in Chapter 7.)

In order to assist in decision-making for people lacking capacity to make decisions, ss.35–41 MCA 2005 provide for advocates to be available in certain circumstances. These are known as Independent Mental Capacity Advocates (IMCAs). The IMCA's role is to ensure that all relevant matters are taken into consideration when making a decision, the views of the person are heard when they can be ascertained, potential conflicts of interests (or, sometimes, ulterior motives) by practitioners and relatives are avoided, and the human rights of the person are at all times respected. The IMCA's independence is crucial, as is their duty to challenge what they see as not being in the best interests of the person. An IMCA *must* be involved where a person who lacks capacity is 'unfriended' (i.e. there is nobody who will represent their interests, or advocate for them), where the decision involves:

- providing, withholding or stopping serious medical treatment;
- moving a person into long-term care in a hospital or care home;
- moving the person to a different hospital or care home.

An IMCA *may* also be involved where there is a safeguarding or protection issue, especially where serious allegations are involved. In this situation, the person need not be unfriended (Williams *et al.* 2013).

Other forms of decision-making

Advance decisions (also known as 'advance directions', or 'living wills') are placed on a statutory footing by ss.24–26 MCA 2005. Section 24 MCA 2005 identifies the key components of an advance decision:

- the person has reached the age of 18 years;
- they have capacity to make the advance decision;
- the advance decision is only effective when the person loses capacity.

An advance decision can only be relied on if:

- the person lacks capacity;
- the proposed treatment is that specified in the advance decision; and
- the circumstances are the same as specified in the advance decision (s.25(4) MCA 2005).

If, after making it, the circumstances and any treatment referred to in the advance decision are present at a time when the person lacks capacity, the treatment should not be carried out.

An advance decision may be oral or written. Obviously, a written advance decision provides better evidence. However, if it applies to life-sustaining treatment it must be in writing and signed by the person making it. Another person must witness the signature. The advance decision must state clearly that it is to apply to the particular form of treatment 'even if life is at risk' (ss. 25(5) and 25(6) MCA 2005).

The wording of s.24 MCA 2005 refers to 'treatment'; this does not include social care decisions. The distinction between the two is sometimes unclear. Food, warmth, shelter and hygiene precautions are all examples of social care. However, artificial nutrition and hydration are medical treatment and, hence, a refusal can be included in an advance decision (*Airedale NHS Trust v Bland*).

The person making the advance decision can withdraw it orally (even if it is written), or in writing, at any time during capacity (s.24(4) MCA 2005). It also ceases to be valid if the person subsequently makes an LPA (see p. 45) that includes giving the attorney the power to decide on treatment anticipated in the advance decision. The MCA 2005 also states that it ceases to be valid if the person 'has done anything else clearly inconsistent with the advance decision remaining his fixed intention'. An example of such an inconsistency is found in case example 2.3.

2.3 HE v A Hospital NHS Trust

case example

In this case, an advance decision stated that the patient, a Jehovah's Witness, was not to receive a blood transfusion even if her life was threatened; she then became engaged to an adherent of Islam. This, alongside other evidence, demonstrated inconsistency with the terms of the advance decision, which meant that it was not valid.

The terms of an advance decision should usually be followed.

Understandably, some doctors are concerned about following advance decisions when they see that they could improve, or even save, the life of the person. To take account of this concern, s.25(4) MCA 2005 provides that an advance decision is not applicable to the treatment in question if:

> there are reasonable grounds for believing that circumstances exist which [the patient] did not anticipate at the time of the advance decision and which would have affected his decision had he anticipated them.

This provides considerable leeway for doctors. Family circumstances may have changed (for example, the arrival of a child or grandchild). The person may have entered a relationship following the making of the advance decision. The medical intervention refused in the advance decision because of the side effects and poor prognosis may now have no lasting side-effects and a very good prognosis.

Lasting Powers of Attorney

The MCA 2005 introduces LPAs. They replace the previous Enduring Power of Attorney, which only applied to property and financial decisions. There are two types of LPA, both of which may be made simultaneously. The first relates to *property* and *financial matters*. The second type relates to *health and welfare matters* (s.9(1) MCA 2005). Unlike a *property and financial* LPA, an LPA concerning *health and welfare matters* can only come into effect if the donor loses capacity. The latter are of greater interest to social work practitioners. The thinking behind an LPA is that, during capacity, a person creates one to empower somebody else to make decisions if they lose capacity. It is essential that the proper forms, provided by the Office of the Public Guardian, are used. Under an LPA, a person can appoint one or more people to act as their attorney. This gives the attorney the power to make legally binding decisions on the person's behalf in the event that they lose their capacity. The attorney may be a relative, friend or a professional. Before it can be invoked, the LPA must be registered with the Office of the Public Guardian. The provisions relating to LPAs are in ss.9–13 MCA 2005.

A number of matters identified in the Code may be included in a *personal welfare LPA*. These matters include:

- where the person making the LPA (known as the 'donor') should live;
- aspects of day-to-day care;
- consent or refusal to medical treatment (if this is to apply to life-sustaining treatment, it must expressly include this) (s.11(8) MCA 2005);
- arranging for the donor to be assessed for community care services, etc.;
- exercising rights to personal information about the donor.
(Department of Constitutional Affairs 2005, para. 7.21).

An LPA may be very specific as to what the attorney can do, or it may be drafted in general terms.

For the social work practitioner, a number of key points should be remembered. First, is the person claiming to be the attorney really an attorney? Second, if they are the attorney, does the LPA actually give them responsibility for making this decision? Has the subject matter of the decision (e.g. moving into residential care) been specifically excluded? Third, social care practitioners should always be alert to the possibility of LPAs being used in an abusive way. Any concerns should be reported through the local safeguarding procedures (see Chapter 7, p. 154). The Office of the Public Guardian has a general supervisory role over the working of LPAs.

> **Exercise 2.6**
>
> Consider whether it is lawful and/or appropriate for a social worker to agree to act as an attorney for one of their service users under a Lasting Power of Attorney?

Court of Protection

The Court of Protection has jurisdiction in matters relating to the MCA 2005. In cases where a person lacks capacity in relation to welfare matters, the Court has the power either to make, by order, a decision on behalf of the person lacking capacity; or to appoint a deputy (s.16 MCA 2005). A deputy may be a relative, friend or a professional (such as, a social worker). However, advice issued by the Department of Justice suggests that the appointment of a social worker should usually be avoided, as it might give rise to a potential conflict of interest (s.16(4)(a) MCA 2005). A decision of the Court is to be preferred to the appointment of a deputy, particularly if it is a single issue (e.g. sterilization s.16(4)(b) MCA 2005). However, there may be circumstances when a series of decisions is required over a period. Understandably, the courts are reluctant to be too involved in the daily decision-making process: to do so would be expensive and would not benefit the individual. In these circumstances, the court may appoint a deputy with responsibility for making the decisions specified in the order. The powers conferred on the deputy should be as limited in scope and duration as is 'reasonably practicable in the circumstances' (s.20(1) MCA 2005).

There are restrictions on the authority of a deputy:

- The deputy cannot make a decision if he or she 'knows or has reason to know' that the person has capacity (s.20(1) MCA 2005).
- The deputy cannot refuse to consent to life-sustaining treatment – decisions of this nature are usually decided by the court (s.20(5) MCA 2005).
- A deputy cannot be given the power to do anything that the person has already given to an attorney under a valid LPA (s.20(4) MCA 2005).

As with an LPA, social work practitioners must check that the person claiming to be a deputy was appointed as such, and that the decision in question falls within the scope of the order of the court.

The implications of the *Bournewood* case

Article 5 of the ECHR states that everyone 'has the right to liberty and security of person. No one shall be deprived of his liberty save in the following cases and in accordance with a procedure prescribed by law'. In the words of the ECHR, the term 'following cases' includes persons of 'unsound mind'. The powers of detention under the MHA 1983 are justified in that they are aimed at people of 'unsound mind', and a procedure exists (the MHA 1983) that prescribes the process and includes safeguards. Of course, people with a mental disorder enter hospital as voluntary or informal patients and, in many cases, that is appropriate. However, what of a person who lacks capacity to enter and remain in hospital? This arose in a case that preceded the MCA 2005: *R v Bournewood Community and Health NHS Trust ex parte L*.

> **2.4 *R v Bournewood Community and Health NHS Trust ex parte L***
>
> *case example*
>
> In the *Bournewood* case, L, who was autistic and had no ability to communicate, was admitted to a mental health unit in a hospital as an informal patient. He had always been incapable of consenting or refusing medical treatment. The hospital decided that there was no need to detain him under the MHA 1983 because he was fully compliant and did not resist admission. The case went to the House of Lords (as it then was) which concluded that he had not been deprived of his liberty because he had not attempted to leave the hospital. The House of Lords said that there was no need to detain him formally as he was an 'informal patient' under s.131 MHA 1983. An informal patient was one who, though lacking capacity to consent, did not object to being in hospital. His treatment and care within hospital could be justified under the doctrine of necessity and was in his best interests. They held that he had not been unlawfully deprived of his liberty.

This decision caused considerable concern for civil liberties organizations, on several grounds. First, it was unreal to think that L was not 'detained'. It is quite likely that if he attempted to leave the hospital, the holding power under s.5 MHA 1983, would have been used to prevent him from leaving (see Chapter 6, p. 126). The idea of a person lacking capacity being 'fully compliant' is nonsensical. Compliance is a very common way of expressing consent; capacity is a prerequisite of compliance-based consent. In addition, there were very few, if any, safeguards in this informal process. Whatever may be said about the compulsory powers under the MHA 1983, it does provide safeguards: stated criteria, fixed periods of detention, statutory review processes and access to the Mental Health Review Tribunal (see Chapter 6, p. 132), which are not available to the informal patient.

With these issues in mind, the case was taken to the European Court of Human Rights as *HL v UK*. The European Court of Human Rights was critical of the House of Lords. On the question as to whether he had been deprived of his liberty, the Court said 'the key factor ... is that the healthcare practitioners treating and managing [the patient] exercised complete and effective control over his care and movements' and 'he was under continuous supervision and control and was not free to leave'. This deprivation of liberty was in breach of Article 5 of the ECHR. His admission was not 'in accordance with a procedure prescribed by law' as required by Article 5 of the ECHR. Furthermore, he was unable to take proceedings to challenge his detention, unlike the situation had he been detained under the MHA 1983.

Deprivation of Liberty Safeguards

The *HL v UK* decision required the United Kingdom to rethink its law on deprivation of liberty. The outcome was the introduction of the Deprivation of Liberty Safeguards (DOLS), added to the MCA 2005 by the MHA 2007. These provide the 'procedure required by law' under Article 5 of the ECHR. In *G v E*, the court said 'it is our view that the MCA 2005 provides a 'procedure prescribed by law' for depriving such persons of their liberty'.

Depriving someone of their liberty is a serious matter, and the decision to do so should not be taken lightly. The deprivation of liberty safeguards make it clear that a person may only be deprived of their liberty when:

- the person lacks the capacity to decide where to live;
- it is in their own best interests to protect them from harm;
- it is a proportionate response to the likelihood and seriousness of the harm; and
- there is no less restrictive alternative.

DOLS may only be used where a person is being, or is about to be, deprived of their liberty either in a care home or in hospital. They cannot be used to deprive a person of their liberty in their own home; this would have to be done using the inherent powers of the Court of Protection (*CC v KK and STCC*).

A deprivation of liberty is different from a restriction on liberty, although the cumulative effect of a number of restrictions may amount to a deprivation. It does not necessarily entail a person being locked in a room or a building. The European Court in *HL v UK* provided some useful indicators of what is a deprivation of liberty:

- The starting-point must be the specific situation of the person concerned.
- Account must be taken of a whole range of factors arising (such as the type, duration, effects and manner of implementation of the measure in question).
- The distinction between a deprivation of, and a restriction on, liberty is one of degree and intensity, and not one of nature or substance.
- Duration of any restrictions is a relevant factor.

As a result, it is important to treat each case on its own merits, rather than make generalizations.

A Code of Practice has been issued under the MCA 2005 (Ministry of Justice 2008). It provides guidance on what practitioners should look for in order to decide whether a person has been deprived of their liberty:

- Restraint is used, including sedation, to admit a person to an institution where that person is resisting admission.
- Staff exercise complete and effective control over the care and movement of a person for a significant period.
- Staff exercise control over assessments, treatment, contacts and residence.
- A decision has been taken by the institution that the person will not be released into the care of others, or permitted to live elsewhere, unless the staff in the institution consider it appropriate.
- A request by carers for a person to be discharged to their care is refused.
- The person is unable to maintain social contacts because of restrictions placed on their access to other people.

It is important to consider what measures have been taken in relation to the individual and when they are required. The period of time is important; very short periods of isolated control may be a restraint, rather than a deprivation. How do the restrictions affect the individual and why are they necessary? What is the purpose of the control (safety of the person, or simply the convenience of the home or hospital)? It might also be important to hear the views of others (e.g. the family). What do they think of what is being done, or what is intended?

When a person has been deprived of their liberty under these provisions, the following safeguards will apply:

- the appointment of a representative to act on behalf of the person;
- a right of challenge to the Court of Protection against any unlawful deprivation of liberty;
- a right for the deprivation of liberty to be reviewed and monitored regularly.

Exercise 2.7

Scenario 1

Jack is living in a care home. He has dementia and has been assessed as lacking capacity to make most of the important decisions in his life, such as where to live, his personal care and his medical treatment. He also lacks capacity to make decisions about his personal safety. He has recently made sporadic efforts to leave the home and, on one occasion, was found going out of the gate onto a busy road. His nephew and partner visit him twice a month. During these visits, he appears to be content and enjoys looking at old family photographs. However, once they leave he becomes agitated and expresses a desire to 'go home'. He is not aggressive, but the staff are concerned how to respond to his behaviour. It has been decided that it is necessary to act to prevent him from coming to harm, particularly when he says he wants to leave the home. The nephew and partner have been told that their visits will have to stop as they are disruptive and increase the likelihood that he will wander. It has also been decided that, from 6.00 pm onwards, he will be locked in his room until morning, with frequent checks to see that he is safe. During the day, he is to be placed in a chair with a restraining strap to prevent him from getting out of it. Staff would be at hand to make sure that he is taken to the toilet when necessary.

One of the staff has said that this plan may constitute a deprivation of liberty and that a DOLS authorization is necessary. Another member of staff has queried whether what is planned is reasonable and whether a deprivation of liberty could be changed into a restriction that would maximize his liberty, yet ensure that he was safe.

What advice would you give the home?

Scenario 2

Mrs Wilson is 81 and has had difficulties with her memory for the past three years. Following an emergency admission to hospital after a fall, she spent over eight weeks on an acute medical ward. During her stay at the hospital, she became incontinent, increasingly immobile, confused, unable or unwilling to feed herself, and occasionally aggressive. The medical tests, including a CT scan, were inconclusive, but the nursing assessments suggested that Mrs Wilson's nursing needs were both complicated and multiple. The discharge team recommended that she should be transferred to a nursing home. Her husband, who is 93, is devoted to his wife but admits that, even with a comprehensive package of care, he would be unable to care for her at home unless her condition became significantly better. He is, himself, suffering from a serious and deteriorating medical condition and, although able to look after himself with family assistance, he also has difficulty retaining information. Indeed, he has been the victim of exploitative financial abuse by door-to-door traders. As a result, his daughter has recently executed a Power of Attorney in relation to both parents.

Mrs Wilson has now been admitted to a nursing home chosen by her family. Her en suite room is well-furnished and she seems to regard her placement as an extension of her hospitalization. She makes only occasional reference to a desire to go home – occasionally to the home in which she lived as a child. Her husband visits daily. He is concerned that there is no improvement in her condition and that she is kept in her room and, occasionally in bed, all day. When questioned about this, the staff explain that Mrs Wilson is often resistant to being dressed and washed, and that she seems content to be in bed. As the bed has cot-sides, Mrs Wilson is not able to leave the bed. The family wonder what medication, if any, is being prescribed and whether Mrs Wilson, in spite of her apparent reluctance, could be encouraged to engage in communal eating and other activities.

1. What advice would you give the family?
2. Would your answer be different if it was confirmed that Mrs Wilson is being prescribed medication to make her compliant and passive?

Conclusion

Whilst the MCA 2005 has been well-received by service users and their carers (Manthorpe *et al.* 2009), there is also evidence to suggest that, in practice, there is little conformity with its provisions. Disappointingly, the evidence suggests that few *'practicable steps'* are taken, other than oral discussion, to assist the individual decision-maker as required in s.1(2) MCA 2005. Also, neither guidance nor training have fully addressed the need for assessment of capacity to be carried out in a culturally sensitive way. Practitioners should be aware of the importance of capacity whilst, at the same time, avoiding stereotypical assumptions based on, for example, age and mental illness.

chapter 3
Referral and Assessment

In this chapter, you will learn about:

- Referrals
- The duty to assess
- The assessment process
- Needs and wants
- Assessment following discharge from hospital
- The single assessment for older people
- Mental health service users
- People with learning disability

Remember to consult The Legal Toolbox on pp. xiii–xx. This will help you to understand processes and procedures referred to in this chapter.

Referrals

Access to social care is by means of a *referral* (which may be a self-referral) to a Council with Social Service Responsibility (CSSR). It is a referral that, where the conditions set out in s.47 National Health and Community Care Act 1990 (NHSCCA 1990) are met, triggers access to an *assessment* of a person's need for one or more social services. As can be seen from Figure 3.1, referrals come from many quarters.

The nature of the *access process* varies from one CSSR to another but, however made, this initial contact is often crucial in influencing the outcome and an individual's later experience of community care support. Although there is a dearth of recent research on how CSSRs respond to referrals, it appears that, where social workers are attached to multidisciplinary teams and/or primary health teams, they are likely to receive a broader range of referrals (Corney and Bowen 1980). CSSRs should be careful neither to make access so difficult as to deny individuals the right

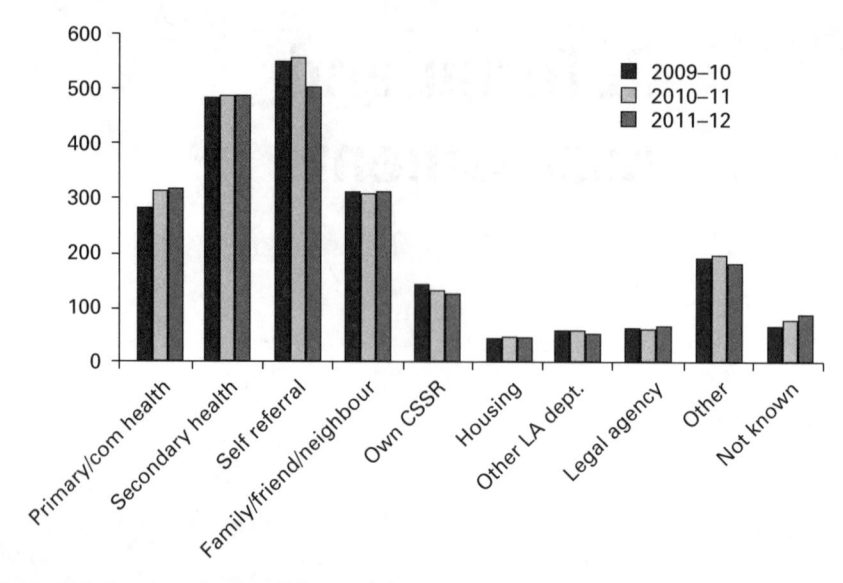

Figure 3.1 Origins of referral for social care services
Source: Health and Social Care Information Centre (2013a).

to an assessment, nor to screen people out of the process inappropriately. It is increasingly common, however, for CSSRs to provide a single access point to social services, or, in some instances, to all local authority services.

'Putting people first' (Department of Health 2010a) discussed the importance of the first contact and highlighted:

> the inexperience of staff making judgements, that people's needs (and the willingness and ability of their carers) are often insufficiently explored, and that people are screened out too early or not given adequate signposting to other sources of support.

The person responsible for the first point of contact must be suitably trained to ensure that they do not screen people out too readily on insufficient information.

Call centres have certain advantages but, in its recent report, the Audit Commission noted:

> Call centres … can save money by reducing the potential demand for formal assessment through providing accurate information and correctly routing enquiries. But they can add to costs if the initial assessment closes down too quickly, or provides inadequate information that leads to poor decisions by people or their carers. This will generate costs later if councils have to intervene in emergencies or when earlier action would have been more cost-effective. (Audit Commission 2012, para. 89)

As will be seen, CSSRs must err on the side of assessing a person, rather than screen them out an early stage. Financial considerations are not relevant to the decision to assess the need for community care services.

In some situations, people may be diverted to a body that is more appropriate. Anecdotally, it seems that a number of calls for social services are queries about social security benefits. The important point to remember is that the initial point of contact should be designed to determine whether the person appears to be in need of community care services; it is not a part of the assessment process.

The duty to assess

One of the few clear – though restricted – rights that exist under community care law is to be found in s.47(1) NHSCCA 1990. This states that:

> where it appears to a local authority that any person for whom they may provide or arrange for the provision of community care services may be in need of any such services, the authority:
>
> (a) shall carry out an assessment of his needs for those services; and
> (b) having regard to the results of that assessment, shall then decide whether his needs call for the provision by them of any such services.

CSSRs may not delegate their assessment duty to another body or person unless a specific arrangement exists under s.75 National Health Service Act 2006, or s.113 Local Government Act 1972. The current assessment process is the outcome of the Griffiths report (Griffiths 1988) which aimed to correct the perverse incentive that had existed since the National Assistance Act 1948 (NAA 1948) in favour of residential care, rather than care in the person's home. The previous situation meant that many people were in state-funded residential care when they could have continued living in their own homes.

The Griffiths report identified a number of shortcomings in the law at that time; these included:

- no real choice between residential and domiciliary care;
- the tendency to concentrate on available services, rather than actual need;
- a near monopolistic supply of community care services by CSSRs;
- inadequate registration and inspection machinery;
- the patchy and uneven development of services.

The government White Paper 'Caring for People: Community Care in the Next Decade and Beyond' (Department of Health 1989) picked up on these concerns and laid down six objectives for a reformed law:

> promoting the development of domiciliary, day and respite care services to enable people to live in their own homes if feasible and sensible;
> ensuring that service providers make practical support for carers a priority;
> making proper assessments of need and good case management the cornerstone of high quality community care services;
> promoting the development of a flourishing independent sector alongside good quality public services;
> clarifying the responsibilities of agencies thus making it easier to hold them to account.

These objectives influenced the drafting of the NHSCCA 1990. However, the legislation failed to tackle the second objective and did little to resolve the problem identified in the final objective. In addition, as will be seen, much of the NHSCCA 1990 relies on the muddle of legislation that has emerged since 1948. In one sense, the NHSCCA 1990 was a radical piece of legislation; in another sense, it was more of the same.

The NHSCCA 1990 does not define 'assessment'; s.47(4) enables the Secretary of State to give directions on how an assessment shall be carried out. These are found in the Community Care Assessment Directions (Department of Health 2004a). The Directions identify a number of key principles:

- the CSSR must consult the person, consider whether the person has any carers and, if appropriate, consult those carers;
- the CSSR must take all reasonable steps to reach agreement with the person and, if appropriate, any carers of that person, on the community care services that they are considering providing to meet their needs;
- the CSSR must provide information to the person and, if appropriate, any carers of that person, about the amount of the payment (if any) that the person will be liable to make in respect of the community care services which they are considering providing to him.

Although s.47 NHSCCA 1990 appears to provide an unqualified right to be assessed, there are two restrictions:

- It must *appear* to the CSSR that the person *may be in need of services*;
- The *apparent need* must be for *community care services* and not for any other type of service. Community care services are defined by s.46(3) NHSCCA 1990 (see Chapter 4, p. 69).

The right to an assessment is a free-standing right. Anyone who fits the criteria set out in s.47 is entitled to an assessment regardless of whether they will be eligible for any services. The fact that the CSSR will not provide any services because the person's financial means exceed the maximum amount allowed does not deny a person the right to an assessment. A person who will be self-funding still falls within s.47. An assessment is helpful for self-funders and their families as they can use it to help purchase appropriate services.

A CSSR cannot refuse to assess somebody because it thinks that it will not be able to afford to provide any services the person may need. To do this would be unlawful.

> **case example**
>
> ### 3.1 *R v Bristol City Council ex parte Penfold*
>
> In the case of *Penfold*, the High Court held that it was unlawful to sift out assessments where there was no likelihood of the CSSR meeting any of the needs. There was benefit in assessing someone even though there was no hope of services being provided; an assessment would provide a clearer understanding of unmet needs.

What is the threshold for deciding whether a duty to assess arises? The section does not impose a high threshold – it says when a person 'may be in need of any such services'. A CSSR should err on the side of assessment if there is some evidence of current or imminent need. However, a need that may arise in the future should not be too remote or speculative. For example, a person could not expect an assessment if they think that, in five years' time, they will be of an age that they may need services. This point was also emphasized in the *Penfold* case (see above).

> **Exercise 3.1**
>
> Identify three situations where a person 'may appear' to be in need of community care services.

The assessment process

'Putting people first' (Department of Health 2010a) provides helpful guidance on the assessment process. The first point to recognize is that the purpose of an assessment is to:

> identify and evaluate an individual's presenting needs and how these needs impose barriers to that person's independence and/or well-being. Information derived from an individual's assessment

> should be used to inform decisions on eligibility. (Department of Health 2010a, para.78)

The importance of listening to the person is emphasized in the guidance. It states:

> The assessment process should be person-centred throughout and also consider the wider family context. Councils should recognise that individuals are the experts on their own situation and encourage a partnership approach, based on a person's aspirations and the outcomes they wish to achieve, rather than what they are unable to do. Professionals should fully involve the person seeking support by listening to their views about how they want to live their lives and the type of care and support that best suits them and by helping them to make informed choices. This includes identifying the support the person needs to make a valued contribution to their community. (Department of Health 2010a, para. 83)

In carrying out an assessment, it is important to be aware of the person's family context, and of any other individuals who may be affected by the process and its outcome. It is also important to consider the possible significance of the person's cultural background and such issues as their language needs. The characteristics of an individual relevant to the assessment process include their mental capacity and whether they appear to be suffering from a mental disorder. Such issues should be borne in mind throughout the assessment process (see Figure 3.2). As a

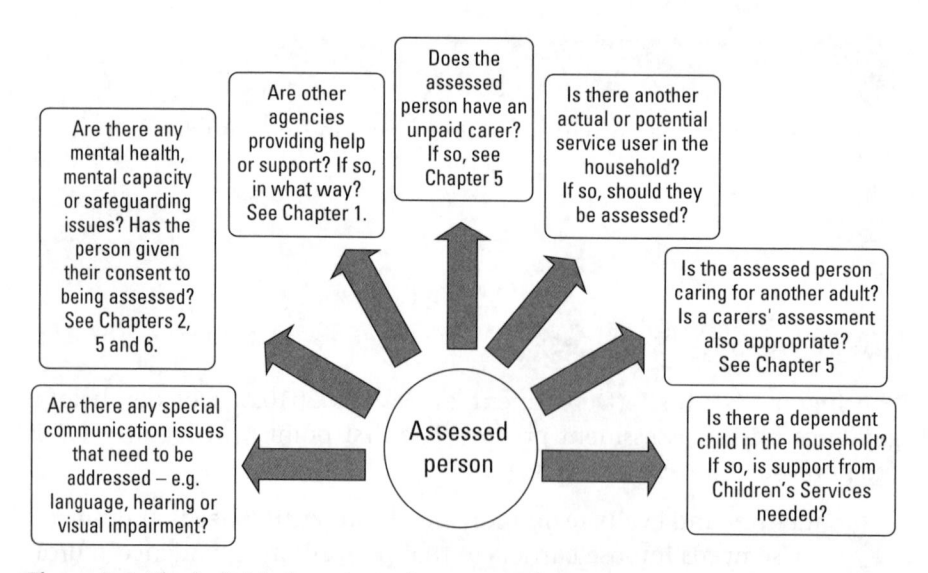

Figure 3.2 The individual context of an assessed person

result, it may become necessary to defer the completion of the assessment in order that such matters can be taken into account, and also whether other practitioners and agencies are, or should be, involved in the person's case.

> **Exercise 3.2**
>
> The importance of language in relation to such issues as identity formation and social interaction, as well as communication, is well-documented.
>
> 1. To what extent, if any, do you consider that a service user from an ethnic minority background has a right to receive an assessment in the language of their choice?
> 2. What are the practical implications for a CSSR in meeting such a request?
>
> (Pugh and Williams 2006).

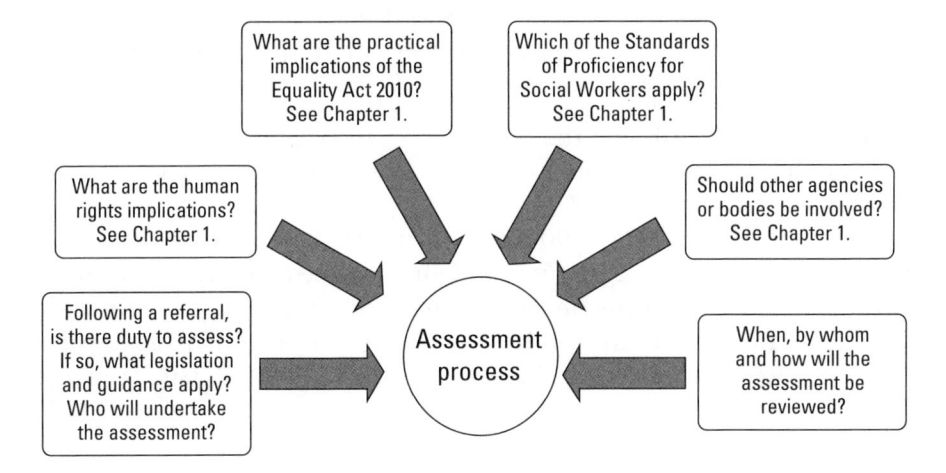

Figure 3.3 The broader context of making an assessment

It is also important, in carrying out an assessment, to bear in mind other relevant legislation and guidance (see Figure 3.3). These can include the Human Rights Act 1998 (HRA 1998) (see Chapter 1, p. 7), the Equality Act 2010 (EA 2010) (see Chapter 1, p. 13), and the Standards of Proficiency for social workers (see Chapter 1, p. 23).

Needs and wants

Need is a difficult word to define in the context of social care. The dictionary definition of need is 'of necessity, necessarily, unavoidably'

(*Oxford English Dictionary* 2011). At a very general level, we 'need' hydration and nutrition; we need warmth; we need clothes; we need social interaction. However, the extent to which those 'needs' should be met, or can be met, through publicly funded social care intervention is less clear. Furthermore, the way in which any needs are met through social care is also complex and often controversial. What is clear, however, is that the word 'need' in its everyday sense has to be adapted or reconstructed to reflect the legal context within which it is used. We have to think in terms not only of 'need', but also 'legal need'. This can be seen in the use of the terms 'presenting need' and 'eligible need' in the guidance.

The revised guidance on eligibility criteria published by the Department of Health distinguishes between:

> *Presenting need* – that is, 'issues and support needs' identified when people contact or are referred to a CSSR social services department.
>
> *Eligible needs* – that is, any presenting needs that come within the CSSR's eligibility criteria. The authority will meet these needs after taking resources into consideration. (Department of Health 2010a, para. 47)

This distinction reinforces the requirement to separate resource considerations from the assessment process – assessment and eligibility are different.

Although the NHSCCA 1990 refers to 'need', that does not mean that the *preferences* or *wants* of the person being assessed are irrelevant. In *R v North Yorkshire CC ex parte Hargreaves*, the CSSR's failure to take into consideration the views of the service user was held to be unlawful, particularly as this was in breach of the existing guidance issued by the Secretary of State under s.7 Local Authority Social Services Act 1970 (LASSA 1970). Preferences do not necessarily have to be accommodated, but taking them into consideration is central to the assessment process.

Need is not confined to material need. In *R v Avon CC ex parte M* the court had to consider whether 'need' included psychological need. It held that it did:

> The law is clear. The council have to provide for the applicant's needs. Those needs may properly include psychological needs. Where they do, it is not right to describe the payment in meeting those needs as 'forcing the authority to pay more than the usual amount it would be prepared to pay for the individual concerned'. The authority would simply be paying what the law required, and not being forced to pay more. (see pp. 271–2)

Exercise 3.3

Scenario

Two sisters have lived together in the family home all their lives. Following an assessment by the CSSR, it is recommended that one of the sisters should enter a residential care home. She has been offered a place in a care home 30 miles away. There are currently no vacancies in a home which is nearer than that. The public transport system is poor and the care home is not on a direct bus route from the family home. The sister remaining at home also has mobility problems. In responding to the CSSR offer, the two sisters say that they need to be close to each other and to see each other on a daily basis as they have done all of their lives. The CSSR argues that this is not a 'need' but, rather, a 'desire or preference'. Furthermore, they say that they are unable to offer a placement nearer the family home.

1. Do you consider that the sisters' request is based on a need or is it simply a want or desire?
2. What other legislation is relevant in determining this issue?

Confusingly, s.47 NHSCCA 1990 is not the only means by which a person may be assessed for community care services. Section 4 Disabled Persons (Services, Consultation and Representation) Act 1986 (DP(SCR)A 1986) requires that when requested either by a 'disabled person', or by a person who provides a disabled person with a 'substantial amount of care on a regular basis' (other than somebody employed to do so), a CSSR must decide whether the disabled person's needs require services under s.2(1) Chronically Sick and Disabled Persons Act (CSDPA 1970). Implicit in this provision is the need to assess the person. So, a disabled person, or their unpaid carer, may request an assessment under the DP(SCR)A 1986 alongside any right they may have to an assessment under the NHSCCA 1990. Assessments of unpaid carers are discussed in Chapter 5.

To add to the confusion, if, when assessing a person under s.47(2) NHSCCA 1990 it appears to the CSSR that the person is 'disabled', it must then make a decision as to what services are required under s.4 DP(SCR)A 1986. The person does not have to request that the DP(SCR)A 1986 is used. They must be informed by the CSSR of their rights under that Act.

The rationale for this dual system, if ever there were one, is now lost in time. In its White Paper 'Caring for our future: reforming care and support' (Department of Health 2012a), the government proposes a single duty to assess. Section 9 of the Care Act 2014 imposes a duty to assess 'where it appears to a local authority that an adult may have needs for care and support'. This would be a very welcome reform.

What happens if the person refuses to be assessed? Does this mean that the CSSR is relieved of its duty under s.47 NHSCCA 1990, or s.4 DP(SCR)A 1986? The law is unclear on this matter. The wording of s.47 NSHCCA 1990 imposes a duty so, arguably, the existence of that duty does not depend on the permission of the person. However, two difficulties arise. First, is it possible to undertake a proper assessment if the person refuses to participate or, indeed, is hostile? Second, even though an assessment may be undertaken in such circumstances, services could not be imposed on the person without their permission. The Court of Appeal in *R v Kensington and Chelsea Royal Borough Council ex parte Kujtim* said that 'the duty of the local authority is not absolute in the sense that it has a duty willy-nilly to provide such accommodation regardless of the applicant's willingness to take advantage of it'.

The government White Paper (Department of Health 2012a) recommends that the CSSR should be relieved of its duty to assess if the person refuses an assessment, unless they lack capacity to make that decision and an assessment is in their best interests. Under Clause 11 of the Care Act 2014, it is proposed that an assessment should be undertaken if the person who is refusing is experiencing, or at risk of experiencing, abuse or neglect.

Assessment following discharge from hospital

A report by BUPA highlights concern over the ability of current residential care provision to meet the needs of an ageing population (BUPA 2011). It points out that some 81,000 care home places could be lost by 2020 at the same time as demand is likely to increase by 18,000. This would lead to a loss of almost 100,000 care home places. A consequence may be that an increased number of older people will have to be admitted to hospital, thus placing greater pressure on the NHS. This is (unfortunately) often referred to as 'bed blocking'.

Setting aside the pressures on the NHS, keeping a person in hospital longer than is necessary is an attack on their dignity and autonomy. However, discharge from hospital may be delayed because the necessary community or residential care has not been arranged. This has resulted in a great deal of finger-pointing with health bodies accusing CSSRs of failing to act with sufficient urgency to make arrangements for community care services. CSSRs point out that they have inadequate financial resources to make the necessary arrangements. Amidst considerable political concern, the Community Care (Delayed Discharges etc.) Act 2003 (CC(DD)A 2003) was introduced. This Act introduced a new system whereby CSSRs will be responsible for the costs of keeping a person in hospital if discharge is delayed by their failure to make arrangements for community care services.

The CC(DD)A 2003 was based, in part, on the thinking behind reforms in Sweden that provided financial incentives to reduce delayed discharges (Styrborn 1995).

This is only one of the reasons for delays in discharge, however. Bryan's study of delayed discharge found that:

> delayed transfers could occur at any stage in the discharge process, but that the main bottlenecks were associated with gaining approval for public financing of social care services, securing placements in residential care homes, resolving family disputes over possible arrangements and arranging both NHS sub-acute beds or domiciliary care assistance. The sheer complexity and bureaucracy involved in the discharge process was an overriding concern and an important contributory factor to delays that occur. (Bryan 2010)

The policy behind the CC(DD)A 2003 as stated in the CSSR circular that was issued following its introduction was to:

> strengthen joint working and encourage clear and timely communication with new statutory duties on the NHS and councils;
> improve assessment and provision of community care services for people in hospital by introducing financial incentives; and
> encourage development of new service capacity which can facilitate patient transfer to community settings which promote independence or prevent unnecessary admission. (Department of Health 2003)

The CC(DD)A 2003 imposes a charge on CSSRs if a care package is not in place when the patient is deemed fit to be discharged from hospital. It applies to a patient referred to in the Act as a 'qualifying hospital patient'. A qualifying patient is a patient in an NHS hospital (or an independent hospital funded by the NHS) who is receiving acute care; it does not include privately-funded treatment. Acute care is defined as intensive medical treatment provided by a consultant for a limited time, after which the patient no longer benefits from it. It does not include maternity care, mental health care or palliative care.

An initial responsibility on the hospital is to assess whether the patient meets the criteria for NHS funded continuing care. If the patient meets the criteria, the delayed discharge provisions do not apply. NHS continuing health care is a package of care that is funded and arranged by the NHS. It may be provided in a number of different settings and these include a person's own home, or a care home. In order to qualify for continuing health care, the person must have a 'primary health need'. In assessing a person, the nature of the needs, their intensity, complexity and unpredictability will be considered. If a person has eligible continuing health care needs, the NHS must meet them without charge (Department of Health 2012b).

If the patient is not eligible for continuing NHS-funded care, then under s.2 CC(DD)A 2003, the hospital must give notice to the CSSR in whose area the patient is ordinarily resident at the time. If the patient does not appear to have an ordinary residence (e.g. he or she is a traveller), the notice must be given to the CSSR in whose area the hospital is situated. The notice must inform the CSSR that the patient may need community care services if they are to be discharged safely. Before doing this, the hospital must consult the patient and any known carer of the patient, if it is practicable to do so (s.2 CC(DD)A 2003). The importance of encouraging patients to be involved cannot be over-emphasized. One study suggests there is scope for improving the involvement of patients in planning their discharge from hospital (Swinkels and Mitchell 2009). Research shows that some patients do not participate because of the perceived expertise of professionals and disempowerment resulting from poor health, low mood, dependency, lack of information and the complexities of the discharge processes.

The giving of notice by the hospital is important, as the CSSR has no duty to monitor a patient who is in hospital in order to see whether they might need a s.47 NHSCCA 1990 assessment (*R (on the application of B) v Camden London Borough Council and others*. Once notice has been given, the CSSR is required to carry out an assessment of the patient's needs 'with a view to identifying any community care services that need to be made available in order for it to be safe to discharge' them. After consulting with the hospital, it must then decide which of those services it will provide for the patient on discharge. Similarly, the CSSR must assess any carer where they request an assessment, or have in the previous twelve months of the date of the notice, or at any time since that date, asked for a carer's assessment under s.1 Carers and Disabled Children Act 2000 (CDCA 2000) (see Chapter 5, p. 103). The purpose of the carer's assessment is to identify services that may be provided for the carer in order to achieve a safe discharge. The assessment of carers is discussed more fully in Chapter 5.

The hospital must then notify the CSSR of the date on which it proposes to discharge the patient. The delayed discharge regulations require the hospital to give at least one day's notification of the discharge (see r.7 and Schedule 1 Community Care (Delayed Discharges etc.) Act (Qualifying Services) (England) Regulations 2003. It may be withdrawn because, for example, the patient's condition worsens and discharge is no longer appropriate. If the notice is withdrawn, then the CSSR is no longer liable to pay under the scheme (s.5 CCDDA 2003). The CSSR will be liable to pay a daily rate (£100 or £150 depending on the area) if discharge is delayed in the following circumstances:

- the patient has not been discharged and the CSSR has not complied with its duty to carry out the assessment and decide what community care services should be made available (s.6(2)(a) CC(DD)A 2003); or
- it is not possible to discharge the patient because:
  □ the CSSR has not made available the services it has assessed the patient as needing in order to achieve a safe discharge; and/or
  □ the CSSR has not made available services for the carer which it assessed them as needing in order to achieve a safe discharge (s.6(2)(b) CC(DD)A 2003).

It is debatable whether the CC(DD)A 2003 has been successful in reducing the number of delayed discharges. It should be noted that that the imposition of the charge is not compulsory; hospitals can decide not to impose it. There is evidence that not many hospitals choose to impose the charge and, instead, work collaboratively with CSSRs to reduce or prevent delays (Godden *et al.* 2009). The study by Godden *et al.* identified a reduction in delayed discharges, but this predated the CC(DD)A 2003. It found that bed-days lost in 2006/07 because of delayed discharges accounted for only 1.6 per cent of all bed-days. It was also found that 68 per cent of delays were attributed to the NHS and not to CSSRs. It is also possible that delayed discharges cause problems elsewhere in the NHS (Clover 2013).

> **Exercise 3.4**
>
> Wales has chosen not to introduce the charging provisions for delayed discharges from hospital. In the light of the discussion in the preceding section, do you consider this decision to be wise or unwise?

The single assessment process for older people

Guidance and advice has been issued in relation to the assessment of specific client groups. Practitioners need to be aware of such specialist provisions and of their legal status. Some guidance is issued under s.7 LASSA 1970 (see Chapter 1). Other guidance is not issued under s.7 and its precise legal status is unclear. In 2001, the National Service Framework for Older People set out a number of standards designed to ensure fair, high-quality, integrated health and social care services for older people

(Department of Health 2001a: i). Standard 2 aims to 'ensure that older people are treated as individuals and they receive appropriate and timely packages of care which meet their needs as individuals, regardless of health and social services boundaries', and also to ensure that:

> NHS and social care services treat older people as individuals and enable them to make choices about their own care. This is achieved through the single assessment process, integrated commissioning arrangements, and integrated provision of services, including community equipment and continence services. (Department of Health 2001a: 23)

Standard 2 seeks to address one of the most basic problems in delivering care to people; namely, the divide between social services and health care. As has been discussed (p. 55), the White Paper *Caring for People: Community Care in the Next Decade and Beyond* (Department of Health 1989) identified the need to clarify responsibilities between agencies as one of its priorities. Achieving greater integration has been notoriously difficult to achieve, particularly between health and social care (Henderson 2012). A number of reasons may be suggested. Structural reasons are often put forward – the NHS provides health care whereas CSSRs provide social care. Budgets are distinct and each agency will seek to transfer responsibilities to other agencies to reduce costs. Cultures are different, in part stemming from different training. The language used is different – 'patient' and 'service user' (Community Care 2005). However, despite these difficulties there are some good examples of interdisciplinary working; for example, in Community Mental Health Teams (Lymbery and Postle 2007: 150–2; Cole 2012).

The single assessment process (SAP) is designed to facilitate greater inter-agency working. It is rare for a person's needs to fall neatly into one or other category. In addition, during an assessment people may have to provide the same information to different agencies. Not only is this wasteful of resources, it also adds to the stress imposed on the person being assessed. Agencies may be reluctant to share information, sometimes based on misunderstandings of data protection law or confidentiality. This may lead to the provision of poorer care. The Guidance notes that:

> many frail older people will have numerous separate assessments per year with the majority of the information being repeated on each assessment. The single assessment process will help to minimise this unnecessary duplication, while allowing a full assessment to be built up over time. It will also reduce paperwork by providing a single assessment summary (preferably based on electronic records) for health and social care. (Department of Health 2002: 3)

The SAP must be supported by commissioning arrangements and service provisions that are integrated across agencies. Arguments about who should be responsible for undertaking a particular task should not delay assessment, neither should it delay the provision of services. The Department of Health Guidance identifies a number of stages in the process:

(i) Publishing information about services
(ii) Contact assessment, including the collection of basic personal information. This may, in some cases, be all that is necessary.
(iii) Overview assessment – which is more detailed
Specialist assessment – where a specific need, such as a health problem is present
(iv) Comprehensive assessment – which is likely to consider such issues as: personal care and hygiene, disease prevention, safety, mental health, and senses such as sight, hearing and communication
(v) Evaluating assessment information
(iv) Deciding what help should be offered, including:
eligibility decisions
care planning
monitoring
reviewing.
(Department of Health 2002: 4)

Mental health services users

Another of the client groups for which guidance exists consists of individuals who suffer from a mental disorder. As with all those who satisfy the statutory definition of 'disabled' (see Chapter 1, p. 18), they qualify for a community care assessment under s.47 NHSCCA 1990. In addition, however, those who have received, or are receiving, secondary services (i.e. specialist mental health services) may also qualify for additional support and services on the basis of the care programme approach (CPA) (Department of Health 2008a). Eligibility for the programme will not be triggered by a specific statutory provision, but those subject to guardianship or to a Community Treatment Order (CTO) will be presumed to fall within this guidance (see Chapter 6, p. 130). It sets out the general considerations to be taken into account when considering whether an individual qualifies for the programme. These include such issues as:

- severe mental disorder (including personality disorder) with a high degree of clinical complexity;
- a current or potential risk (such as suicide, self-harm or harm to others);

- a current or significant history of severe distress/instability or disengagement;
- the presence of non-physical co-morbidity;
- multiple service provision from different agencies;
- a current or recent detention under the provisions of the MHA 1983, or referral to a crisis/home treatment team;
- significant reliance on carer(s), or having significant caring responsibilities;
- experiencing disadvantage or difficulty as a result of such issues as parenting responsibilities or unsettled accommodation/housing issues.

People with learning disability

The original specific provision for people with learning disability had relatively limited impact on the life of adults with learning disability, and the services they received remained patchy in quality (Joint Committee on Human Rights 2008). The current guidance 'Valuing people now' (Department of Health 2010b) is supported by a delivery plan identifying a number of priorities. Learning Disability Partnership Boards exist in every CSSR to ensure that the provision for people with learning disability is embedded within each authority by improving planning and commissioning across all services. The plan also acknowledges the insufficient awareness of the particular needs of people with learning disabilities from minority ethnic communities.

Conclusion

Prompt and effective assessment is the key to ensuring good practice; the challenge for social workers is how to reconcile the identified legal needs with the management and provision of community care service entitlement (see Chapter 4). The process of assessment is, of itself, a form of intervention (Payne 2009) and, as such, must be carried out sensitively and within the parameters set out in the relevant law. The confusion that may result from overlapping guidance adds to the social work challenge but, by putting people first and by giving individuals the benefit of any reasonable doubt, practitioners are able to comply with the law in a manner that is consistent with their professional values and most likely lead to optimum outcomes.

chapter 4
Community Care Services

In this chapter, you will learn about:

- Determining the need for community care services
- Eligibility criteria – fair access to care
- The provision of community care services
- The legal definition of community care services
- The nature of community care services
- The delivery of community care services
- The role of the voluntary sector
- The role of the private sector
- Direct payments
- Changes since the Community Care (Direct Payments) Act 1996
- Direct payments, capacity and mental disorder
- Making use of direct payments
- Person-centred planning
- Personal budgets
- Registration and regulation
- Care Quality Commission
- Paying for domiciliary care
- Paying for residential care
- Self-funders
- Issues of choice
- Proposals for change

Remember to consult The Legal Toolbox on pp. xiii–xx. This will help you to understand processes and procedures referred to in this chapter.

Determining the need for community care services

How does a CSSR determine whether to provide services for a person who has been assessed? If services are to be provided, what is their nature and extent? The case of *R v Gloucestershire County Council and another ex parte Barry* discussed s.2 Chronically Sick and Disabled Persons Act (CSDPA 1970) (although its discussion of 'need' has a wider application).

4.1 *R v Gloucestershire County Council and another ex parte Barry*

case example

In this case, B, who was 79 years of age and severely disabled, lived alone in his own home and had no contact with his family. In 1992, Gloucestershire CSSR assessed his needs. Services were then provided under s.2(1) CSDPA 1970: namely, home care help twice a week for shopping, collecting his pension, laundry and cleaning, and meals on wheels four days a week. Under s.2(1) CSDPA 1970 if a local authority is satisfied that it is necessary to make arrangements in order to meet the needs of a chronically sick or disabled person, it was the 'duty of that authority to make those arrangements'. In 1994, the CSSR told B that it would no longer be able to provide services to meet his full needs as assessed because it had suffered a cut of £2.5 million in its budget.

B sought a judicial review of the decision, claiming the authority acted unlawfully in withdrawing the services without first reassessing his needs. The court refused the application, holding that, in carrying out a reassessment, the local authority was entitled to take into account available resources. B appealed to the Court of Appeal, arguing that 'needs' depended on the nature and extent of the disability; they could not be affected by the local authority's ability to pay for them otherwise its duty would become a mere power. The Court of Appeal declared that, in assessing whether it was necessary to make arrangements in order to meet B's needs, the authority was not entitled to take account of the resources available to it. Gloucestershire appealed to the House of Lords.

The House of Lords allowed the appeal. It held that a person's need for services could not be identified in a vacuum – regard had to be given to the ability of the authority to pay for them. B argued that his 'needs' had not changed since he was first assessed in 1992, therefore the obligation under s.2 CSDPA 1970 remained in place despite the cuts in central government funding. Gloucestershire argued that, in deciding what his needs were in 1994, they were entitled to take account of the reduction in funding. The House of Lords decided that resources were relevant in identifying any need that should be met, but that need should be measured against an agreed local eligibility criteria, which takes account of the budget.

The result of this decision is that a person may, in everyday language, be in 'need' of something, but this does not necessarily mean that they have a 'need' that should be met by the CSSR. In assessing an applicant's need for a service, the degree of that need, and the necessity to make arrangements to meet it, they had to balance:

- the severity of the applicant's disabling condition against
- the cost of the arrangements, and
- the availability of resources.

The ability to take account of resources in assessing need under the CSDPA 1970 appears to undermine the purpose of the section; on the face of it, the section states that if a person has a need and it is necessary to meet that need, then the need must be met. Lord Nicholls in the House of Lords said that a CSSR must exercise its functions in a responsible manner. He pointed out that, during the argument before the court:

> some emphasis was placed upon a submission that if a local authority may properly take its resources into account in the way I have described, the s.2(1) duty would in effect be limited to making arrangements to the extent only that the authority should decide to allocate money for this purpose. The duty, it was said, would collapse into a power. I do not agree. A local authority must carry out its functions under s.2.(1) in a responsible fashion. In the event of a local authority acting with *Wednesbury* unreasonableness ... a disabled person would have a remedy. (For *Wednesbury* unreasonableness, see p. 167.)

So, if the person's needs were such that a failure to meet them would put that person at risk of death or serious injury, the CSSR would not be able to claim that it did not have a duty to provide services. No reasonable CSSR would turn its back on a person in that situation.

Despite this limitation, the decision is not a welcome one for those who believe that people should have rights within the social care system. One consequence of the decision was that CSSRs devised eligibility criteria in order to demonstrate that the allocation of social care resources was done as fairly and transparently as possible (Schwehr 1997). At first, each authority devised its own eligibility criteria. This resulted in fragmentation. The government's White Paper 'Modernising Social Services' was critical of this. It states that:

> Decisions about who gets services and who does not are often unclear, and vary from place to place. Eligibility criteria are getting ever tighter and are excluding more and more people who would benefit from help but who do not come into the most dependent categories. Decisions about care can still be service driven, and concentrate on doing things for people according to what is available, rather than tailoring services to the needs of

individuals and encouraging those who are helped to do what they can for themselves. (Department of Health 1998)

> **Exercise 4.1**
> 1. Do you think that the Gloucestershire decision is a reasonable one?
> 2. Is there a rational basis for CSSRs having eligibility criteria in determining the need for community care services for an individual?

Eligibility criteria

In an attempt to achieve great uniformity and to avoid creating a postcode lottery on social care, the government introduced guidance in 2003 on eligibility criteria for community care. This was designed to assist CSSRs to devise and implement criteria that met those concerns. These criteria are now found in guidance issued by the Department of Health (Department of Health 2010a). This replaces earlier guidance in use since 2002 and incorporates a number of changes. First, assessments were now to be outcome-based, rather than needs-based; that is, to relate to the desired outcome of the provision of a service. Second, the emphasis was now on personalization and support planning, rather than care planning. This fits in with the personalization approach to social care (see p. 84).

A number of key messages are included in the revised guidance. There is now an explicit emphasis on:

- rights, anti-discrimination, and social inclusion;
- self-assessment;
- early information on resource allocation to assist self-directed support, personalized budgets, and the management of risk;
- importance of first contact;
- community wellbeing; and
- information-sharing between agencies.

In undertaking an assessment under the revised guidance, two aspects of risk must be considered. It is essential that practitioners work within their CSSR adult safeguarding procedure; it is also necessary to use the CSSR risk assessment procedures in assessing the nature and degree of risk. Compliance with CSSR procedures is essential and practitioners must be aware of the dangers of working outside them.

The eligibility criteria constitute a single process designed to determine eligibility for social care support. In deciding whether somebody is eligible for services, risks to independence in the short, medium and long term must be considered. It also requires that local budgetary considerations are taken into consideration; increasingly, the criteria are being used to allocate scarce resources at a time of rising demand. Although the context within which the revised guidance operates is different, (e.g. the development of personalized budgets), the criteria remain the same as they were under the old guidance. Four bands are identified: critical, substantial, moderate and low; each band has its own set of criteria (see Table 4.1).

A number of general points should be made concerning the application of the criteria. In the first place, it requires practitioners to make a professional judgement about where within the criteria a person should be placed. This may result in professional disagreement, which practitioners should discuss and seek to resolve (see Chapter 1, p. 24).

The wording of each band is important. Note, for example, that the *critical* band uses words such as 'vital' and 'serious'. The *substantial* band softens the language a little and uses words such as *partial*, *majority* and *many aspects*. The *moderate* band refers to 'several aspects', whereas in the low band reference is made to 'one or two'. It is important to appreciate the changes in wording and to use the language of the criteria band to justify the conclusion. It is also important to note that not every need that a person may have will fall within one category. Some of a person's needs may be *critical*, whereas others may be *low*. What matters is the overall assessment of the person.

Each band uses the term 'cannot or will not be sustained'. An assessment is not merely a snapshot of the situation on the day of the assessment. For example, in a situation where an unpaid carer is struggling to cope because of their own ill health or disability, it would be inappropriate to conclude that all is well simply because on the day of the assessment everything was working reasonably well. The situation may be very fragile and could collapse overnight. Unless some support is given to the carer, the person being cared for is placed at an unacceptable risk.

As will be seen in this chapter, other significant changes are taking place in the provision of community care services and are designed to maximize choice and control by service users. In addition, the future funding of community care is being discussed at a political level, following the publication of the Dilnot report on fair funding (Dilnot *et al.* 2011). The Law Commission's report on adult social care also makes a number of proposals for change (Law Commission 2011).

Assessments will try to predict needs and identify outcomes. They will always be subject to review and, if necessary, to amendments. The guidance recognizes that needs are likely to change over a period of time, and the timing of any review should be agreed with the service user and, where appropriate, their carer. It states that reviews should (see p. 75):

Table 4.1 Criteria used for the allocation of resources for the vulnerable elderly

Critical band: - **Life is, or will be, threatened**; and/or - **Significant** health problems have developed or will develop; and/or - There is, or will be, **little or no** choice and control over **vital** aspects of the immediate environment; and/or - **Serious** abuse or neglect has occurred or will occur; and/or - There is, or will be, an inability to carry out **vital** personal care or domestic routines; and/or - **Vital** involvement in work, education or learning cannot, or will not, be sustained; and/or - **Vital** social support systems and relationships cannot, or will not, be sustained; and/or - **Vital** family and other social roles and responsibilities cannot, or will not, be undertaken
Substantial band: - There is, or will be, only **partial** choice and control over the immediate environment; and/or - **Abuse or neglect** has occurred, or will occur; and/or - There is, or will be, an inability to carry out the **majority** of personal care or domestic routines; and/or - Involvement in **many aspects** of work, education or learning cannot, or will not, be sustained; and/or - The **majority** of social support systems and relationships cannot, or will not, be sustained; and/or - The **majority** of family and other social roles and responsibilities cannot, or will not, be undertaken
Moderate band: - There is, or will be, an inability to carry out **several** personal care or domestic routines; and/or - Involvement in **several** aspects of work, education or learning cannot, or will not, be sustained; and/or - Social support systems and relationships cannot, or will not, be sustained; and/or - **Several** family and other social roles and responsibilities cannot or will not be undertaken
Low band: - There is, or will be, an inability to carry out **one or two** personal care or domestic routines; and/or - Involvement in **one or two** aspects of work, education or learning cannot, or will not, be sustained; and/or - **One or two** social support systems and relationships cannot, or will not, be sustained; and/or - **One or two** family and other social roles and responsibilities cannot, or will not, be undertaken

> Establish whether the outcomes identified in the support plan are being met though current arrangements.
> Consider whether the needs and circumstances of the service user and/or their carer(s) have changed.
> Support people to review their personal goals and consider what changes if any should be made to the support plan to better facilitate the achievement of agreed outcomes.
> Ensure that the risk assessment recorded in the care plan is up to date and identify any further action that needs to be taken to address issues relating to risk.
> Demonstrate a partnership approach across agencies and with the service user as well as their family and friends if they choose.
> Support people to strengthen their informal support networks.
> Support people to increase their productive role in their community.
> Help determine the service user's continued eligibility for support.
> The outcome of any review must be recorded and shared with the service user. (Department of Health 2010a, paras 141–51)

Exercise 4.2

Consider the application of the eligibility criteria to the following situations:

Scenario 1

Mr A, a 35-year-old man described as having mild learning disability, is living alone in a one-bedroom flat. His parents have supported him until recently but are now feeling too old and frail to continue. There is concern that Mr A is socially isolated, has no daytime occupation and has limited independence skills. He cannot use public transport but is able to make his way on foot around his locality, including visiting his parents who live a mile away. He can prepare simple meals but is not adept at using either a cooker or a washing machine and, until recently, his mother did most of his domestic chores, including providing a cooked meal each day. Mr A manages his own money but, again, this has been with considerable parental support. Mr A has expressed the wish to move back to his parents' home as he is lonely and afraid that they are abandoning him. His parents cannot agree to this, which has caused friction in their relationship. Mr A has now started to be uncooperative in his behaviour.

Scenario 2

Mr C is a 62-year-old man with severe learning and physical disabilities. He uses a wheelchair and needs a hoist and tracking for personal care. He lives in a specialist nursing home and has regular contact with his parents, who live nearby and take him out on family visits. His parents want Mr C to attend church every Sunday but are unable to take him themselves. The nursing home cannot provide staff to facilitate such attendance unless the fees are increased to provide for this additional one-to-one support. Mr C needs two-to-one support for personal care and one-to-one support for feeding. The remainder of the time he has support on the basis of two staff to five residents.

Scenario 3

Mr I is aged 36 and lives alone. He has both a learning and physical disability. His marriage broke down six months ago and, since that time, he has had trouble maintaining the cleanliness of his flat. He seems to have recovered emotionally from the break-up (which may have been helped by the fact that no children were involved). However, Mr I is unwilling to participate in his usual social activities. His friends continue to call and offer whatever support they think he will accept. In addition, support staff visit three times a week to help him with his laundry, heavy housework and shopping, and to make sure he pays his bills. A local day care centre has been suggested to him, but he is undecided about the offer. Without continued support, and until he lets his friends back into his life, Mr I could struggle at home.

The provision of community care services

On completion of an assessment, a decision must be taken as to whether the person being assessed is in need of social care services. Such services can be vital in ensuring that an individual is able to enjoy the basic human right of living in dignity and with maximum autonomy. Provision of social care is widely used, particularly by older people. It may be provided at an assessed person's home, or in a residential setting (such as a care home, or a nursing home). However, a current trend in this area is the constant tightening up of eligibility criteria because of reductions in public expenditure, which places significant pressure on CSSRs and practitioners, as well as causing considerable concern to services users and their carers (Alzheimer's Society 2011). One consequence of a more demanding application of the criteria is that services are provided only at crisis point.

The legal definition of community care services

Regrettably, the current law on adult social care is far more complex than, for example, the law on children's services. Community care services are defined in s.46(3) National Health and Community Care Act 1990 (NHSCCA 1990) as services under the following legislation:

- Part III National Assistance Act 1948;
- s.45 Health Services and Public Health Act 1968;
- s.254 and Schedule 20 National Health Service Act 2006 and
- s.117 Mental Health Act 1983.

As mentioned in Chapter 3, this list demonstrates that the NHSCCA 1990 did not change the nature of the services provided as part of adult social care; it simply changed the mechanisms for assessing and providing services. As a result, the law does not provide an easily accessible overview of the services that people may receive following an assessment under s.47 NHSCCA 1990.

The approach recently recommended by the Law Commission is radically different from that under the current law (Law Commission 2011). Under the Care Act 2014, what are currently known as 'community care services' would be defined as any of the following:

(a) accommodation in a care home or in premises of some other type;
(b) care and support at home or in the community;
(c) counselling and other types of social work;
(d) goods and facilities;
(e) information, advice and advocacy.

The new law would also include a list of outcomes that should be achieved under a general duty to promote wellbeing. These include:

- health and emotional wellbeing;
- protection from harm;
- education, training and recreation;
- the contribution made to society, and
- securing rights and entitlements.

The nature of community care services

The types of service that can be provided under the current law are presented in Table 4.2.

Table 4.2 The types of community care service available under the current law

Service	Legislation	Comment
National Assistance Act 1948 (NAA 1948), Part III		
Residential accommodation	s.21	– For persons aged 18 years or over who by reason of age, illness, disability, or any other circumstances, are in need of care and attention that is not otherwise available to them – Residential accommodation for expectant and nursing mothers who are in need of care and attention which is not otherwise available to them
Welfare arrangements	s.29	– Informing people of services available under the section – Providing instruction to help people overcome the effects of disability – Workshops where people may be engaged in suitable work and hostels – Providing suitable work in their own homes or elsewhere – Assistance in disposing of the products of their work – Providing recreational work at home or elsewhere
Health Services and Public Health Act 1968 (HSPHA 1968)		
Promoting the welfare of older people	s.45	– Provision of meals in the home and elsewhere – Inform older people of available services and identify those in need of them – Help in travelling to and from home in order to participate in CSSR or similar services – Assistance in finding suitable households for accommodating older people – Provision of visiting and advisory services and social work support – Provision of practical assistance in the home (home adaptations) – Contribution towards the cost of employing a warden in warden-assisted housing schemes – Provision of warden services for occupiers of private homes
National Health Service Act 2006 (NHSA 2006)		
Services provided by CSSR social services authorities	s.254 and Schedule 20	– Local social services authorities have the following functions: • care of expectant and nursing mothers (not including accommodation) • prevention, care and after-care, including provision of services in respect of people received into guardianship under the Mental Health Act 1983 (MHA 1983) • home help and laundry facilities.
Mental Health Act 1983 (MHA 1983)		
	s.117	This section imposes a duty on Clinical Commissioning Groups (CCG) and the local CSSR to provide after-care services for anyone discharged from detention under s.3 of the MHA 1983. Services are to be provided, often in co-operation with voluntary bodies, until the authorities are satisfied that they are no longer needed. The scope of the duty under s.117 is unclear. The MHA 1983 does not specify what services are to be made available under the section or the duration of the duty.

> **case example**
>
> ### 4.2 R (K) v Camden and Islington Health Authority
> In this case, the court said that the precise nature and extent of the services provided under s.117 Mental Health Act 1983 were within the discretion of the CSSR.

It is clear, however, that the CSSR and the CCG have a duty to provide services under s.117 and that they cannot charge the recipient (*R v Harrow London Borough Council ex parte Cobham*). When a person receives such services, however, the authorities have only a limited duty of care, as was discussed by the court in the *Clunis* case in case example 4.3.

> **case example**
>
> ### 4.3 Clunis v Camden and Islington Health Authority
> In this case, the plaintiff killed a man in an unprovoked attack; he pleaded guilty to manslaughter by reason of diminished responsibility. He brought an action against the authority on the grounds of a breach of their alleged duty of care on the grounds that, if it were not for this breach, he would not have committed the crime. The case was difficult and involved a general rule that you cannot base such a claim on your own wrongful act. However, the court did say that it would not be fair or reasonable to impose the common law duty on the authority in such circumstances.

Age UK provide examples of services that may be available:

> assistance in the home – home help/care or a personal assistant;
> respite in various forms;
> day care;
> night-sitting services;
> care in a care home;
> provision of aids and equipment to help with daily living tasks and for home safety;
> provision of home adaptations;
> pre-prepared meals delivered to an individual;
> advice and information;
> preventive and rehabilitation services;
> services to meet psychological, social and cultural needs;
> services for carers;
> assisting in placement in various types of supported housing;
> community transport; and
> services in conjunction with health and other services where needs overlap.
> (Age UK 2010)

Community Care Services 79

A 'disabled person' may also be assessed under s.2 CSDPA 1970. Specific services may, in addition to the above, be provided under the CSDPA 1970. In broad terms, they cover the following:

- practical assistance in the home;
- the provision of, or help in obtaining, wireless, television, library or similar recreational facilities;
- the provision of lectures, games, outings or other recreational facilities outside the home, or assistance in taking advantage of available educational facilities;
- the provision of facilities for, or assistance in, travelling to and from home to participate in services under s.29 NAA 1948 or, with the approval of the authority, any similar services;
- the provision of assistance in arranging for the carrying out of home adaptations or the provision of any additional facilities designed to achieve greater safety, comfort or convenience;
- facilitating the taking of holidays;
- the provision of meals in the home or elsewhere;
- the provision of, or assistance in obtaining, a telephone.

The language used in s.2 CSDPA 1970 is somewhat dated, but important services fall within its remit.

The delivery of community care services

If a CSSR decides that services need to be provided, the duty to provide is primarily the responsibility of the CSSR in which the person is 'ordinary resident'. The definition of ordinary resident is unusually complex and generates considerable disagreement between CSSRs as to which one is responsible. Lord Scarman in *R v Barnet LBC ex parte Shah* defined it as 'a man's abode in a particular place or country which he has adopted voluntarily and for settled purposes as part of the regular order of his life for the time being, whether of long or short duration'. The Ordinary Residence Guidance makes it clear that it is a question of fact; intention, and length and continuity of residence are relevant (Department of Health 2011). The Supreme Court has recently questioned the test in Shah in the case of *In Re A*. The case involved the habitual residence of a child. Baroness Hale felt that the Shah test should be abandoned in the case of the child in favour of the approach adopted by the European Court. The European Court adopts a test which reflected some degree of integration by the child into a social and family environment (para. 54). The future implications of this for ordinary residence in relation to adults is unclear, but if an adult case went to the Supreme Court it is possible, indeed likely, that it would seek to move away from the Shah test.

A community care service will either be provided directly by the CSSR for the area, or the authority may facilitate the provision of the service by the independent sector – either a voluntary organization or a commercial undertaking. In the past, it was usual for the local CSSRs to provide most of the community care services directly using their own care homes or domiciliary services. This was seen as restricting the range of available services and resulting in a service-led assessment, rather than one that concentrated on the needs of the individual. One of the aims of the NHSCCA 1990 was to extend the nature of community care services by developing a 'market' in community care services. Sir Roy Griffiths, in his review of community care services, pointed to the near monopolistic position of CSSRs (see Chapter 3, p. 55). There is an interesting debate, however, on whether the role of the third sector should be one of support or substitution (Joseph Rowntree Foundation 2005).

The role of the voluntary sector

The role of the voluntary sector in providing community care is not new, but with the creation of the welfare state following World War II, the state displaced, to some extent, the work of charities in providing assistance. The provision of education, welfare, health and unemployment services was seen as the province of government, rather than charities. Following the NHSCCA 1990, the role of the voluntary sector was enlarged, albeit often by grants or contracts with CSSRs. The implications of the arrangements for this sector are complex. For example, there may be a potential conflict between the role of a service provider in service design and also their role as advocates. The coalition government's Big Society continues the trend set by the Labour government with its emphasis on volunteering and support for charities. Davies warns of the dangers for the voluntary sector of these recent developments:

> In a period that combines an intensification of competition for government funding with a general economic downturn, there is a serious danger that some voluntary organizations will collapse, or be pushed aside by private sector companies, that large providers will edge out smaller providers and national will replace local provision. In such circumstances, voluntary organizations will aim to ensure that proximity to the state through the expected expansion of public service delivery opportunities does not result in the mission drift and incorporation feared by critics of the contract culture, and that innovative advocates of the community interest are not transformed into instrumental, target-driven service providers. (Davies 2011: 647)

The role of the private sector

The provision of community care services by the private sector (or 'for-profit' organizations) has also increased since the 1990s. Drakeford refers, in particular, to the increase in private provision in residential care. He concludes that the introduction of the market economy into residential care has:

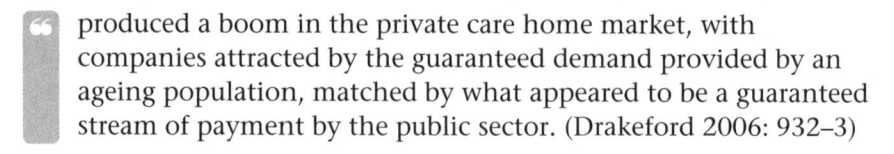

> produced a boom in the private care home market, with companies attracted by the guaranteed demand provided by an ageing population, matched by what appeared to be a guaranteed stream of payment by the public sector. (Drakeford 2006: 932–3)

The Southern Cross debacle illustrates the dangers that risky business models can create in a 'market' where protection for vulnerable people is paramount (Scourfield 2007). The adult social care market is estimated to be worth about £15 billion per year. It is a large employer of some 1.75 million people. Some providers are very large and are often private equity firms.

Direct payments

Historically, the payment of money to service users was not permitted; rather, needs were met through the provision of services. This did not resonate with the promotion of independence and choice. Service users had little input into the service provided or who provided it and when. A new approach to the delivery of community care was introduced by the Community Care (Direct Payments) Act 1996 (CC(DP)A 1996). The thinking behind direct payments was that, instead of a CSSR providing or facilitating the provision of services, people should be given a cash equivalent to enable them to arrange their own services. Direct payments are part of the community care scheme and are only available if the person is assessed as needing community care services. Proponents of direct payments argue that this provides them with greater control over when, how and by whom services are provided.

Changes since the Community Care (Direct Payments) Act 1996

Since their introduction under the CC(DP)A 1996, a number of changes have been made to the scheme. CSSRs are placed under a duty to offer direct payments where the person is eligible (Department of Health 2009a) with older people also now included. The number of people receiving direct payments in England increased substantially between 2005–06 (37,000) and 2011–12 (143,000) (Health and Social Care Information Centre 2013a). The primary legislation is now the Health and Social Care Act 2001 (HSCA 2001). Department of Health guidance on direct payments was published in 2009 (Department of Health 2009a). Direct payments are one component of a broader development in social care law; namely, personalization, which will be discussed later in this chapter.

Direct payments, capacity and mental disorder

Initially, the recipient of direct payments needed to have the mental capacity to consent to receiving them (in that the service user had to have the ability to accept the payment in lieu of services). Neither was it possible for a third party to consent on behalf of a person who lacked capacity (*Morgan v Phillips*). The Health and Social Care Act 2008 (HSCA 2008) extended the availability of direct payments to people who may be lacking in capacity. It also extended the duty to offer direct payments to people with mental health problems.

For people who lack capacity under the Mental Capacity Act 2005 (MCA 2005) (see Chapter 2), a payment can now be made to a 'suitable person' who is willing to act on their behalf. This may be a person with an LPA, or a deputy appointed by the Court of Protection (see Chapter 2, p. 46). It may also be that family members or friends are the providers of care for the person. However, for people with a mental disorder, the take-up of direct payments has been low (Newbigging and Low 2005). CSSRs now have the power (but not a duty) to make direct payments to anyone who is under an obligation to accept services under the MHA 1983; for example, under a Community Treatment Order (CTO) (see Chapter 6, p. 130). Their discretionary nature reflects concern that difficulties could arise in making direct payments in relation to services that have been imposed on a person. If the CSSR does not offer direct payments, it must give its reasons in writing to the service user and also make them aware of the complaints procedure (see Chapter 8, p. 162). With respect to any other services not covered by an imposed condition, the CSSR has a duty to offer direct payments (Department of Health 2009a, paras 207–12).

Direct payments have now been extended to the provision of services to a disabled person where they have parental responsibility for a child under s.17A Children Act 1989 (CA 1989) and to the parents of disabled children. A direct payment may be made to an informal carer following an assessment under s.1 Carers and Disabled Children Act 2000 (CDCA 2000), if the CSSR has decided to provide them with services. Carers have the right to be assessed (see Chapter 5) and CSSRs may provide them with assistance if they are providing 'regular and substantial care' for a person who may be in need of community care services. Other than for a short period of respite care, residential care cannot be funded by direct payments.

The direct payments provisions also cover certain categories of people within the criminal justice system.

Making use of direct payments

People can make use of their direct payments in a number of ways (such as for the purchase of any equipment that may be needed). Typically, a direct payment may be used to employ a care worker or personal assistant. Usually, partners, spouses and close relatives cannot be employed using direct payments as the relationship is deemed to be personal, rather than professional. In exceptional cases, however, a CSSR may authorize such a payment. Employing people creates a complex legal relationship involving employment law, and health and safety. This may prove a disincentive for many people. As an alternative, they may consider making use of an agency (e.g. a voluntary organization) to provide a care worker. This avoids many legal complexities; it also provides some reassurance that the worker is trained appropriately and is a suitable person to provide personal care. Direct payments are one way in which service users can exercise choice as part of the recently introduced personalization agenda.

Person-centred planning

The government pledged that it would transform adult social care. In 'Putting people first' (Department of Health 2010a), it proposed a new approach to the provision of community care services. It recognizes the existing shortcomings of community care provision and stated that:

> The time has now come to build on best practice and replace paternalistic, reactive care of variable quality with a mainstream system focussed on prevention, early intervention, enablement, and high quality personally tailored services. In the future, we want people to have maximum choice, control and power over the support services they receive. (Department of Health 2007: 2)

The idea of giving people greater control over their care through the payment of money, rather than the direct provision of services, is not new. The Independent Living Fund (ILF) was established in 1988 to support people with disability living in their own homes. Money is provided to pay for personal assistants. The coalition government has proposed winding down the ILF and transferring its responsibilities to CSSRs. The ILF scheme has now been closed to new applicants and will be completely phased out by 2015. Direct payments have also paved the way for greater emphasis on personal control. This goes beyond traditional CSSR support and attempts to take a more holistic approach. The government has, however, committed itself to the personalization agenda, a key component of which is personal budgets. Giving people greater control over the way in which their needs are addressed is often referred to as 'self-directed support'. The Department of Health states:

> Put simply, person-centred planning is a way of discovering what people want, the support they need and how they can get it. It is evidence-based practice that assists people in leading an independent and inclusive life. Person-centred planning is both an empowering philosophy and a set of tools for change, at an individual, a team and an organizational level. It shifts power from professionals to people who use services. (Department of Health 2010c)

Personal budgets

A personal budget is a sum of money given to a service user who is assessed as having eligible social care needs. Within that budget, the person is allowed to decide how they wish to use that money to achieve the identified outcomes. The idea of personal budgets has been grafted onto the existing system. This means that the sum of money identified in the personal budget is arrived at using the same assessment process and resource allocation system as for directly-provided services. The ways in which the person is able to exercise control and choice is through:

- direct payments (see p. 83);
- a virtual budget – that is, a budget that is managed by a CSSR, but in accordance with the service user's wishes;
- a third-party account holder who manages the budget on behalf of the service user and in accordance with their wishes (an Individual Service Fund);
- a trust managed by trustees who may be relatives, friends, carers or possibly a professional (e.g. a lawyer). The beneficiary of the trust is the service user.

Whereas, usually, direct payments are controlled and managed by the service user, the other methods relieve them of that responsibility whilst, at the same time, enabling them to exercise choice and control. The outline of the process is presented in Figure 4.1.

Once they are in place, the arrangements should be reviewed to ensure that the indicative budge is adequate and that there are no safeguarding issues or risks that need to be addressed. As with all community care arrangements, there must be regular reviews.

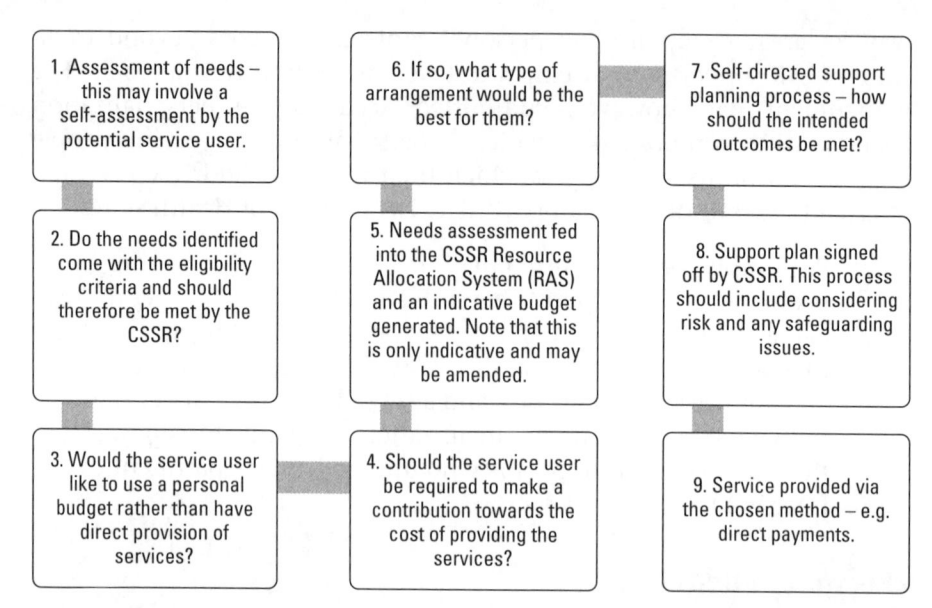

```
┌─────────────────────┐     ┌─────────────────────┐     ┌─────────────────────┐
│ 1. Assessment of    │     │ 6. If so, what type │     │ 7. Self-directed    │
│ needs – this may    │     │ of arrangement would│     │ support planning    │
│ involve a           │     │ be the best for     │     │ process – how       │
│ self-assessment by  │     │ them?               │     │ should the intended │
│ the potential       │     │                     │     │ outcomes be met?    │
│ service user.       │     │                     │     │                     │
└─────────────────────┘     └─────────────────────┘     └─────────────────────┘
          │                           │                           │
┌─────────────────────┐     ┌─────────────────────┐     ┌─────────────────────┐
│ 2. Do the needs     │     │ 5. Needs assessment │     │ 8. Support plan     │
│ identified come     │     │ fed into the CSSR   │     │ signed off by CSSR. │
│ with the eligibility│     │ Resource Allocation │     │ This process should │
│ criteria and should │     │ System (RAS) and an │     │ include considering │
│ therefore be met by │     │ indicative budget   │     │ risk and any        │
│ the CSSR?           │     │ generated. Note that│     │ safeguarding issues.│
│                     │     │ this is only        │     │                     │
│                     │     │ indicative and may  │     │                     │
│                     │     │ be amended.         │     │                     │
└─────────────────────┘     └─────────────────────┘     └─────────────────────┘
          │                           │                           │
┌─────────────────────┐     ┌─────────────────────┐     ┌─────────────────────┐
│ 3. Would the service│     │ 4. Should the       │     │ 9. Service provided │
│ user like to use a  │     │ service user be     │     │ via the chosen      │
│ personal budget     │     │ required to make a  │     │ method – e.g.       │
│ rather than have    │     │ contribution towards│     │ direct payments.    │
│ direct provision of │     │ the cost of         │     │                     │
│ services?           │     │ providing the       │     │                     │
│                     │     │ services?           │     │                     │
└─────────────────────┘     └─────────────────────┘     └─────────────────────┘
```

Figure 4.1 An outline of the process for deciding on personal budgets

Exercise 4.3

What are the advantages and risks or dangers of direct payments and personal budgets?

Registration and regulation

As discussed (p. 76), one means of providing community care is care in a residential setting. The Registered Homes Act 1984 (RHA 1984) introduced a system of registration and inspection for residential care homes and nursing homes run by independent providers. CSSR services were not subject to the legislation. Indeed, it was CSSR inspection units who were responsible for enforcing the law against private providers. The legislation was, in many respects, an ineffective way of ensuring and enhancing the quality of residential care (Brammer 1994). The White Paper 'Modernising social services' was critical of the existing regulatory framework:

> The existing arrangements for regulating care services have developed in a piecemeal fashion. Responsibilities for regulating the various services for adults and children are divided between CSSRs, health authorities and the Department of Health centrally.

> Other services – notably councils' own care homes, small children's homes and domiciliary care (care given to people in their own homes) – are not subject to any regulation (Department of Health 1998).

Following a review of regulation by the government in 1997, the Care Standards Act 2000 (CSA 2000) introduced a new approach to registration and inspection.

The CSA 2000 made a number of significant changes to the regulatory framework, which applied to all care homes, regardless of whether they were private or owned by the CSSR. Compliance standards were introduced and all care homes had to meet those standards. Inspectors had wider powers than under the RHA 1984. The HSCA 2008 replaced the CSA 2000 and is now the main legislation for England.

The HSCA 2008 covers residential accommodation (not, in itself, defined) for people who require 'nursing' or 'personal care'. These are defined in the regulations (Health and Social Care Act 2008 (Regulated Activities) Regulations 2010). 'Personal care' is defined by regulation 2 as:

> Physical assistance given to a person in connection with:
>
> (a) Eating or drinking, toileting, washing or bathing, dressing, oral care, the care of skin, hair and nails ... or
> (b) The prompting, together with supervision, of a person, in relation to the performance of any of the activities listed in paragraph (a), where that person is unable to make a decision for themselves in relation to performing such an activity.

'Nursing care' means any service provided by a nurse involving:

> (a) The provision of care; or
> (b) The planning, supervision or delegation of the provision of care, other than any services which, having regard to their nature and the circumstances in which they are provided, do not need to be provided by a nurse.

The HSCA 2008 includes domiciliary care services as well as care homes. Paragraph 1 of Schedule 1 includes, as a regulated activity, 'the provision of personal care for persons who, by reason of old age, illness or disability are unable to provide it for themselves, and which is provided in a place where those persons are living at the time the care is provided.' It also applies to nurses' agencies, private hospitals, private clinics and private voluntary hospices.

These are legalistic definitions of personal and nursing care, and ignore some of the broader human rights aspects of residential care. A number of rights under the European Convention on Human Rights (ECHR) are relevant. The right under Article 3 not to be subjected to inhuman or degrading treatment is an obvious right. Sadly, as will be seen, treatment in a minority of care homes can fall below acceptable standards and amount to inhuman treatment. The right to liberty under Article 5 is also relevant. The Deprivation of Liberty Safeguards (DOLS) (see Chapter 2, p. 48) were introduced to ensure that only in exceptional circumstances can people be deprived of their liberty in a care home. Article 8 is particularly important. Private life must be respected in a care home. Article 8 protects a person's home. Although a resident in a care home may have left what might have been their family home for many years, this does not mean that they cease to have a home and are simply hotel guests. Their space in the care home is now their home and worthy of protection under Article 8. The right to family life also forms part of Article 8. What provision is there in the home for a resident to meet their family in private or, in the case of an older person, for their grandchildren to visit? In addition, is the person placed in a home that is many miles away from their original community and their family? Does this interfere with their right to enjoy family life and, if so, what can be done to alleviate this? Living in a care home does not reduce the obligation of the state to protect human rights (Williams 2011).

Evidence also suggests that the removal of an individual, particularly an older person, from one placement to another can have a significant impact on their wellbeing and life expectancy. Given this situation, it may not be surprising that a number of home closures, resulting in the transfer of the residents to new placements, have given rise to a series of legal actions based on breaches of the ECHR.

Care Quality Commission

The regulatory authority for England is now the Care Quality Commission (CQC). Not only does it regulate social care (residential and domiciliary), it also regulates many aspects of health provision (e.g. maternity and midwifery, termination of pregnancies, family planning services, diagnostic and screening procedures). The CQC also monitors mental health services – in particular, care provided for people detained under the MHA 1983. Providers of any regulated activity must register with the CQC. In order to register, the provider must meet certain standards of provision. It is against these standards that providers are inspected and monitored. The legal framework for inspection and registration is found in the HSCA 2008 and the related regulations (The Health and Social Care Act 2008 (Regulated Activities) Regulations 2010). The CQC has published 'Essential standards of quality and safety', which provides guidance (Care Quality Commission 2010a). This document attaches outcomes to the regulations. Outcome is central to the process and contains the following:

- Respecting and involving people who use services
- Consent to care and treatment
- Care and welfare of people who use services
- Cooperating with other providers
- Meeting nutritional needs
- Safeguarding people who use services from abuse
- Cleanliness and infection control
- Management of medicines
- Safety and suitability of premises
- Safety, availability and suitability of equipment
- Supporting workers
- Assessing and monitoring the quality of service provision
- Complaints
- Fees
- Staffing
- Statement of purpose
- Records.

Three types of inspection are used: scheduled, responsive and themed. Scheduled inspections are routine inspections; responsive inspections are carried out where there has been concern about the quality of the provision (e.g. following a series of complaints) and themed inspections look at a particular aspect of a service across a number of registered providers.

The CQC is a public authority and is, as such, subject to the duty under s.6 HRA 1998, to act in a way that is consistent with the ECHR. Issues such as dignity, privacy, liberty, freedom of religion and no discrimination in the enjoyment of the ECHR rights must feature prominently in the registration and inspection process. A recent report by the CQC illustrates the way in which it goes about reporting on issues, such as dignity, respect and compassion within residential, nursing and domiciliary care (Care Quality Commission 2012).

The CQC has recently attracted a considerable amount of criticism. In its ninth Annual Accountability Report on the CQC, the House of Commons Health Committee reported that the compliance activity by the CQC had fallen to a low level during 2010–11 (House of Commons Health Committee 2011). It concluded that the registration process had not been properly tested before being rolled out. There was also concern that the bias in its work had moved away from the core function of inspection to concentrating on the introduction of registration for primary and social care providers (Dyer 2011). The Committee concluded that the fact that:

> inspections fell by an unacceptable 70% demonstrates a failure to manage resource and activity in line with the main statutory objective of the CQC to 'protect and promote the health, safety

and welfare of people who use health and social care services'. In the current climate of financial constraint and reorganisation of the health service it is more important than ever to have a regulator that maintains a clear focus on its primary duties. In this instance that did not happen. (House of Commons Health Committee 2011: para.15)

The effectiveness of the inspection process for care homes is questionable. A number of highly-publicized incidents of abuse and neglect in care homes raise doubts as to whether, alongside the excellent care that the majority of homes provide to residents, there are some whose standards fall far below the basic expectations of the regulatory framework and those of the ECHR. Initially, the courts held that, for private providers of residential care, the HRA 1998 did not apply, since they were not public authorities within s.6 of that Act. This was held to be the case even if the CSSR was paying the home's fees.

4.4 YL v Birmingham City Council

This case concerned a care home resident aged 84 who suffered from Alzheimer's disease. The home was owned by a private company but funded largely by the CSSR under the NAA 1948. For various reasons, the relationship with the home broke down, and it was proposed to move the resident to another home. This was challenged under Article 8 of the ECHR and s.6 HRA 1998. The Court held, on a 3 to 2 majority, that there was a difference between a CSSR with a statutory duty to arrange care and accommodation and a private care home providing such services. The private provider was not a public authority.

This is a strange conclusion, given that the independent sector provides the majority of residential care. It would mean that a person placed in a CSSR-owned care home would be directly protected by the HRA 1998, whereas someone in an independent home would not. This decision attracted a great deal of criticism (Baxter and Carr 2007; Palmer 2007; Williams 2008). The government's response to the outcry, and this apparent injustice, was minimalist. Section 145 HSCA 2008 provides that, where a private or voluntary sector care home provides residential care 'under arrangements made with a CSSR', the provider is to be treated as coming within s.6 HRA 1998, and, therefore, under a duty to act compatibly with the ECHR. This section does not apply to self-funders in residential care. Thus, we may have the situation in which some residents in a home are protected directly by the ECHR while others are not. Independent agencies providing domiciliary care do not fall within this provision.

The situation also raises issues in relation to adult protection, such as the case referred to in a recent *Panorama* TV programme that highlighted the serious abuse of an 80-year-old Alzheimer's sufferer in a care home in London (BBC 2012). This exposure of abuse resulted in the conviction of a care worker for assault. The CQC was criticized, in that it had rated the home as 'excellent'. Following the incident, the CQC made two visits to the home and concluded that 'people who use the service, are protected from abuse, or the risk of abuse, and their rights are respected and upheld'. Sadly, any regulatory regime will not be totally effective in eradicating abuse and neglect, and in identifying unsuitable practitioners. However, the current system fails in a number of ways and requires fundamental review and a more rights-based approach. (See also Chapter 6 on Adult Protection, as well as the problems disclosed in a number of Serious Case Reviews (SCRs), including the report on abuse at Winterbourne View private hospital (Flynn 2012).)

Paying for domiciliary care

A key difference between health and social care is that services provided by the National Health Service are invariably free at the point of delivery, whereas social care is not necessarily free. In certain situations, service users may be required to pay for, or contribute to, the cost of any social care that they receive. A significant number of people pay for their own care because they are ineligible for CSSR support. These are often referred to as 'self-funders' (see p. 93). Section 17(1) Health and Social Services and Social Security Adjudications Act 1983 (HSSSSAA 1983) says that a CSSR *may* recover 'such charges (if any) as they consider reasonable'. It is necessary to note that they *may* and not *must* charge. The section applies to the following domiciliary care provisions:

- s.29 NAA 1948 (welfare arrangements for disabled people);
- s.2 CSDPA 1970 (services for disabled people);
- s.45 HSPHA 1968 (welfare of old people);
- Schedule 20 NHSA 2006, or Schedule 15 NHS (Wales) Act 2006 (prevention of illness; care and after-care; home-help facilities);
- s.2 CDCA 2000 (carers' services).

CSSRs cannot charge for general social work advice or support services, occupational therapy, or assessment of need under, for example s.47 NHSCCA 1990. As noted, services under s.117 MHA 1983 are free (*R v Manchester City Council ex parte Stennett and Two Other Actions*), as is intermediate care. Intermediate care is the provision of services aimed at preventing unnecessary or prolonged hospital stay or long-term residential care. Such provision is time-limited, typically not longer than six weeks, but often as short as one or two weeks, or less. The provision of community equipment (i.e. additional facilities aimed at promoting independence and an optimum quality of life) must also be provided free of charge, as with any minor adaptations to property of less than £1000. Community equipment may be provided by the health services, by a CSSR or jointly from their pooled resources.

Under s.17(3) HSSSSAA 1983, if a person benefits from a service and satisfies the service that they have insufficient resources to make it practicable to pay for it, the CSSR must consider this in deciding what to charge. They must not charge more than it appears 'reasonably practicable' for the person to pay. The discretion to charge resulted in wide variations in the charging policies of CSSRs. A study by the Joseph Rowntree Foundation (2009) identified significant inconsistencies across six CSSRs. No two CSSRs adopted the same policy; one CSSR had two charging systems; the levels of difficulty varied; and there was no consistency in how authorities defined 'income', or whether to take into consideration welfare benefits.

This was unsatisfactory. In response to these concerns, the government issued statutory guidance in 2001 (Department of Health 2001b). This guidance does not require CSSRs to charge for domiciliary services. However, if they elect to do so, the policy has to be reasonable and fair.

Guidance has been issued on how to develop such policies. For example, the use of flat rate charges should be kept to a minimum; as a minimum, the same capital limits as for residential care charges should be applied, although a more liberal rule may be adopted; and consideration should be given to the effect of charges on net income, which should not be reduced below a defined basic level of pension credit or income support, plus 25 per cent. Section 17 HSSSSAA 1983 does not preclude a CSSR from imposing charges on those in receipt of social security benefits. Savings and capital may be taken into consideration, although only up to the rates applicable for residential care (see below).

Paying for residential care

Unlike the discretionary power to charge for domiciliary care, s.22 NAA 1948 states the CSSRs '*shall* recover from him the amount of the payment which he is liable to make' in accordance with the section. This applies whether the care home in question is owned by the CSSR or an independent provider. The regulations are complex and overly legalistic.

For 2013/14, a person with capital assets valued at over £23,250 is not eligible for financial support from the CSSR. Any capital below the upper limit, but above the lower limit of £14,250, is subject to what is known as a 'tariff income'. The tariff income is intended to reflect a notional return on the capital sum. For every complete £250 or part thereof over the lower limit, a tariff income of £1 per week is generated. So, for example, if the person has capital of £15,250 (i.e. £1000 over the lower limit) a tariff income of £4 per week is generated. Income will also be taken into consideration. For the purpose of the charging provision, 'income' includes pensions, annuity income, trust income and rental income. Any tariff income must be added to this.

In order for a resident in a care home to have some money to spend, there is a personal expenses allowance of £23.90 per week (the figure for 2013/14). A care home cannot make use of this as a means of making a resident pay more for their care. For example, the care home cannot charge the resident an extra amount to cover anything that is included in the CSSR contract with the home, or which is required to satisfy any eligible needs.

Self-funders

As with domiciliary care, many people are required to pay for all of their own residential care. One estimate is that 44.9 per cent of older people in residential care in England are self-funders. Current evidence suggests that the numbers are likely to increase in future. In addition, some 170,000 older people are currently funding the home care they receive (Social Care Institute for Excellence 2011). Compared with those who qualify for publicly-funded support, self-funders are often at a considerable disadvantage in not having clear information about their options, and in not having access to the support of an advocate in helping them achieve their preferences (Melanie Henwood Associates 2010). It seems that all too often, self-funders are left to fend for themselves. Their vulnerability is compounded by the fact that a number of the remedies outlined in Chapter 8 may not be open to them. However, it should be noted that, since October 2010, self-funders in residential care in England who are dissatisfied with the outcome of a complaint have been able to require an investigation by the local government ombudsman (see Chapter 8, p. 163) under s.34A-T Local Government Act 1974 (LGA 1974).

Issues of choice

The CSSR must respect a person's choice with regard to the care home in which they are to live. The regulations state that the care home offered to the person must be suitable for their assessed needs. A care home preferred by the person must not cost the CSSR more than they are prepared to pay for someone with that person's needs, although in *R v Avon County Council ex parte M* it was held that a person's need may require more expensive provision than the CSSR would usually pay. This was in relation to an out-of-county placement of a man with learning disability. It must also be available and the person in charge of the home must be willing to accept the placement.

If a person's choice is to live in a home that is more expensive than the one offered by the CSSR, a third party (a relative, friend, or perhaps a charitable organization) may make what is known as a 'third-party top-up'. Essentially, this means that the third party must make good the difference between what the CSSR provides plus what the person is liable to pay, and the fee charged by the home. The arrangement requires the third party to enter into a contract with the CSSR for the payment of the top-up. A resident cannot enter into a top-up agreement other than in very specific and exceptional cases (Department of Health 2004b).

Proposals for reform

As noted (see p. 73), the Law Commission has published a report on Adult Social Care. The Commission's work was motivated by the confused state of the current law. It noted the 'disparate range of legislative provision' which, it argues, 'reflects the different policy imperatives and understandings that have been carried out at various times in the period since 1948' (Law Commission 2011). Much of our law depends on legislation passed in the immediate post-war period; namely, the NAA 1948. The legislative framework is unclear, confusing and in need of reform. This lack of clarity is added to by the guidance issues under s.7 LASSA 1970. The Law Commission proposed a single adult social care Act supported by regulations and a single code of practice. The guidance provided by s.7 would no longer be used in adult social care. There would be an overarching statutory principle that 'adult social care must promote or contribute to the wellbeing of the individual'. Adult social care would be provided at two levels. A universal level would be part of the provision of services to the local community, which would be used to prevent or delay a person needing personal social care. Then there would be a duty to assess a person who may have needs that could be met by community care services. Regulations would be made setting out the eligibility framework that CSSRs would be required to use in devising their own eligibility criteria. There would be a single duty to undertake a carer's assessment. Community care services would no longer be defined by reference to other pieces of legislation, but would include residential accommodation; community and home-based services; advice, social work, counselling or advocacy; and financial or any other assistance. There would be greater portability of services to meet the needs of people who may move from one CSSR area to another. These, and other recommendations, will provide a more accessible law, which will be of benefit to practitioners, service users and carers.

Another significant challenge is how future social care is to be funded. The growing demand for social care services, partly as a result of the good news that people are living longer, has placed considerable strain on CSSR budgets. The charging provisions outlined above are thought to be unfair and may vary across different CSSRs. The Dilnot review concluded that the current funding system was not fit for purpose (see p. 73). It was unfair, unsustainable and did not allow people to make reasonable provision for their future social care. The review made a number of recommendations for a future funding model.

To protect people from extreme care costs, the review recommended capping the lifetime contribution for adult social care costs that any individual is required to make at £35,000. After that point, the state would be responsible for funding the social care. People who enter adulthood with an existing social care need would be eligible for free support from the state and would not be subject to a means test. People should contribute a standard amount to cover their general living costs, such as food and accommodation, in residential care. The annual figure proposed was £7,000–£10,000. To encourage people to plan ahead for their later life, the Dilnot review recommended that the government invest in an awareness campaign.

Although these proposals are far from perfect, they make an important contribution to the debate on future funding. There is a sense of urgency given the existing strains on social services budgets and the general disquiet over the current arrangement. The government has responded to the Dilnot review with its own proposals (Age UK 2013).

Conclusion

In the Queen's Speech, delivered on the 9 May 2012, the government pledged that a 'draft Bill will be published to modernise adult care and support in England (Hansard HL 2012). The Care Act 2014 was recently passed by Parliament. It is anticipated that implementation will commence in 2016. Transition to the new system will, to say the least, be challenging. The main change in the Bill is the consolidation of the array of legislation into one coherent and consistent statute. This, in itself, will make it easier for practitioners to navigate, and for service users and carers to know their rights. The current state of adult social care law is, to say the least, confusing and confused. Reform of the law will be welcome, although this will not tackle the chronic underfunding of social care, which is likely to continue for many years to come.

chapter 5 Carers

In this chapter, you will learn about:

- The contribution of carers
- Carers and human rights
- Who is a carer?
- The legal definition of a carer
- Carers and community care
- Assessment of carers
- Disabled Person (Services and Consultation and Representation) Act 1986
- Carers (Recognition of Services) Act 1995
- Carers and Disabled Children Act 2000
- Carers (Equal Opportunity) Act 2004
- Provision of services
- The legal consequences of caring
- Young people as carers
- The law and young carers

Remember to consult The Legal Toolbox on pp. xiii–xx. This will help you to understand processes and procedures referred to in this chapter.

The contribution of carers

Care by professional carers is only one part – a relatively small part – of the totality of care provided in England. The 2011 Census collected data on unpaid carers in the United Kingdom. It revealed the extent to which social care depends on unpaid carers (sometimes referred to as 'informal carers') and the potential cost to the state if that care were no longer provided. The term 'carers' (rather than 'unpaid carers') will be used throughout this chapter, and covers care provided by people such as family members, friends or neighbours, rather than professionals or third-sector bodies. The 2011 Census reports that there are approximately 5.8 million people providing care in England and Wales. This means that one tenth of the population (10.3 per cent) provides care; in 2001, it was 10.0 per cent. Of those providing care, 3.7 million provide 1–19 hours per week, 775,000 provide 20–49 hours and 1.4 million provide 50 hours or more unpaid care.

The carer/cared-for relationship is a complex one. People care for a range of different reasons, including love, concern and basic human decency. A sense of duty may arise out of a family relationship, neighbourliness, or friendship. The type of care provided in the person's own home will include the provision of personal care (washing, dressing and toileting), help in getting in and out of bed, assistance with mobility and, in some cases, administering medicine (Carers UK 2009). The overwhelming majority of carers provide excellent care, often at great personal and financial expense. There is a difficult judgement to be made about the extent to which the carer/cared-for relationship should be placed within a formal legal context. If the legal context is too demanding, it may either require a degree of expertise and knowledge that it would be unreasonable to expect of a carer, or will simply act as a disincentive to undertake the role. However, as will be seen (p. 106), a number of legal duties and obligations arise from the caring role.

Carers and human rights

It is tempting to think of human rights solely in the context of the service user. However, carers have human rights, and these must also be acknowledged and respected by service providers and practitioners. For example, carers have a right to a family life under Article 8 of the ECHR. Carers may well sacrifice their private life, their home and their family life in order to care. Similarly, their health and financial wellbeing may be affected by the responsibilities of caring.

Who is a carer?

Of carers across the UK, 58 per cent are women. There is a 50 per cent likelihood that women will be a carer by the time they are 59; for men, this is 75 years. Ethnicity may increase the likelihood of being a carer; for example, Bangladeshi and Pakistani men and women are three times more likely to provide care compared with white British men and women (Carers UK 2009).

Trying to cost the provision of care is difficult. In 2002, it was estimated that the cost of providing replacement for the care provided by carers in England was £46.66 billion; by 2007, this had risen to £70.52

> **Box 5.1 Impacts experienced by carers**
>
> **Financial***
> - 72% of carers are worse off because of caring, rising to 83% among those aged 45–54
> - 58% are worse off because of the extra costs of disability
> - 54% have given up work to care
> - 49% end up subsidizing the costs of the disability of the person they care for because of inadequate disability benefits
> - 21% have to reduce the hours they work
> - 28% find the charges for services too high
>
> * Typically carers retire from employment eight years earlier than non-carers, resulting in implications for earning capacity and pension contributions.
>
> **Health**
> - Carers' health is affected by their worsening financial circumstances and reducing essential expenditure
> - 62% worry about their financial circumstances most or all of the time
> - Working age carers tended to worry far more (75% among those aged 35–44), as do those on Income Support (84%)
> - 53% say that the worry is affecting their health
>
> **Benefits**
> - 61% receive Carer's Allowance
> - 28% receive Income Support
> - 24% receive Tax Credits
> - 43% receive a pension
> - 23% of those over 60 receive Pension Credit
>
> *Source*: Carers UK (2007).

billion. By comparison, in 2006/07, the annual spending on the health services in England was £82 billion and the annual spending on social services in 2005/06 was 19.3 billion (Buckner and Yeandle 2007).

In its 2007 report, Carers UK provided a profile of carers that identifies some of the difficulties that this group encounters (see Box 5.1).

The legal definition of a carer

To qualify as a carer under the law, there are two basic requirements. First, the individual must be providing a service for a person who appears eligible for community care services. The service in question could include advocacy and emotional support, as well as the kinds of personal care services that CSSRs provide (see Chapter 4). Second, under s.1 Carers and Disabled Children Act 2000 (CDCA 2000), the carer must be providing, or intending to provide, a *substantial amount of care on a regular basis*. A carer could, therefore, be entitled to a carer's assessment even if they had not been acting as a carer prior to the user's need for services, as long as the carer's intentions are evident. Thus, a would-be carer could be engaged from an early stage in planning services for a potential user. This is an important consideration, especially in the context of such events as discharge from hospital (see Chapter 3) or intermediate care (see Chapter 4, p. 91).

According to the Community Care Guidance (Department of Health 1993, appendix 4, para. 8), although the terms 'substantial' and 'regular' are not statutorily defined, CSSRs should be prepared to interpret the terms widely and take proper account of individual circumstances. Thus, it is not simply the time spent each week caring that has to be considered but the actual impact that the caring role has on a particular carer. Similarly, regular care need not necessarily mean 'often', since the guidance recognizes that some individuals will have fluctuating needs whilst other situations may involve a carer in a lifelong commitment. In other words, the guidance stresses the subjective nature of the exercise; that is, the need to look at the carer in their particular circumstances and milieu. Difficulties may arise for those who perform their caring role at a distance, or whose situation is made more difficult because they are responsible for the care of more than one person. It should also be noted that, where more than one carer is involved in the caring role, it should not be assumed that it is solely the 'main' or 'primary' carer who provides the cared-for person with substantial and regular care. There can be more than one carer falling within the definition.

Exercise 5.1

Which of the following, if any, fall within the legal definition of carer and would qualify for a carer's assessment?

- A neighbour who calls in every day to check whether her visually impaired friend is safely out of bed.
- A nephew who visits every second week to attend to the garden of his disabled uncle. The uncle has always been very proud of his garden and becomes very upset if the garden is neglected
- A niece, who lives 50 miles away and does not drive, phones her 80-year-old aunt regularly to check on her wellbeing. She makes a difficult and slow rail and bus journey every month to clean the house and launder the aunt's sheets. Her aunt has recently been diagnosed with

Parkinson's disease. The niece is 70 years of age and is herself arthritic.
- Two sisters have lived together in the family home all their lives. They have always shared responsibility for running the home. Both retired from full-time employment 15 years ago. One of the sisters has always been partially disabled, but now has additional health problems that have increased gradually since retirement. As a result, the other sister is being called on to do more household tasks, with increasing responsibility for the care of her sister. Up to this point, there has been no CSSR involvement. Their doctor is, however, becoming increasingly concerned about the effect this is having on the health of the sister who is not disabled.
- A widowed mother and her adult son who has learning disability live together. The son is able to attend a day centre, but cannot live independently. His grandmother lives in the neighbouring village some five miles away. She expects her daughter to call on her every day to prepare the evening meal and becomes very angry if she does not. Because of her dual responsibilities, the mother is unable to work full-time but is employed part-time as a hospital cleaner. She is finding it increasingly difficult to maintain her job, which she enjoys, whilst at the same time supporting both her son and the grandmother.

Carers and community care

Because of the considerable contribution made by carers, it is important for social workers who work in the field of community care to be aware of the powers and duties that a CSSR may have in relation to them, and to consider whether these apply in a particular situation. Often, awareness of the presence of a carer occurs when the person being cared for undergoes an assessment or a review (see Chapter 3, p. 57).

The White Paper that preceded the NHSCCA 1990 (see Chapter 3, p. 55) identified the needs of carers as an important priority (Department of Health 1989). Regrettably, carers are nowhere mentioned in the 1990 Act. However, they are often central to the provision of care for a service user and it would be difficult to ignore their input and continued ability to care. The ability of a carer to continue to provide support is an important part of the assessment process when applying the eligibility criteria

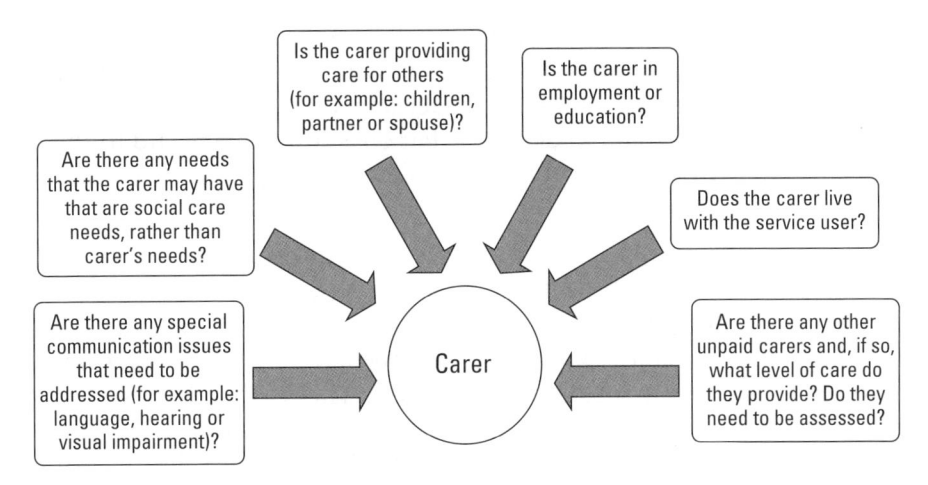

Figure 5.1 Assessing carers' needs

(see Chapter 4, p. 72). This is recognized in the Community Care Policy Guidance which states:

> In assessing the carer's ability to care or to continue care, care managers should not assume a willingness by the carer to continue caring, or continue to provide the same level of support. They may wish to bear in mind the distinction between caring about someone and caring for them. (Department of Health 1995)

Assessment of carers

As with service users, assessments of carers are complex and involve a number of factors (Figure 5.1).

These complexities arise largely as a result of the legislation being introduced as private members bills – and thus developed piecemeal. As a result, reform is now much needed, since there are currently no fewer than four separate Acts that apply to carers, which often overlap.

Disabled Persons (Services and Consultation and Representation) Act 1986

Section 8 Disabled Persons (Services and Consultation and Representation) Act 1986 (DP(SCR)A 1986), states that where:

> (a) a disabled person is living at home and receiving a substantial amount of care on a regular basis from another person ..., and

Carers 101

> (b) it falls to a CSSR to decide whether the disabled person's needs call for the provision by them of any services for him under any of the welfare enactments,
> (c) the CSSR shall, in deciding that question, have regard to the ability of that other person to continue to provide such care on a regular basis.

Two points should be noted. First, the duty is imposed on the CSSR to consider the ability of a carer to continue to provide care. Although, this is not related directly to the needs of the carer, it does at least ensure they are not invisible in the process. Second, the term 'substantial amount of care on a regular basis' is used. This is not defined in the DP(SCR)A 1986, and is vague and open to interpretation. The phrase resurfaces in subsequent carer legislation. It vagueness is unhelpful, given that the existence of any carer's rights is dependent on it.

Carer (Recognition of Services) Act 1995

The first piece of legislation concerned solely with carers, as such, was the Carers (Recognition of Services) Act 1995 (C(RS)A 1995). To avoid duplication, if a carer's assessment is made under this Act, then s.8 DP(SCR)A 1986 (noted above) does not apply. The C(RS)A 1995 enables a carer to request a CSSR to carry out an assessment of their ability to provide, and continue to provide, care. However, two conditions must be satisfied. First, the CSSR must be carrying out a s.47 NHSCCA 1990 assessment in order for the carer to be entitled to an assessment. This might present problems if the cared for person is perfectly content with the level of care that the carer is giving and does not consent to an assessment under s.47 NHSCCA 1990. In effect, the person being cared for can deny the carer the right to an assessment by refusing to undergo an assessment under s.47 (see Chapter 3. p. 62). The second point involves the language of the DP(SCR)A 1986; namely, that the carer must provide or intend to provide 'a substantial amount of care on a regular basis' (e.g. when the person leaves hospital and returns home).

The C(RS)A 1995 also includes carers where the person being cared for is being assessed under two other pieces of legislation. First, the CSSR may be assessing the needs of a disabled child under Part III Children Act 1989 (CA 1989). This provision applies to children who may be in need under s.17 CA 1989. Second, the CSSR may be assessing somebody under s.2 Chronically Sick and Disabled Persons Act 1970 (CSDPA 1970). As noted in Chapter 4 (p. 80), this section deals with the provision of welfare services for people who are disabled. If, in either of the cases, a carer provides or intends to provide a 'substantial amount of care on a regular basis' (s.1(1) C(RS)A 1995), the carer can request the authority to undertake a carer's assessment (s.1(2)(b) C(RS)A 1995).

Thus, a carer's assessment may be attached to an assessment of the cared-for person under the NHSCCA 1990, the CA 1989, or the CSDPA 1970. Following a carer's assessment, the CSSR must take into account the results of the decision in determining the package of care for the cared-for person. If, when making a cared-for person assessment under one of the above statutes, it appears to the CSSR that there may be a person entitled to a carer's assessment but that this has not been requested, the CSSR has the duty to inform that carer of their right under the C(RS)A 1995.

When undertaking a carer's assessment, the CSSR must consider whether the person works or wishes to work, or is undertaking, or wishes to undertake, education, training or any leisure activity. To add further confusion to this area of law, when making an assessment under s.1(2a) C(RS)A 1995, the CSSR may take into account, as far as it considers it to be material, an assessment under the Carers and Disabled Children Act 2000 (CDCA 2000).

Carers and Disabled Children Act 2000

The C(RS)A 1995, together with the DP(SCR)A 1986, gave limited support to carers. However, they fell far short of giving carers any real rights within the care system. More was required. A common-sense approach to reforming this area of law would have been to repeal the existing provision on carers and introduce a consolidated and consistent piece of legislation. Sadly, this did not happen. New legislation was introduced in the form of the CDCA 2000. However, it was to co-exist with the legislation already discussed.

The CDCA 2000 makes one very significant change. Under this Act, if a carer aged 16 years or older provides a 'substantial amount of care on a regular basis' for another person aged 18 years or over, they *may ask* the CSSR to assess their ability to provide, or to continue to provide, care. The CSSR must then undertake the assessment if they are satisfied that person cared for is someone for whom they *may* provide community care services. The significance of this provision is that the cared-for person need not be having an assessment under s.47 NHSCCA 1990. The carer's assessment is a free-standing right and not contingent on the cared-for person being assessed. Note that the CSSR is under a duty to make the assessment, but has discretion whether or not to provide services.

As noted, an assessment under the C(RS)A 1995 must take account of any assessment under the CDCA 2000; the reverse is also true. A carer's assessment under each piece of legislation must have regard to an assessment under the other. As with the C(RS)A 1995, consideration must be given to whether the carer works; or is undertaking training, education or leisure activity, or wishes to do so (ss.1(2) and (3a) CDCA 2000).

Section 6a CDCA 2000 requires CSSRs to inform a carer of their right to a carer's assessment. If they think that a person is a carer and would be entitled to an assessment if requested, then they must be informed of that right (where necessary, in an appropriate format, or minority language). The duty does not apply if the CSSR has previously carried out a carer's assessment, has already informed them of their right to an assessment, or has assessed the carer under s.4(3) CC(DC)A 2003. This section requires the CSSR, in certain circumstances, to undertake a carer's assessment prior to the cared-for person's discharge from hospital.

Carers (Equal Opportunity) Act 2004

To complete the suite of legislation on carers, reference must be made to the Carers (Equal Opportunity) Act (C(EO)A) 2004. As well as making some changes to the two earlier pieces of legislation already discussed, it makes changes to the legal rights of carers. One important change is the need for different authorities to cooperate in planning services for carers under the C(RS)A 1995 and the CDCA 2000. Under these two Acts, a CSSR can request the following authorities for assistance in the planning process:

- another CSSR;
- any local housing authority;
- the National Health Service Commissioning Board; and
- any clinical commissioning group.

If requested, these authorities must 'give due consideration' to the request. This falls short of a clear duty to cooperate.

Exercise 5.2

Refer to the scenarios set out in Exercise 5.1.

Which of the human rights under the ECHR should apply to carers? (See pages 7–13.)

Provision of services

Section 2 CDCA 2000 outlines the services that local authorities should consider providing for a carer following an assessment. As with the provision of community care services to the cared-for person, the CSSR has a discretion whether to provide the services or not. In the light of the assessment, the CSSR must consider the following:

- whether the carer has needs in relation to the care that they are providing, or intend to provide;
- if so, whether they could be satisfied wholly or partly by the provision of services that the authority may provide;
- if so, should they provide the service?

The CSSR has some discretion regarding the form that service may take, but it must be sure that it will help the carer provide care for the cared-for person. It may take the form of a community care service provided by the CSSR to the cared-for person, if both the carer and the cared-for person agree. For example, where a carer has difficulties lifting a disabled person, equipment may be provided as part of the care plan, which will clearly benefit the carer as well as the cared-for person.

Section 3 CDCA 2000 introduced the idea of vouchers, issued by a local authority. Vouchers enable carers to take a break from the caring role. They can be used to enable the cared-for person to receive services for a limited period of time from elsewhere, in lieu of the care otherwise provided by the carer. Regulations under the CDCA 2000 outline the details (Carers and Disabled Children (Vouchers) (England) Regulations 2003). The vouchers may be 'money vouchers' (which specify the sum that may be spent on the replacement care and can only be issued to the person being cared for), or they may be 'time vouchers'. A time voucher will specify the services for which the voucher may be redeemed; it may also specify which supplier is authorized by the CSSR to provide it. A time voucher may be issued to the person cared for or to the carer, provided the cared-for person consents or lacks capacity to consent.

A voucher must be redeemed within one year in order to obtain the services either from the CSSR itself, or from a supplier with whom it has entered a contract to supply community care services. Additionally, a preferred supplier i.e. not the CSSR or a supplier with whom they have entered a contract) may be chosen by the voucher holder. However, in the case of a time voucher, the preferred supplier must provide the same service as that specified in the voucher, and must also provide it at a cost that the CSSR would expect to pay, and on its usual terms and conditions. If it is a money voucher, the preferred supplier must agree to the authority's usual terms and conditions. Third-party top-ups are possible to cover services that are additional to, or more expensive than, those that can be obtained using the voucher. Top-ups cannot be used to obtain additional services directly from the CSSR. The top-up can only be paid by somebody other than the service user or the CSSR. A voucher can only be used for residential accommodation for periods of up to 28 consecutive days, and for no longer than 120 days in any twelve-month period.

Under s.17(2)(e) HSSSSAA 1983 the CSSR may, in providing services under the CDCA 2000, make a charge they consider 'reasonable'.

Special provisions apply where the CSSR is providing services either to the cared-for person under community care legislation, or to the carer under the CDCA 2000 (but not to both). If the authority decides to provide an additional service to whomever is not receiving any, and it is a service that could be provided under community care legislation or the CDCA 2000, the authority must decide who is to receive the service. This also applies if the CSSR is not providing services to the carer or cared-for person, but proposes to do so, and the services proposed could be provided either to the carer or to the cared-for person; again, the CSSR must identify the recipient of the proposed service. Finally, if both carer and cared-for person are receiving a service and the authority proposes to provide an additional service that could be provided to either, it must decide who is to receive such service (ss.4(2),(3),(4) CDCA 2000).

> **Exercise 5.3**
>
> Refer to the scenarios set out in Exercise 5.1.
>
> If a carer's assessment is carried out, what services might be provided and to whom?

The legal consequences of caring

People may care for both good and ulterior reasons; a pretence of caring may mask abuse – in particular, financial abuse. Practitioners should be aware of the potential for caring relationships to be abusive. Chapter 7 (p. 146) identifies a number of criminal offences that may be committed against people at risk. Unlike the situation in some other countries, there is no general duty in the United Kingdom for one adult to care for another (*Shepherd* 1862). This is in contrast to the law on children and young persons. Section 1 Children and Young Persons Act 1933 makes it an offence for anybody having responsibility for a child under 16 years to wilfully assault, ill-treat, neglect, abandon, or expose or cause them to be assaulted, ill-treated, neglected, abandoned, or exposed' in a manner likely to cause them unnecessary suffering or injury to health (including injury to or loss of sight, or hearing, or limb, or organ of the body, or any mental derangement).

Nevertheless, the law imposes duties, in some circumstances, on people who have assumed a caring role, albeit not as professional carers. As discussed in Chapters 2 and 6, both the Mental Capacity Act 2005 (MCA 2005) and the Mental Health Act 1983 (MHA 1983) impose criminal liability on carers who wilfully neglect people. In addition, common law recognizes that, in some circumstances, not to care for someone, or to provide poor care, may be criminal. The cases of *Instan* and *R v Stone* illustrate the issues.

5.1 *Instan* and *R v Stone*

Instan

The accused lived with her aunt who suffered gangrene in the leg. The accused did not provide any food or medical attention for her and eventually the aunt died, the death being hastened by the lack of care. The conviction for manslaughter was upheld on appeal. Lord Coleridge said:

> that it was the clear duty of the [carer] to impart to the deceased so much as was necessary to sustain life of the food which she from time to time took in, and which was paid for by the deceased's own money for the purpose of the maintenance of herself and the prisoner; it was only through the instrumentality of the prisoner that the deceased could get the food. There was, therefore, a common law duty imposed on the [carer], which she did not discharge.

R v Stone

The accused and his partner failed to care for his sister who was anorexic and in need of constant care. They were convicted of manslaughter. When she came to live with them, they had initially made efforts to care for her, but failed to continue the care. It was, therefore, reasonable to conclude that they assumed an ongoing duty of caring for her, which they could have discharged either by obtaining help or by caring for her themselves.

Another duty imposed on carers derives from s.5 Domestic Violence, Crime and Victims Act 2004 (DVCVA 2004), which makes it an offence to cause or allow the death or serious physical harm of a vulnerable adult where the accused person was a member of the same household and had frequent contact with the vulnerable adult. This offence was designed to tackle the problem of members of households doing nothing to prevent the abuse of children or vulnerable adults taking place in the home. The accused may be the person who causes the death or violence, or they may be somebody who was aware of the risk of violence and failed to take reasonable steps to prevent it. This does not apply to visitors having a caring role for the victim. Both membership of the household and frequent contact have to be established. Section 5 DVCVA 2004 applies where the person was aware of the risk of serious physical harm and foresaw the occurrence of the unlawful act or course of conduct that resulted in death. However, it also applies when they were unaware of the risk, but ought to have been aware of it and ought to have foreseen the occurrence of the act. The responsibility is to take steps that could reasonably have been expected to protect the vulnerable person (*R v Khan and Khan*).

> **Exercise 5.4**
>
> **Scenario**
>
> A husband and wife have his mother living with them. The mother is suffering from dementia and her behaviour is becoming progressively more demanding and physically aggressive, especially towards her daughter-in-law. As the husband is in full-time employment and often away from home on business, the daughter-in-law has the main caring responsibility. She is finding this very stressful, particularly when her husband is absent and not available to provide support. On such occasions, she feels that the only way to cope is by locking her mother-in-law in her bedroom for long periods of time. The previous week, her mother-in-law had attacked her with a tray. She reacted by pushing her mother-in-law away, who then fell against a wardrobe, injuring her head badly. A friend of the mother-in-law saw the injury and reported her concerns to the CSSR.
>
> What are the possible legal and social work implications in this case?
>
> You should also refer to Chapter 3, p. 53, and Chapter 6, pp. 112.

Young people as carers

In some cases, the primary carer is a child or young person. Because of the overlap between the legislative responsibilities towards vulnerable adults and the law relating to children in need, it is important for practitioners in both adult and children's services to be aware of the needs of young carers. A survey of 4,000 school children by the BBC found that one in twelve had moderate or high levels of caring responsibilities, four times the official figures of 175,000. On this basis, it was estimated that there were some 700,000 young carers in the UK (BBC News 2010). It appears that about 13,000 are caring for more than 50 hours a week and that their average age is 12 years (Carers Trust undated).

Few parents want their children to be carers but it can happen for many reasons (such as families being isolated, afraid of outside interference or unsupported). In many cases, the dividing line between 'helping around the house' and providing personal care to another person can be extremely narrow, and many children find themselves gradually taking on progressively more responsibility for a near relative, such as:

- a parent with a physical illness, disability, mental health problem or dependency on alcohol or drugs;
- a frail, elderly grandparent who has a health problem or who is disabled;
- a brother or a sister with a health problem or disability.

Around 3 million children in the UK have a family member with a disability. More than a half of young carers live in one-parent families and almost one third care for someone with mental health problems (Barnardo's 2006).

Young carers and services

The situation outlined raises problems for those working in children's services and adult services in both health and social care (Aldridge and Becker 1993). Child carer invisibility is a cause for concern (Jenkins and Wingate 1994). One reason for this is the failure of children's services and adult services to work together. Another is the fear among some families that, if children's services are involved, a young carer might be taken into care under the CA 1989. Closer working between the two branches of social care is essential to ensure that young carers and those for whom they provide care are supported and enabled to live in their own homes. In its report on adult social care, the Law Commission (2011) recommended greater integration between the relevant services.

The general approach is that CSSRs should, where appropriate, provide services to parents, rather than place the responsibility of caring on young people. However, a delicate balance has sometimes to be struck between the rights of a child to support in reducing the caring burden and the reluctance of some families to accept intervention and support. Even in those cases where a decision is made to focus support on the child as opposed to the parent, close monitoring of the situation should take place to ensure that the child does not become fixed in their role as carer to the detriment of their education and future prospects. A number of charitable organizations (e.g. the Children's Society and Barnado's) have developed specialist support services for young carers. These organizations claim that many young carers struggle educationally, are often bullied for being 'different', and are afraid to ask for help as they fear letting the family down or being taken into care (Association of Directors of Social Services and Association of Directors of Children's Services 2009). As Cooklin (2010) indicates, some children often try to hide their fears from outsiders, partly out of loyalty and partly due to the fear that they may be 'taken away'.

CSSRs need to be aware of potential professional gaps in supporting young carers. The CA 1989 promotes partnership between parents and CSSRs, and the challenge for practitioners is to ensure that they are regarded by families as a resource to provide support and assistance, rather than bodies to be feared (Herring 2011: 581). As The Children's Society recognizes, the challenge may be daunting, given the age and acute vulnerability of the young people involved (such as those from refugee and asylum-seeking families).

The law and young carers

The legislation that applies to young carers is complex and, as with the law relating to adult carers, is equally in need of consolidation. The Care Act 2014, when implemented, will arguably further complicate the issues (Clements and Bangs 2012), and may even undermine existing rights. As the law currently provides, a young carer may qualify for assessment as a *child in need* under s.17 CA 1989, or as a carer either under the C(RS)A 1995 or the CDCA 2000. To qualify as a *child in need*, the carer applicant would need to show that his health or development is likely to be significantly impaired; to qualify for a carer assessment, the young carer would need to show that he/she was providing *substantial* and *regular care*. However, given that the guidance emphasizes that the term *significant* should be interpreted in the context of the individual actually providing the support, and that children and young persons should not be expected to take on similar levels or responsibilities as adults, it is highly unlikely that their contribution would be regarded as insufficient to meet the statutory criteria.

Only the CDCA 2000, however, provides a right to services and that Act applies only to those who have attained the age of 16 or over. Thus, in circumstances where a very young carer may be in need of services, the only current legal option would be to provide services under the CA 1989. Where eligibility criteria to children's services are restrictive, very young carers may not be eligible for support and are often unlikely to receive an assessment until a crisis occurs. Reform of the law is needed. One possibility might be to incorporate provisions into the CA 1989 that would address the needs of young carers. The case for statutory reform and a robust social services response is overwhelming, given the compelling evidence of social need.

Exercise 5.5

Scenario

A divorced father experiences episodes of profound depression. His ex-wife has emigrated with her new partner. During such episodes, his 14-year-old son assumes responsibility for running the home and caring for his younger siblings. As a result, he regularly misses school and when he does attend is lethargic and non-attentive. The school is very concerned about the welfare of the son and the younger siblings.

What action, if any, could be taken in these circumstances?

Conclusion

The government White Paper 'Caring for our future: reforming care and support' contains a number of commitments to improve the legal rights of carers. These include:

- transforming support for carers by legislating to extend the right to a carer's assessment, and provide an entitlement to public support;
- a national minimum eligibility threshold for support for carers, as for people who use services;
- earlier identification of carers, along with greater choice and control over their own lives, and better support to balance work, education or leisure activities with their caring role. (Department of Health 2012a)

Carer rights embedded in adult social care legislation will go some way towards realizing the ambitions of the Griffiths Report (see Chapter 3, p. 55) to make carer support an integral part of community care provision. As the statistics at the beginning of this chapter indicate, carers make a huge contribution towards the working of adult social care but do so at great personal expense. The need for greater support and clearer rights for carers is beyond dispute.

chapter 6 Mental Health Law

In this chapter, you will learn about:

- Admission to hospital under the Mental Health Act 1983
- The Mental Health Act Code of Practice
- Key definitions
- Learning disability
- Treatability
- Appropriate medical treatment
- The practitioners involved in the admission process
- The nearest relative
- Informal admission under the Mental Health Act 1983
- Formal admission for assessment
- Formal admission for treatment
- Formal admission for assessment in cases of emergency
- The application process
- Admission of patients already in hospital
- The medical treatment of detained patients
- Removal to a place of safety
- Guardianship
- Community provision
- Community Treatment Orders
- Leave of absence
- Hospital Managers
- Mental Health Review Tribunals

Remember to consult The Legal Toolbox on pp. xiii–xx. This will help you to understand processes and procedures referred to in this chapter.

Introduction

Many of the procedures set out in the MHA 1983 (such as compulsory admission to hospital) involve an Approved Mental Health Professional (AMHP)). However, for a number of reasons, it is important that other social workers are aware of the processes and potential for using the MHA 1983, not least because of the incidence of mental health problems within the community. For instance, the Office of National Statistics has estimated that, at some point in their lives, one in four British adults is likely to experience at least one diagnosable mental health problem (e.g. anxiety, depression, eating problems, dementia, personality disorders, bipolar disorders and schizophrenia) (NHS Confederation (Mental Health Network) 2011). Many people who suffer from mental health problems and who are in need of help and support live in the community. As a result, they are likely to receive the help and support they need in the form of social care services under the provisions of the NHSCCA 1983 (see Chapter 4, p. 77), or s.117 MHA 1983 (see p. 78), or through treatment in the NHS from the general practitioner services, or at a hospital outpatient clinic.

Compulsory admission into hospital can also occur via the criminal court system, under ss.37 and 41, Part 3 of the Act, on the grounds of the defendant's mental disorder. Social workers will have a part to play in such admissions, and may also play a significant role in the supervision of ex-offenders when discharged from hospital. However, this chapter concentrates on Parts I, II, IV, 4A and VII of the MHA 1983, often referred to as the 'civil law process'.

Admission to hospital under the Mental Health Act 1983

It may become apparent while assessing a person for community care services that the person is suffering from a mental disorder to such a degree that they need hospital care or treatment, or that a person's mental condition has deteriorated while receiving care in the community. Although most such admissions will be informal and voluntary, the MHA 1983 also empowers AMHPs to authorize a person's detention in hospital for a specified period.

The MHA 1983 is a highly intrusive piece of legislation that permits action to be taken that is contrary to a person's normal right to self-determination and choice. It is essential, therefore, that the human rights of those who are being detained, or who are at risk of detention against their will, are respected. Although the ECHR does not proscribe compulsory deprivation of liberty, certain safeguards apply to reduce the

> **Exercise 6.1**
>
> Evidence shows that certain social groups are proportionately more likely to be subjected to compulsory powers of detention.
>
> 1. Which groups do you think these might be?
> 2. Why do you think these groups are at greater risk of compulsory admission to hospital?
>
> (See Austen and Jeffrey 2007: 296; McKenzie and Bhui 2007: 649–50; Campbell 2010: 2398–413; Golightley 2011: 8–20.)

risk of the power being used unlawfully. The key article of the ECRH is Article 5. The relevant part of the Article states:

> Everyone has the right to liberty and security of person. No one shall be deprived of his liberty save in the following cases and in accordance with a procedure prescribed by law …
>
> (e) the lawful detention of … persons of unsound mind.

Various points arise. The starting point is that everyone has the right to liberty – the fact that a person has a mental disorder (or, indeed, lacks mental capacity (see Chapter 2) does not, of itself, justify detention. If the state wishes to interfere with an individual's right to liberty, two matters need to be present. First, there must be a legal procedure outlining the circumstances in which a detention can take place and this must contain essential safeguards for the individual. In England, the MHA 1983 is the 'legal procedure' relied on by the state. Second, the purpose of the detention must fall within the specific areas mentioned in Article 5. For present purposes, the relevant area is that the person is of 'unsound mind'. This is an unfortunate term, reflecting the fact that the ECHR was drafted in the early 1950s when mental health terminology lacked refinement and any degree of precision. Cases, such as *Winterwerp v Netherlands*, heard before the European Court of Human Rights make it clear that the term is not capable of precise definition and will change as more is known about mental health. It stated that 'unsound mind' is a developing concept that should reflect contemporary thinking, rather than reflecting the time when it was drafted. The Court has also made it clear that any detention must be in a hospital or other suitable institution authorized for such detention (*Ashindene v United Kingdom*).

Concern about the human rights deficit in the MHA 1983 as it was originally enacted, (and as illustrated, for example, by the *Bournewood* case (see Chapter 2, p. 47), plus concern over its incompatibility with the Human Rights Act 1983 (HRA 1983), led to the introduction, for consultation, of a draft Mental Health Bill in 2002. However, there was strong opposition to its proposals. A second draft Bill was published in 2004, but this was again subject to intense criticism. In 2006, the government abandoned the Bill and decided to confine itself to amending the MHA 1983 by means of the Mental Health Act 2007 (MHA 2007). It could be argued that clever drafting was used to give the government what it wanted from the draft Bills, but through a process of amendment rather than new legislation.

The purpose of this brief history is to raise awareness of the controversial nature of mental health legislation and the complexities that inevitably arise in legislating in respect of people with a mental disorder. Is legislation capable of dealing with the complexities of mental health? What is the correct balance between protecting the public from 'dangerous people' and the right to liberty of the individual? What is the purpose of detention under the MHA 1983? Is it merely to 'get the person off the streets' or is it to treat them for their mental disorder? If it is to treat the individual, what is meant by 'treatment'? How should the legislation protect people against the abuse or misuse of any power under the MHA 1983?

As seen in Figure 6.1, a significant number of people are detained under the MHA 1983. The statistics show a disproportionate number of detained patients coming from areas with a high incidence of social exclusion, unemployment and low income. Women; members of ethnic communities; deaf people; those suffering from schizophrenia, affective disorder and addictions are also more likely to be compulsorily detained (Lawlor *et al.* 2012).

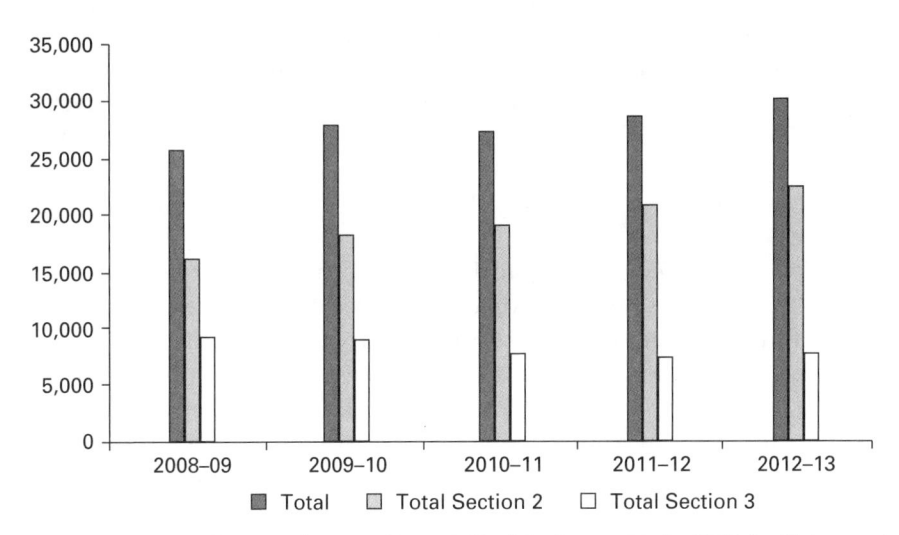

Figure 6.1 Detentions under the Mental Health Act 1983 in NHS facilities and independent hospitals by legal status, 2008–09 to 2012–13
Source: Health and Social Care Information Centre (2013b).

Exercise 6.2

1. What strategies should a CSSR develop in order to combat these disproportionate rates of admissions?
2. Discuss the statistics in the context of the Equality Act 2010 (see Chapter 1, p. 13).

The Mental Health Act Code of Practice

In addition to the MHA 1983, a Code of Practice has been published by the Department of Health under s.118 MHA 1983 (Department of Health 2008b). Although the Code is not legally binding as such, practitioners (doctors, approved clinicians (see p. 121), managers and staff of hospitals, and AMHPs) must have regard to it. (A separate code is published for use in Wales). In Chapter 1 of the Code, five guiding principles are identified. Those who are at risk of being subjected to the powers of the MHA 1983 are entitled to the protection afforded by the five principles.

Principle 1 – the purpose principle: Any act undertaken under the MHA 1983 must be done for the purpose of minimizing the undesirable effects of mental disorder by maximizing the safety and wellbeing of patients, promoting their recovery and protecting others from harm. Wellbeing includes both mental and physical wellbeing.

Principle 2 – the least restrictive principle: Any restriction imposed on a person must be limited to the minimum restriction of their liberty, having regard to the purpose for which it is imposed. This is often referred to as the 'least restrictive alternative'. It links with the doctrine of proportionality (discussed in Chapter 1). Unfortunately, the lack of alternative provision and/or the shortage of resources in the community undermine this principle. What might appear, on the face of it, to be too extreme an action may, in reality, be all that can be done within existing resources.

Principle 3 – The respect principle: Respect is central to the working of the MHA 1983. People's needs are diverse and will be informed by race, religion, culture, gender, age, sexual orientation and disability. The person's views, wishes and feelings should be followed wherever this is practicable and consistent with the reason for taking the decision. As with mental capacity, care should be taken not to rush to conclusions based on personal attributes that may not conform to what others may consider to be 'normal'.

Principle 4 – the participation principle: People must be involved in decisions that are made about them. So far as is possible, decisions must be taken with them and not about them. Carers and family members should also be involved unless the practitioner is satisfied that they do not have the person's welfare at heart. Their views should be taken seriously although, ultimately, the practitioner has the responsibility for making the decision.

Principle 5 – the effectiveness, efficiency and equity principle: Resources available to practitioners must be used effectively, efficiently and in an equitable way to meet the needs of the person and to achieve the purpose for which the decision was taken. Of course, practitioners have to recognize that in addition to their duty to the individual, they have a wider duty towards all people who may be in need of help.

These five principles are very important. If challenged, a practitioner should be able to show how that they took all the principles into account in arriving at their decision. According to the Introduction to the Code of Practice (para.vi), they should record any departure from the Code since it could become the basis of a legal challenge. It is sensible, therefore, for a practitioner to seek advice before acting contrary to its provisions (Department of Health 2008b). This has been reinforced by the Court of Appeal in the case of *R v Mersey Care NHS Trust*. The question before the Court was whether the Trust's seclusion policy breached Articles 3 and 8 of the ECHR. It was held that the Code should be observed by all hospitals unless they had a good reason for departing from it in relation to an individual patient. In this case, it was the Code that ensured that rights under the ECHR were protected.

In individual cases, different weight will be given to each of the principles. Every case is different. In some situations, less weight will be given, for example, to the person's point of view, or that of the family or carers. A practitioner must be able to provide evidence for their decision.

Key definitions

A number of key definitions are contained in the MHA 1983. Central to the working of the MHA is the definition of 'mental disorder'. It is understandably difficult to capture such a complex concept in a few words. Either a detailed and exhaustive definition is required (which invariably misses out certain things), or the definition needs to be general with discretion for the practitioner to make a judgement. The MHA 1983 adopts the second approach. Section 1(2) defines a 'mental disorder' as meaning: *any disorder or disability of the mind.*

This definition applies throughout the MHA 1983. The original MHA 1983 referred to categories of mental disorder. These definitions have now been abolished and this single legal definition applies. It is arguable, however, that the definition is unacceptably wide.

> **Exercise 6.3**
>
> 1. Do you consider the current definition of 'mental disorder' to be too broad?
> 2. Does the definition give too much discretion to practitioners when deciding whether a person has a mental disorder?

The original MHA 1983 contained a provision that 'promiscuity or other immoral conduct, sexual deviancy or dependence on alcohol or drugs' were not to be considered as implying that person may be suffering from a mental disorder. Section 1(3) MHA 1983 makes it clear that dependence on alcohol or drugs is not to be considered a disorder or disability of the mind. However, it may be a component of a dual diagnosis; that is, a diagnosis of mental disorder, as well as dependence on alcohol or drugs. The reference to promiscuity or other immoral conduct and sexual deviancy is removed from the amended MHA 1983.

Learning disability

What about people with a learning disability? Are they included within the MHA 1983? The answer is that they are only partially included. Under the terms of the MHA 1983, a person with a learning disability does not have a 'mental disorder' unless it is 'associated with abnormally aggressive or seriously irresponsible conduct' on their part. The courts will take a very restrictive view of whether conduct falls within this definition. In *Re F (Mental Health Act guardianship)* [2000], the court did not regard a woman's determination to return home to an abusive environment as 'seriously irresponsible' conduct.

The need to demonstrate abnormally aggressive or seriously irresponsible conduct in cases of learning disability does not apply to two particular provisions of the MHA 1983:

- Admission for assessment under s.2 MHA 1983 (see p. 124).
- Section 136 MHA 1983 – this involves removal to a place of safety by the police (see p. 128).

In these cases, a learning disability alone will suffice. One point should be noted – the mental disorder must be associated with the behaviour and not the cause of it (e.g. the behaviour might arise from physical distress that manifests itself in the person's conduct, or difficulties of communication (Department of Health 2008b, paras 34, 6–34). Learning disability is defined as:

> a state of arrested or incomplete development of mind which includes significant impairment of intelligence and social functioning.

Exercise 6.4

Scenario

Damion, a young man in his twenties with a learning disability, is living with his grandparents. Until recently, he seemed to be coping well with life with the help of anti-depressant medication. However, his grandparents recently contacted the local CSSR because of their considerable concern about him. He has begun to act strangely, is staying up all night and, when challenged, shouts abuse. He has even threatened to set himself and his room on fire if anyone intrudes on his privacy and has visited a local garage to buy petrol. When his grandparents contact the garage to ask that no more petrol is sold to him, he threatens to kill them. He accuses his grandparents and the neighbours of spying on him and of working for the secret services. The grandparents are convinced he has petrol hidden in his room but are denied access. An AMHP and doctor respond to the grandparents' pleas for help. When they visit, they find that Damion has locked himself in his room. He repeats his threat to set the house on fire and to kill himself if approached.

How would you apply the principles (set out on p. 116) to this case?

Treatability

The original MHA 1983 required that, in order for a patient to be detained, their mental disorder had to be treatable. This led to concern about people with dangerous severe personality disorders (DSPDs). It is important to understand that only a tiny proportion of people with mental health problems can be in any way regarded as dangerous. However, people with a DSPD have been held responsible for a number of high-profile killings (such as that by Michael Stone, a violent psychopath). As Stone's condition was thought not to be treatable, he was not detained and consequently was able to kill.

Concern over the need to show treatability became a major feature of the debate on reform. If certain types of mental disorder were considered untreatable, the question arises as to why anybody with that disorder should be detained in a hospital. Many argue that detention is appropriate as the only effective way of protecting the public. This is highly contentious. The contrary argument is that it is unfair to the individual to be detained in hospital for something that is not treatable.

Appropriate medical treatment

The MHA 1983 circumvents this debate by redefining 'treatment' and by removing the treatability test. It introduces the concept of 'appropriate medical treatment'. This is defined as:

> medical treatment which is appropriate taking into account the nature and degree of the mental disorder and all other circumstances. (s.3(4) MHA 1983)

This is a less than helpful definition – although it is clear that it does not require anyone to say what is likely to happen as a consequence of the treatment (unlike the old style treatability test).

Treatment is defined as:

> medical treatment the purpose of which is to alleviate, or prevent a worsening of, the disorder or one or more it is symptoms or manifestations. (s.145(4)) MHA 1983)

Medical treatment *includes*:

> nursing, psychological intervention and specialist mental health habilitation, rehabilitation and care. (s.145(1) MHA 1983)

The effect of these broadly-based definitions of mental disorder, treatment, appropriate treatment and medical treatment is to widen the range of people who may potentially come within the terms of the MHA 1983. Presumably, this is a response to the concerns (real and imagined) over the ability of the previous law to deal with cases such as that of Michael Stone.

The practitioners involved in the admission process

The MHA 1983 involves a number of different practitioners and imposes duties and responsibilities on them. Depending on the issue, not only may an AMHP be involved but also, as mentioned above, other social work practitioners who work more generally with adults in the community. Nevertheless, the key practitioners in this context are AMHPs who are approved as such by the local CSSR under s.114 MHA 1983. They must undergo special training before they can practice as AMHPs. The details of their training and qualifications are laid down by Health and Care Professions Council (s.114ZA MHA 1983). An AMHP must demonstrate to the local authority that they have 'appropriate competence in dealing with persons who are suffering from mental disorder' (s.114(3) MHA 1983).

Under the MHA 1983 before it was amended by the MHA 2007, only social work practitioners were eligible to become ASWs (the terminology used in the original MHA 1983). The amended MHA 1983 has opened up the category of practitioners who may be approved as an AMHP. In addition to social workers, an AMHP may now be an occupational therapist, nurse or psychologist. Doctors, however, are not allowed to become AMHPs. It is important to note that, although these additional categories of practitioner may be employed by another body, they must be approved by a CSSR. Their duty when acting as AMHPs is to follow the provisions of the MHA 1983 and the Code. Since AMHPs are a public authority for the purposes of the HRA 1998 (see Chapter 1, p. 7), they must act in a way that is compatible with the ECHR.

Other practitioners who have responsibilities under the MHA 1983 are the approved clinicians; that is, practitioners who have been approved by the Secretary of State to carry out certain statutory functions. As with AMHPs, the MHA 1983 has opened up the categories of those who may act in this role. As a result, the category of approved clinician may now include not only a medical practitioner, but also a chartered psychologist, nurse, social worker and occupational therapist. They must undergo appropriate training before they can carry out this role. When acting as approved clinicians, practitioners are performing a function of a public nature and are therefore bound to act in a way that is compatible with the ECHR (Department of Health 2008b, para. 23.39).

An approved clinician may also be the responsible clinician; that is, the doctor with overall responsibility for an individual detained patient, or a patient who is subject to a Community Treatment Order (CTO) (see pp. 130–1). Certain functions under the MHA 1983 can, nevertheless, be carried out by any qualified medical practitioner; for example, the provision of one of the two medical recommendations that must be provided in relation to an application to detain a patient under s.2 MHA 1983 or s.3 (see p. 124).

The nearest relative

A legacy of the history of mental health legislation is the role of the nearest relative. As will be seen, the nearest relative can play a significant role under the MHA 1983 and may be made privy to confidential information about the health of the person who may be detained. The idea of a legally authorized pecking order of relatives perhaps reflects a world in which family structures were different and families were expected to undertake the caring role.

Mental Health Law

> **6.1 *JT v UK***
>
> In this case, the European Court of Human Rights considered the case of a woman detained under the MHA 1983. She had a difficult relationship with her mother and made allegations of sexual abuse against her step-father. Under the original MHA 1983, her mother was designated as her nearest relative and, consequently, had a right to be involved in decision-making regarding her daughter. The daughter did not want the mother to know where she was. At the time, there was no way that the daughter could remove the mother as nearest relative, unless the mother consented. Although a friendly settlement was reached, the case illustrates that in some cases the concept of the nearest relative works against the best interests of the detained patient. The UK government agreed that it would change the law to arrange for the nearest relative to be replaced where the patient reasonably objects.

Section 26 MHA 1983 lists the people who can become the nearest relative:

- Husband, wife or civil partner
- Son or daughter
- Father or mother
- Brother or sister
- Grandparent
- Uncle or aunt
- Nephew or niece.

> **Exercise 6.5**
>
> Read the case of *TTM v Hackney LBC and East London NHS Foundation Trust* where the local authority was held liable for a patient's unlawful detention as a result of an AMHP's flawed and incomplete process of consultation.
>
> What lessons does the case contain for practitioners?

Under s.29 MHA 1983, an application can be made to the court for an order to replace the nearest relative identified in the list with someone whom the court considers to be suitable and who is willing to act in that role. To meet the concerns identified in the case of *JT v UK*, the patient or someone on behalf of the patient may apply for such an order.

More broadly, practitioners must involve carers and family where that is appropriate. Paragraphs 2.39–42 of the Code provide guidance on the involvement of carers.

Informal admission under the Mental Health Act 1983

If a person has legal capacity, informal and consensual admission is more appropriate than compulsory admission. In fact, s.131 MHA 1983 makes it clear that nothing should be construed as preventing informal admission where it is appropriate. Nevertheless, Bindman *et al.* (2005) found that one third of patients who had been admitted informally had felt highly coerced during the admission process. The majority were uncertain that they were free to leave hospital. This is despite the fact that para. 2.45 of the Code of Practice stresses that informal patients should be made aware of their legal position and rights.

Practitioners should ensure that persons making the decision to enter hospital voluntarily are in possession of the necessary information and that no undue pressure is placed on them to comply with the wishes of professionals or family. For example, the person should not be threatened with compulsory admission if they fail to 'consent' to informal admission. However, informal admission may not be appropriate, even if the person has capacity. It may be that their mental state or experience suggests that they will change their mind about voluntary admission in circumstances where there would otherwise be a risk to their own safety or that of others (Department of Health 2008b, paras 4.9–4.12).

Whether or not a person has legal capacity to make the decision to enter hospital voluntarily is determined by applying the test under the MCA 2005 to that decision (see Chapter 2, p. 29). The relationship between the MCA 2005 and the MHA 1983 is complex. Where admission to hospital for assessment or treatment for mental disorder is necessary and the person lacks capacity to consent or refuse, an application should be made under the MHA 1983. If the treatment is for a physical condition, or a mental illness that falls outside the powers of detention under the MHA 1983, and the person lacks capacity to make the particular decision, the provisions of the MCA 2005 apply. It is important to realize that the two pieces of legislation are not interchangeable. The interface between the two Acts was discussed by the court in *GJ v The Foundation Trust*.

6.2 *GJ v The Foundation Trust*

case example

GJ was aged 65. He had a diagnosis of vascular dementia, and amnesic disease due to alcohol. He also suffered from diabetes and was prone to hypoglycaemic attacks. A standard authorization for Deprivation of Liberty authorization was made (see Chapter 2, p. 48) and subsequently renewed. An application had been made to the Court of Protection. The judge held that GJ could not be detained under the Deprivation of Liberty Safeguards for the treatment of his mental disorder, but could be detained in order to receive care and treatment for his physical disorder (diabetes). As such, he was eligible to be deprived of his liberty.

At all times, practitioners should remember the need to adopt the least restrictive course of action, the need for proportionality (see Chapter 1, p. 8) and the very strong message from the European Court of Human Rights in *HL v UK* (see Chapter 2, p. 39) concerning unlawfully depriving people who lack capacity of their liberty. (See also the Care Quality Commission 2010b.)

Formal admission for assessment under s.2 Mental Health Act 1983

The requirements for an application for compulsory admission for assessment under s.2 MHA 1983 are:

- the patient is suffering from a mental disorder;
- the mental disorder is of a nature or degree warranting detention in hospital for assessment (plus perhaps medical treatment) for a limited period; and
- the patient ought to be detained in the interests of their own health or safety, or to protect others.

The application must be supported by two medical recommendations, each of which must confirm that these conditions have been met. The detention may last for a period of up to 28 days.

Formal admission for treatment under s.3 Mental Health Act 1983

The requirements for an application for admission for treatment under s.3 MHA 1983 are:

- the patient is suffering from a mental disorder of a nature or degree that makes it appropriate for them to receive medical treatment in a hospital;
- it is necessary for the patient's health and safety, or for the protection of others, that they should receive such treatment and it cannot be provided unless they are detained; and
- appropriate medical treatment is available.

Again, the application must be supported by two medical recommendations confirming that these conditions have been met. Admission under s.3 MHA 1983 is initially for six months.

Formal admission for assessment in cases of emergency under s.4 Mental Health Act 1983

On occasion, it may be necessary to make an emergency application in respect of a patient as circumstances may make it difficult to follow the full procedure under either s.2 or s.3 MHA 1983. This is possible under s.4 MHA 1983. However, it is limited to cases of urgent necessity. It cannot be used simply because it is more convenient for the AMHP, the doctors, or the hospital. The requirements for an emergency application are:

- The application must contain a statement that it is of urgent necessity for the patient to be admitted for assessment under s.2 MHA 1983 but that compliance with the requirements of s.2 would involve unreasonable delay;
- Only one (not two) medical recommendation is required. Ideally the one medical recommendation should be made by a doctor who has previous knowledge of the patient. The medical recommendation must confirm that the requirements of s.2 MHA 1983 have been satisfied. Typically, an emergency admission would take place if it proves impossible to get a second doctor to see the patient in a situation that is volatile and there is a risk of harm to the patient, or to other people.

An emergency application only lasts for up to 72 hours from the point at which the patient is admitted to hospital. During that time, the necessary second medical recommendation must be obtained and the application for the assessment process is then completed. If the second medical recommendation is not forthcoming, the patient can no longer be detained.

The application process

Before considering the other way in which a person may be detained under the MHA 1983, the mechanics of the application processes need to be discussed. Note the following points:

- Applications may be made by an AMHP or the nearest relative (this illustrates the critical role that the nearest relative may play under the MHA 1983).
- An application cannot be made by an AMHP if it would give rise to a potential conflict of interest. Regulations have been made outlining the circumstances in which a conflict may arise. These cover financial, business, professional or personal relationship conflicts. The regulations also apply to any doctor involved in the admissions process (Mental Health (Conflicts of Interest) (England) Regulations 2008).

- The application is addressed to the manager of the hospital to which the admission of the patient is sought.
- If an application under s.3 MHA 1983 is made by an AMHP, the AMHP must take all practicable steps to inform the nearest relative that an application has been made and that the nearest relative has the right to apply for the discharge of the patient under s.24 MHA 1983.
- For an application under s.3 MHA 1983, the AMHP should consult (not merely inform, as under s.2 MHA 1983 the nearest relative. An application may not be made by an AMHP if the nearest relative has notified them (or the appropriate CSSR) that they object to the application being made. This does not apply if the AMHP thinks that it would not be 'reasonably practicable or would involve unreasonable delay' (e.g. the nearest relative is abroad on holiday and cannot be easily contacted.
- Whoever makes the application must have seen the patient within the previous 14 days, even at weekends and during public holidays (*R (Modaresi) v Secretary of State*).
- The doctors making the recommendation must have personally examined the patient.
- One of the medical recommendations must be by a doctor who has been approved by the Secretary of State as having special experience in the diagnosis or treatment of mental disorder; that is, an approved clinician. These are known as 's.12 doctors'.
- At least one of the doctors should have had a previous acquaintance of the patient.
- Standard forms are available for the admission process.

Admission of patients already in hospital under s.5 Mental Health Act 1983

On occasion, a person may already be in hospital as an informal patient, either for treatment for their mental disorder, or for a physical condition. In these situations, it may be possible to detain them temporarily if they attempt to leave, where it is thought that formal detention under the MHA 1983 might be necessary. Alternatively, the patient may be in hospital under s.2 MHA 1983, and it is felt that they should be detained under s.3.

Where the patient is in hospital as an in-patient (for a mental condition, or other condition), a doctor or the approved clinician may initiate a process whereby the patient will be detained in hospital for up to 72 hours pending an application under the MHA 1983. If the patient is in hospital receiving treatment for a mental disorder, a nurse (approved for this purpose) may authorize the detention of the patient in the hospital for a period of up to six hours. It must appear to the nurse that it is necessary – because of the patient's mental disorder, for their health or safety, or for the protection of others – that the patient is prevented from leaving. It must also not be practicable for the nurse to access a doctor or clinician in time to prevent the patient from leaving. The important thing about this process is that it is designed to ensure that the patient can be assessed under the MHA 1983 to see whether formal admission is appropriate.

The medical treatment of detained patients

The MHA 1983 provides for the treatment of people who are detained. The definitions of 'treatment' and 'appropriate medical treatment' have

Table 6.1 Patient safeguards under the Mental Health Act 1983

	Treatment	Safeguard
s.57	Any surgical operation for destroying the function of brain tissue	Consent of patient and a second opinion from a second opinion appointed doctor (SOAD)
s.58	Treatment not within s.57, or s.58A(1) involving medication if three months or more have elapsed since it was first administered (in the first three months neither consent nor a second opinion is required)	Consent of patient or a second opinion from a SOAD
s.58A	Electro Convulsive Therapy (ECT)	Except for emergencies, ECT must not be given to a person with capacity unless they have consented. Where they lack capacity, ECT can only be given if it is appropriate, would not conflict with an advance decision, a decision by an attorney, a deputy, or the Court of Protection (see Chapter 2, p. 46)
s.62	Urgent treatment for the mental disorder	Treatment is necessary to save a patient's life, or to prevent a serious deterioration
		Is immediately necessary to alleviate serous suffering and it is not irreversible
		Is immediately necessary to prevent the patient from behaving violently or being a danger to self or others and it is not irreversible

been discussed (see p. 120). Given the consequences of some kinds of treatment for mental disorder, the MHA 1983 includes safeguards for the person. Table 6.1 presents the types of treatment and the relevant safeguards.

Removal to a place of safety

Under s.135 MHA 1983 an AMHP may apply to a magistrate for the issue of a warrant authorizing a policeman to enter specified premises, by force if necessary, in order to remove an individual to a place of safety. The grounds for such removal are that the person suffering from mental disorder has been, or is being, ill-treated, neglected or kept otherwise than under proper control or, being unable to care for themself, is living alone. The warrant need not name the person, but must contain the address of the premises. In executing the warrant, the police officer must be accompanied by an AMHP and a doctor. The maximum period of detention is 72 hours.

A similar provision exists under s.136 MHA 1983. This empowers a police officer to remove from a public place to a place of safety any person who appears to be suffering from a mental disorder and appears to be in immediate need of care and control. The purpose of detention, for up to 72 hours, is to allow the person to be examined by a doctor and be interviewed by an AMHP. The 72-hour period runs from when the person arrives at the place of safety. This means that the time at which the person was detained must be recorded. It should be noted, however, that, although the criteria under s.136 may be satisfied, this does not mean that the police are obliged to act.

For the purposes of ss.135 and 136, a 'place of safety' is defined as a hospital, police station, residential establishment, or any other suitable place, the occupier of which is willing temporarily to receive the person. According to the Code of Practice, it is preferable 'as a general rule' for the person to be detained in a hospital. The number of place of safety orders in 2011/12 was 15,240, which was a 6 per cent increase on 2010/11 and more than 2.25 times the number made in 2006/7 (though it should be noted that this may be due to improved recording, as well as an increase in the use of these sections) (*R v Harrow London Borough Council ex parte Cobham*).

Guardianship: s.7 Mental Health Act 1983

One of the key principles of the MHA 1983 is that the least restrictive alternative should be chosen. This recognizes, amongst other things, that Article 5 of the ECHR provides for a right to liberty, which can only be interfered with in limited circumstances. Article 8 of the ECHR also provides a right to private life, family life, home and correspondence. This, too, can only be interfered with in exceptional cases. Under the MHA 1983, a lesser form of intervention than admission to hospital is available; this is known as 'guardianship'. Guardianship does not authorize the detention of a patient, but does impose a legal framework around them. At this point, it is worth remembering that a Deprivation of Liberty Authorization (see Chapter 2, p. 48) may be sought for a person under guardianship.

What are the requirements for guardianship? These are found in s.7 MHA 1983:

- the patient must be suffering from a mental disorder of a nature or degree that warrants guardianship;
- it must be necessary in the interests of the welfare (not the health and safety, as under the admissions processes) of the patient, or the protection of other people.

Two medical recommendations are required, as with applications for admission, one of which must be by an approved clinician (see p. 121). A person will be identified as the guardian. This may be the local CSSR, or an individual (e.g. the nearest relative, or an AMHP). If it is an individual, the local CSSR must accept the guardianship on behalf of that individual. If the application is made by an AMHP, the requirement to consult, rather than merely to inform, the nearest relative applies. For AMHPs and doctors, the conflict of interest provisions (see p. 125) also apply.

What are the effects of a guardianship application? Section 8 MHA 1983 confers three powers on the guardian:

- The power to require the patient to live at a place specified by the CSSR, or the guardian (which could include a care home or the patient's own home). A Deprivation of Liberty Authorisation may be used to reinforce this – although it is essential to remember that the conditions of the MCA 2005 (see Chapter 2) must be satisfied.
- The power to require the patient to attend a specified place for medical treatment (although there is no power to force the patient to undergo the treatment) education, occupation, or training.
- The power to allow access to the patient by a doctor, AMHP, or other specified person.

Although these are limited powers, some small-scale studies suggest that guardianship can usefully meet the needs of particular service users. One study concluded that guardianship was useful in managing elderly patients with organic brain diseases (Watts *et al.* 1990; Grant 1992).

> **Exercise 6.6**
>
> The preceding section has provided an overview of the various options available under the MHA 1983.
>
> 1. Is guardianship a useful power?
> 2. When might it be appropriate to use guardianship rather than compulsory admission to hospital?

Community provision

Social workers (other than social work AMHPs) can find themselves working with a service user who was admitted to hospital under the MHA 1983. Patients who have been discharged from detention in hospital under s.3 MHA 1983 are entitled to after-care under s.117 MHA 1983. This section is unusual in social care law in that it gives a person a right to receive after-care services. A duty is imposed on health and CSSRs to provide after-care until such time as it is thought that they no longer need the services. The section does not specify what those services are to be – that is left to the authorities to decide, subject to their meeting needs relating to the person's mental disorder. However, the level of services must be more than a token gesture towards the duty under s.117 MHA 1983. Unusually for the provision of social care, no charges can be made for such after-care services – to charge is unlawful (*R v Harrow London Borough Council ex parte Cobham*). Neither can s.117 MHA 1983 after-care services be imposed on the person. The CSSR authority also has a duty to assess the person for community care services under s.47 NHSCCA 1990 (see Chapter 3, p. 55). Section 117(3) MHA 1983 refers to the place where the person 'is resident'. This is different from 'ordinary residence' (*R Hertfordshire CC) v LB Hammersmith & Fulham* (2011 EWCA Civ_77).

Community Treatment Orders

A new provision in the current MHA 1983 was the introduction of CTOs, of which there were 5218 in 2012/13 (Health and Social Care Information Centre 2013b). It should be noted that, in the Code of Practice, the term used is 'supervised community treatment' (SCT). One problem with the working of the MHA 1983 is that, following formal admission to hospital, a patient's condition may stabilize and the treatment regime starts to work. If a patient is discharged and fails to take medication or attend out-patient clinics, their condition deteriorates and it may be necessary to readmit them under the MHA 1983. The pattern may be repeated on a number of occasions and is often referred to as the 'revolving door'.

The question that has arisen is whether it should be possible to impose treatment on people in their community. For very good reasons (both in principle and practice), this has been rejected. Instead, the MHA 1983 introduced CTOs – which do not impose treatment on a patient but, rather, provide them with an incentive to comply with their treatment regime. Certain formalities must be complied with, involving the AMHP and the responsible clinician. For the present purposes, it is sufficient to outline the effect of CTOs:

- CTOs may be used for people detained under s.3 MHA 1983.
- A CTO will enable to the person to be discharged from hospital and live in the community if the criteria in s.17a MHA 1983 are satisfied (basically these require the responsible clinician to be satisfied that a patient can live in the community on condition that they are liable to be recalled to hospital if they breach any conditions – the AMHP must agree with the responsible clinician).
- If a CTO is made, a patient can leave hospital but s.3 MHA 1983 admission authorization remains in force, although the clock is stopped. Thus, if the original authorization has three further months to run, it does not cease to have effect when the CTO is made, but the remaining period remains in abeyance and may be reinstated if the CTO is revoked.
- A CTO may be revoked and the remaining period of detention reinstated if the patient violates one of the conditions in the CTO. For example, the responsible clinician may feel that a patient requires treatment that they would not receive in the community.
- If a CTO is not revoked but a patient is recalled, they can be detained for up to 72 hours and, if necessary, treated without their consent. A patient can be released on the CTO at any time during that period.

CTOs are controversial and their success has yet to be assessed. There is a fear that they will become a substitute for providing services (Lawton-Smith *et al.* 2008).

Leave of absence

A patient detained under the MHA 1983 may be granted leave of absence for a short period. At one time, leave of absence was (mis)used as a means of imposing conditions on patients who were given leave of absence for a long period. Under s.17 MHA 1983, the responsible clinician may grant a patient leave of absence, subject to any 'condition that maybe imposed'; for example, where the person is to reside during the period of absence. Leave of absence may be granted either indefinitely, or for a specified period (often to attend a family function). If it a 'longer term leave of absence' (i.e. it is indefinite, or for more than seven days) the responsible clinician must consider whether a CTO would be more appropriate. A longer term of absence may be used to assess a patient's suitability for discharge. Patients detained under s.3 MHA 1983 that are granted leave of absence are also entitled to after-care services under s.117 (see pp. 78 and 130).

Hospital Managers and Mental Health Review Tribunals

Although compulsory detention under the MHA 1983 can be regarded as stigmatizing and discriminatory, the advantage is that the legislation contains certain safeguards that might not be available to an informal patient. For some people, formal detention is protective and enables the patient to have recourse to review mechanisms, as well as other safeguards found in the MHA 1983. Two such safeguards are found in the roles of the Hospital Managers and the Mental Health Review Tribunals (MHRTs).

Under s.25 MHA 1983, the responsible clinician and (subject to restrictions) the nearest relative can discharge a patient. In addition, the section provides that a patient can apply to a panel known as the 'Hospital Managers' for discharge. Usually, a panel will consist of three members and will not contain either a medically or a legally qualified person. Under the Code of Practice, the Hospital Managers may do the following:

- undertake a review of whether a patient should be discharged at any time at their discretion;
- undertake a review if the patient's responsible clinician submits to them a report renewing detention, or extending a CTO;
- consider holding a review when they receive a request from (or on behalf of) a patient; and
- consider holding a review when the responsible clinician makes a report to them barring an order by the nearest relative to discharge a patient. (*Re (O) v West London MH NHS Trust*)

In hearing an application, the Hospital Managers must have regard to the rules of natural justice. This means that they must provide written and oral reasons for their decision (Department of Health (2012c).

In addition to applying to the Hospital Managers, the patient may also apply to an MHRT for discharge. MHRTs are judicial bodies that can order the discharge of a patient from detention or guardianship under the MHA 1983. The MHRT can hear a patient's case either:

- on the application from the patient or the nearest relative; or
- on referral from the Secretary of State; or
- if the MHRT has not reviewed the case within a given period, on referral by Hospital Managers.

Conclusion

Mental health legislation remains controversial. The statutory powers are extensive and highly intrusive. Its use must be seen in the context of Article 5 of the ECHR (see Chapter 1, p. 9). The MHA 1983 provides the procedures required by the Article; whether the ambit of the MHA 1983 is too wide is a matter for much debate. However, for many people, admission under the MHA 1983 provides them with the support they need at difficult times. Similarly, the legislation seeks to protect the public from the small number of people with mental health problems who may be dangerous. The necessary balance between the desirable and undesirable aspects of the MHA 1983 is hard to achieve, and the situation is probably not helped by the stigma that mental illness attracts and the assumptions that are made about it. This is particularly curious, since mental health affects such a high proportion of the population.

Social work has a significant role to play in coordinating services and support to individuals and groups who may have had negative experiences and perceptions of mental health services (Foster 2005). Evidence shows that individuals who receive mental health services intervention greatly value the non-stigmatizing services provided by social work (Social Services Inspectorate 2004). The challenge will be to maintain and facilitate this contribution at a time of considerable change in the way services are organized. In particular, CSSRs will need to ensure that the independence of AHMPs is not compromised and that appropriate training is provided, so that cultural and social issues are properly considered in the context of mental health assessments (Ray and Pugh 2008).

chapter 7
Adult Safeguarding and Protection

In this chapter, you will learn about:

- Vulnerable adults
- What amounts to 'abuse' and 'neglect'?
- National statistics
- What is safeguarding?
- Existing law and procedure
- What does 'No Secrets' require of practitioners?
- Criminal law
- Prosecution
- The criminal justice system
- Civil law
- Adult Safeguarding Boards
- Serious Case Reviews
- Functions of a Serious Case Review
- The Law Commission's report and Scottish legislation

Remember to consult The Legal Toolbox on pp. xiii–xx. This will help you to understand processes and procedures referred to in this chapter.

Introduction

As a social work practitioner, you may witness or become aware of situations where vulnerable adults are being either abused or neglected, or suspect that such abuse or neglect is taking place. This may occur at various stages of the social work process, during referral or assessment, or at any other time while the case is ongoing. As in work with abused and neglected children, this is one of the most distressing areas of social care work.

A major study on the prevalence of elder abuse was undertaken by the National Centre for Social Research, funded by Comic Relief. It covered only those aged 66 years and over who were living in their own homes. The evidence makes disturbing reading and surprised many people who thought that levels of abuse and neglect had previously been overstated. It identified significant elder abuse within the homes of older people involving 4 per cent of those aged 66 years or over (O'Keeffe *et al.* 2007). This could amount to around 342,000 people throughout the United Kingdom (approximately equivalent to the population of Leicester). It is also alarming that the research concluded that only around 3 per cent of cases were known to, and picked up, by adult protection agencies.

Abuse is a clear violation of a person's human rights. Abuse is inhuman and degrading. It sometimes threatens life. It is a violation of a person's right to private life. Victims of abuse are entitled to justice under Article 6 of the ECHR; regrettably, justice-seeking options are rarely pursued, or even considered (Clarke *et al.* 2012).

Vulnerable adults

There is no statutory definition of a 'vulnerable' adult. However, in 2000, the Department of Health published 'No Secrets', a guidance document on developing and implementing policies and procedures to protect vulnerable adults from abuse. The guidance was issued under s.7 Local Authority and Social Service Act 1970 (LASSA 1970) (see Chapter 1, p. 5). It should be noted that, in this important area of social work practice, there is no legislation, only guidance. According to paragraph 2.3 of 'No Secrets', a vulnerable adult is:

> A person aged 18 or over who is or may be in need of community care services by reason of mental or other disability, age or illness, and who is or may be unable to take care of him or herself, or unable to protect him or herself, against significant harm or exploitation.

A number of observations can be made about this odd definition. For CSSRs and others covered by 'No Secrets', it has the advantage of being linked to an already identified or relatively easily identifiable group of people. It applies to anybody 'who is or may be' in need of community care services. This links the definition to s.47 NHSCCA 1990 (see Chapter 3, p. 55). It is arguable that linking vulnerability with the need (actual or potential) for community care services is inappropriate. Why should the existence of such a need be relevant to whether a person requires the protection of safeguarding procedures? Moreover, at various stages in their lives, most people are vulnerable in some way; for example, through illness, loss of employment, or bereavement. However, these are often transient conditions. In any case, a person may be experiencing, or be at risk of, abuse or neglect, but not be in need of any community care services. Does this definition mean that the person is excluded from the protection of the safeguarding procedure?

> **Exercise 7.1**
>
> 1. Who do you think should fall within the definition of 'vulnerable adult'?
> 2. Should there be a link with the need for community care services?
>
> (See also Clements and Thompson 2011.)

A similar debate took place in Scotland in the lead-up to the passing of the Adult Support and Protection (Scotland) Act 2007. A broader definition of the term 'vulnerable' had been proposed. This was eventually rejected by the Scottish Law Commission. Its reasoning is very interesting:

> A much narrower definition of vulnerable was said to be needed, many respondents commenting that at some point in their lives almost everyone was vulnerable in the sense we used in our discussion paper. We appreciate the force of this criticism. A wide definition would place too great a strain on local authority resources and would make it impossible for the local authority to confine its attentions to those genuinely in need of them.
> (Scottish Law Commission 1997)

In fact, the term 'vulnerable adult' has been subject to criticism, on the basis that it might imply that vulnerability is linked to an individual or inherent characteristic of some kind. The Law Commission for England and Wales recommended 'adults at risk' as an alternative term, which they define as:

> (1) a person aged 18 or over and who
>   (a) is eligible for or receives any adult social care service (including carers' services) provided or arranged by a local authority; or
>   (b) receives direct payments in lieu of adult social care services; or
>   (c) funds their own care and has social care needs; or
>   (d) otherwise has social care needs that are low, moderate, substantial or critical; or
>   (e) falls within any other categories prescribed by the Secretary of State or Welsh Ministers; and

(2) is at risk of significant harm, where harm is defined as ill-treatment; or
(3) the impairment of health or development or unlawful conduct which appropriates or adversely affects property, rights or interests (for example, theft, fraud, embezzlement or extortion).

(Law Commission 2011)

What amounts to abuse and neglect?

It is difficult to identify the extent to which vulnerable adults are abused and neglected. In part, this is because, in the past, there has been disagreement on how to define these terms. 'No Secrets' defines abuse as:

> a violation of an individual's human and civil rights by any other person or persons. (Department of Health and Home Office 2000, para. 2.5)

This neatly locates abuse within human rights (see Chapter 1, p. 7). The abuse of a vulnerable person amounts to a violation of their human rights; for example, it can amount to inhuman and degrading treatment, and also a violation of private life. Action on Elder Abuse defines abuse as:

> A single or repeated act or lack of appropriate action occurring within any relationship where there is an expectation of trust which causes harm or distress to an older person.
> This definition has also been adopted by the World Health Organization. (Action on Elder Abuse)

This is helpful, as it recognizes that abuse is so often an abuse of a relationship of trust built on family or professional relationships, or friendship.

'No Secrets' excludes stranger crime other than in exceptional circumstances:

> Stranger abuse will warrant a different kind of response than the response to abuse within an ongoing relationship or care setting. Nevertheless in some instances it may be appropriate to use the locally agreed inter-agency adult protection procedures to ensure that the vulnerable adult receives the services and support that they need. Such procedures may also be used when there is the potential for harm to other vulnerable people. (Department of Health and Home Office 2000, para 21.3)

Abuse may take many forms, including physical abuse, sexual abuse, psychological abuse, financial abuse and institutional abuse. Perpetrators

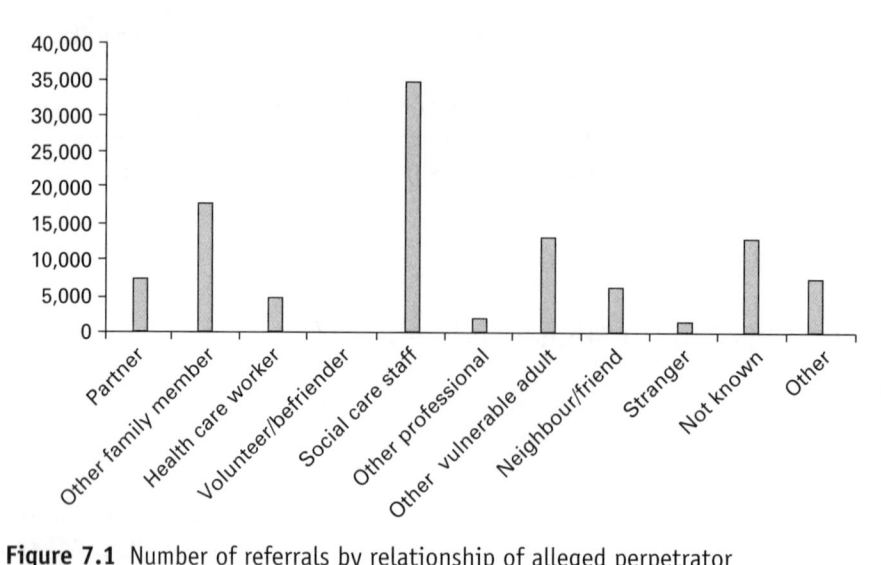

Figure 7.1 Number of referrals by relationship of alleged perpetrator
Source: Health and Social Care Information Centre (2013c).

include family members, informal carers, professionals, friends and neighbours (see Figure 7.1).

National statistics

There is a more systematic collection of statistics now in place at a national level. The Health and Social Care Information Centre has collated data from CSSRs in relation to adults aged 18 years and over in England (Health and Social Care Information Centre 2013a). Although the means by which this data is collected are experimental, it provides an indication of a pattern of abuse of adults at risk. The figures reveal that CSSRs reported 112,000 referrals involving adults where age, gender and client group were known. Referrals were made predominantly by health and social care professionals (see Table 7.1).

For 2012–13, 61 per cent of referrals were in relation to women and 61 per cent for adults aged 65 or over. Of these referrals, 50 per cent were in relation to adults with physical disability (see Figure 7.2).

Table 7.1 Analysis of referrals, repeat referrals and completed referrals by age group

	Referrals			Repeat referrals			Completed referrals	
	18–65	65+	Total	18–65	65+	Total	18–65	65+
	41,905	66,610	108,515	9,070	10,285	19,355	32,450	53,730

Source: Health and Social Care Information Centre 2013c.

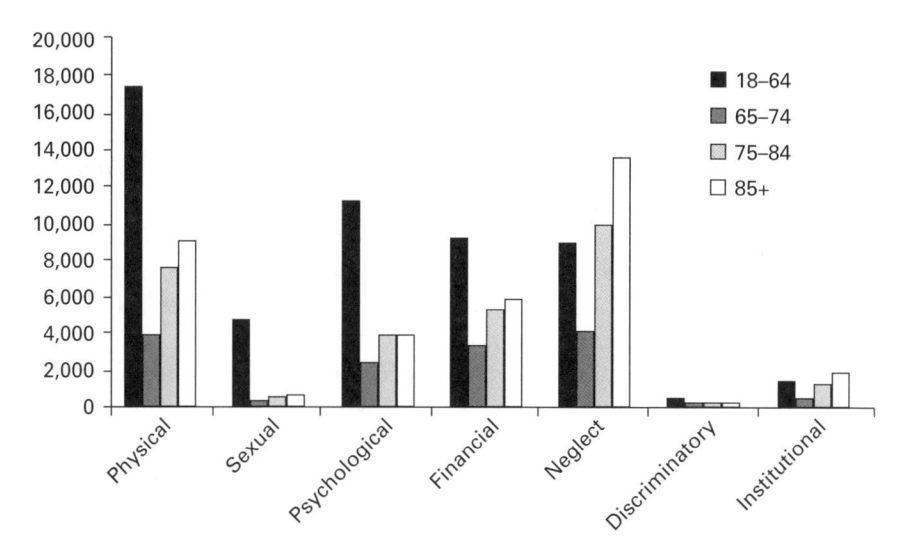

Figure 7.2 Type of abuse by age group
Source: Health and Social Care Information Centre 2013c.

Stigma, vulnerability and family loyalties may be factors affecting referral, but evidence also suggests that a major factor is the low level of awareness of abuse. According to a Commission for Social Care Inspection Report, CSSRs need to do more to 'raise the profile of every citizen's right to be free from abuse' (Commission for Social Care 2008).

> **Exercise 7.2**
>
> 1. What do you think are the reasons for the low level of referral to adult protection agencies?
> 2. What could CSSRs do to remedy this situation?

What is safeguarding?

In its report on Adult Social Care, the Law Commission identified an important distinction between safeguarding and protection. Safeguarding 'relates to the prevention of abuse and a broad focus that extends to all aspects of a person's general welfare'; adult protection 'refers to investigation and intervention where it is suspected that abuse may have occurred' (Law Commission 2011). This may be a useful distinction but it should not lead to over-compartmentalizing the two components. Safeguarding may morph seamlessly into adult protection.

The practitioner's response to cases of suspected abuse or neglect of a vulnerable adult can be based in part – but in part only – on what we know about child protection procedures. However, it is important to sound a note of caution. There is a danger of infantilizing vulnerable adults and treating them as one would a child. A key feature of reaching the age of majority is that the restraints on self-determination that exist, to a degree in childhood, are significantly reduced (see *Gillick v West Norfolk and Wisbech Health Authority and another*; Glendenning 1997; Law Commission 2011). The discussion on human rights (see Chapter 1, pp. 7–10) illustrates the importance of autonomy which is a key aspect of being an adult. We have the right to decide things for ourselves, even though our decisions may not always be what others consider to be in our 'best interests'. We cannot do things that are prohibited by the law. We should not do things that we think are unethical or immoral. Beyond that, no one, particularly a professional, can tell us what to do – although, if we do not follow instructions from, for example, our employer, there will be consequences. Case example 7.1 concerning the exercise of self-determination illustrates the point.

> **7.1 The exercise of autonomy**
>
> *case example*
>
> Jane is 85 years of age. Although she is mentally alert, she is physically frail because of rheumatoid arthritis. She depends for much of her day-to-day care on the help of her neighbour, Mary. Overall, Mary does a good job in looking after Jane. However, Jane has recently noticed that small amounts of money have gone missing from her purse, and that one or two of her valuable ornaments have disappeared. Jane knows that Mary is responsible. When asked by her social worker what she is going to do about this, she replies 'Nothing. Leave it alone. Mary provides me with excellent care and without her, you would put me in a care home because I know that you would not provide me with the hours of home care that Mary does. I don't like the fact that she is stealing but, all things considered, I can live with that.'

This example illustrates the importance of autonomy and self-determination. The key features are that Jane has mental capacity, and that the type and level of abuse are not putting her at serious risk of physical danger.

> *Exercise 7.3*
>
> 1. Consider the above case in the light of what you now know about capacity and autonomy (See generally Chapters 1 and 2.
> 2. What, if anything, should a social worker do in a case such as this?

Clearly, the social worker would need to keep a watching brief on the case and be ready to respond if Jane changes her mind. This may not be a comfortable position to be in, but it is difficult to imagine how it would be possible, at this stage, to go against Jane's wishes by prosecuting Mary. Consideration must be had to the level of risk involved to the vulnerable adult and the proportionality of the response. This does not mean, however, that the social worker should keep the information to herself. As will be seen below, the requirement would be for the social worker to log the information into the safeguarding procedure.

> **Exercise 7.4**
>
> List the factors you consider significant in determining whether instances of abuse should be regarded as 'serious'.
>
> 1. What ethical dilemmas need to be addressed in assessing 'seriousness'? (See Mantell and Scragg 2008.)
> 2. Should CSSRs adopt a no-tolerance approach to the abuse of adults?

Existing law and procedure

In England and Wales, unlike Scotland, there is no single piece of legislation that defines the duties of CSSRs and others in relation to safeguarding adults at risk. There is no adult protection provision, similar to that in s.47 Children Act 1989, which imposes a duty to investigate. Any requirement to investigate has to be based on the duties under s.47 NHSCCA 1990 (see Chapter 3); s.47 NAA 1948; the Mental Health Act (MHA 1983) (see Chapter 6); and the Mental Capacity Act (now MCA 2005) (see Chapter 2).

Reference should be made at this point to s.47 NAA 1948. This section applies to a person who is suffering from grave chronic disease or who (being aged, infirm or physically incapacitated) is living in insanitary conditions and is unable to devote care to themselves, and is not receiving proper care and attention from other persons. Under this section, a CSSR can apply to a magistrates' court for authority to remove the person from their home if it is in their interest to do so, or if it is necessary to prevent injury to the health or serious nuisance to somebody else. The person is to be removed to a place of safety, which is likely to a care home. An emergency procedure also exists under the National Assistance (Amendment) Act 1951. This is an archaic provision that remains in force but is now never used, largely because its use would breach the HRA 1998. In recognition of this, s. 46 of the Care Act 2014 will repeal s.47 NAA 1948.

The problem is that none of the above legislation was specifically designed to address abuse and neglect, although it may be useful in responding to them. In addition, an assessment is different from an investigation of possible abuse or neglect, not least because the latter involves an investigative, rather than therapeutic, approach (*Gillick v West Norfolk and Wisbech Health Authority and another*; Glendenning 1997). In some circumstances, however, the law may impose a duty to investigate in cases of suspected abuse. This may arise, for example, where there is a suspicion of deprivation of liberty. In *A Local Authority v A*, Munby LJ said:

> Where ... a local authority knows or ought to know that a vulnerable child or adult is subject to restrictions on their liberty by a private individual that arguably give rise to a deprivation of liberty, then its positive obligations under Article 5 will be triggered. These will include the duty to investigate, so as to determine whether there is, in fact, a deprivation of liberty.

However, this is not a comprehensive duty. The Law Commission has proposed that new legislation should place a duty on local social services authorities to investigate adult protection cases, or to ensure that an investigation is made by other agencies (Law Commission 2011). Section 34 of the Care Act 2014 states that, where a CSSR has reasonable cause to suspect that an adult in its area:

- has needs for care and support (whether or not the authority is meeting any of those needs);
- is experiencing, or is at risk of, abuse or neglect; and
- as a result of those needs is unable to protect himself or herself against the abuse or neglect or the risk of it,

it has a duty to make such enquiries as it thinks necessary to enable it to decide whether any action should be taken in the adult's case and, if so, what and by whom.

'Abuse' is defined as including:

- having money or other property stolen;
- being defrauded;
- being put under pressure in relation to money or other property; and having money or other property misused.

This definition is not intended to exclude physical, sexual, or psychological abuse.

> **Exercise 7.5**
>
> In the case of *A Local Authority v A*, Munby LJ commented that, although social workers and those engaged in adult protection should act quickly and decisively, they must also guard against being seen as prying or snooping on families they are supposed to help and support.
>
> What justifications can you suggest for intervention in circumstances where an adult is at risk and assessed as entitled to care and support but is refusing such help?

As noted, 'No Secrets' provides multi-agency guidance on how agencies should respond to cases of abuse or neglect. A recent consultation on the review of 'No Secrets' raised a number of concerns on the working of the guidance. The review identified a number of key messages:

- safeguarding requires empowerment – the victim's voice needs to be heard;
- empowerment is everybody's business – but safeguarding decisions are not;
- safeguarding adults is not like safeguarding children; and
- the participation and representation of people who lack capacity is also important.
(Department of Health 2009b: 13)

The review recognized that there were tensions between safeguarding and the rolling out of the personalization of adult social care (see Chapter 4, p. 85), especially around achieving an appropriate balance between choice and risk. More work is required on this issue. Other identified issues include the fact that professionals from across the NHS were struggling to 'own' the concept of safeguarding, the need for Safeguarding Boards to be placed on a statutory footing, the fact that there were reportedly very few successful prosecutions, and concern over the definition of 'vulnerable adult'.

What does 'No Secrets' require of practitioners?

For agencies and practitioners, the first priority must be to ensure the safety and protection of vulnerable adults. Every agency involved in working with a vulnerable adult is required to have an organizational framework in place and to ensure that those who are involved at an operational level both know their role and have access to relevant guidance. Very importantly, 'No Secrets' reminds practitioners of their duty to report *any* suspicion or evidence of abuse or neglect to the person or body identified under their local procedure (Department of Health and Home Office 2000 para 6.4).

Part 6 of 'No Secrets' sets out the procedure to be followed in cases of suspected abuse. The initial purpose is, first, to establish the facts. The collection of evidence is a critical part of the process and will help shape the way in which the allegations are dealt with and, very importantly, whether the criminal law will be used. The process also enables practitioners to assess the person's need for protection, support and redress. This might build on an assessment under s.47 NHSCCA 1990 (see Chapter 3). Once the facts have been gathered and the needs of the person identified, the next step is to decide what should be done in relation to the perpetrator (if the suspicions are founded), whether it is an individual or an organization. Action may take many forms. It might be supportive or therapeutic, or disciplinary; or it might involve the criminal law.

Local procedures should follow the guidance given in 'No Secrets'. The key features are:

- making staff aware of their individual roles, responsibilities, authority and accountability;
- a statement of the procedure for dealing with allegations, including: how to respond to emergencies, the machinery for assessing abuse and deciding whether intervention is required, and the arrangements for reporting to the police urgently if necessary;
- what to do in the event of failure to take necessary action;
- information on points of contact;
- information on recording allegations, investigation and subsequent action;
- a list of sources of expert advice;
- a full description of the channels of inter-agency communication and procedures for decision-making;
- a list of services that may offer victims access to support or redress.
(Department of Health and Home Office 2000, para 5.1)

Practitioners should familiarize themselves with their local procedures. Safeguarding is the business of everyone involved in social or health care. Although an individual practitioner may not be directly involved in investigating cases of suspected abuse, they are often in a position to see abuse happening and should be aware of their responsibilities in such situations.

Whatever the outcome of an investigation, it is important that people who make referrals about suspected abuse know that their concerns have been taken seriously by agencies and practitioners. Protection must be given against the risk of reprisals or retaliation against those who report concerns. The Public Interest Disclosure Act 1998 (see Chapter 8, p. 169) provides for a 'right not to be subjected to any detriment' by an employer for 'whistle-blowers' who follow the procedures outlined in the Act. There is considerable concern that this legislation does not provide adequate safeguards against being victimized for exposing unlawful practices (Hunter 2009).

Any practitioner considering whistle-blowing should ensure that they carefully follow the procedures in the legislation. Advice or guidance should be sought from professional bodies, trades unions and other bodies.

> **Exercise 7.6**
>
> **Scenario**
>
> A whistle-blower, who exposed abuse at a day centre for vulnerable adults with learning disability, spoke of the stress and anxiety she suffered as a result. The complaint related to abuse by members of staff. The whistle-blower, who had been an administrative assistant at the centre for 15 years, said her complaints were ignored. 'I went into social services because I believe passionately in looking after people who can't fight for themselves ... But I have seen my life turned upside down after witnessing vulnerable people being shoved, pushed and denied food and trying to do something about it.' Initially, neither the whistle-blower nor any other staff member reported the incident because 'there had at the times been such intimidation and bullying at the centre that there was a fear of repercussions if anyone made a fuss'. Eventually she reported the abuse to a senior manager, but the lack of managerial understanding of procedure and accountability saw her complaint bounced from one officer to another with no action taken. (Public Services Ombudsman for Wales 2009)
>
> What lessons can be learnt from this example? What policies exist for facilitating whistle-blowing in your local CSSR, and how well are they understood and implemented?

The criminal law

As will be seen (p. 146), many forms of abuse are also criminal offences. Social workers may be involved in the criminal process at various stages and roles. This may include referring the case to the police, taking part in the investigative process, supporting the victim, and acting as a witness in court. The review of 'No Secrets' concluded that there were very few successful prosecutions in relation to safeguarding. Recent figures in England suggest that the rate of prosecution is low, with a total of only

Table 7.2 Range of offences that may arise out of cases of abuse

Offences against the person
Causing or allowing the death of a vulnerable person – *Domestic Violence, Crime and Victims Act 2004* Improper administration of medicine – *s.67 Medicines Act 1968* Murder Assault Grievous bodily harm Actual bodily harm Sexual offences Rape Offences under the Sexual Offences Act 2003
Property offences and financial abuse
Theft Fraud Criminal damage
Mental health and mental capacity
s.127 MHA 1983: It is an offence for a person employed by a hospital or care home to ill-treat or wilfully neglect a patient receiving treatment for a mental disorder as an in-patient or as an outpatient within the hospital or home. It is also an offence to ill-treat or wilfully neglect a mentally disordered person subject to guardianship under the Act. The guardian may commit this offence or any other person having custody or care of the patient – there need not be a legal obligation to care. **s.44 MCA 2005**: It is an offence to ill-treat or wilfully neglect a person who lacks capacity, or whom the perpetrator reasonably believes to lack capacity. The offence may be committed by someone having the care of the person, the donee of a Lasting Power of Attorney, or a deputy appointed by the Court of Protection. (See Chapter 2, p. 46.)
Protection from Harassment Act 1997
A person commits the offence of 'harassment' if they engage in a course of conduct (i.e. on at least two occasions) amounting to harassment, and knows, or ought to know, that it amounts to harassment. The court may impose a restraining order designed to protect the victim from further conduct that amounts to harassment or causes fear of violence. If the person is warned that their behaviour amounts to harassment, this will place them on a warning. It may lead them to modify their behaviour. The Protection from Harassment Act 1997 also provides a civil remedy: a county court or the High Court may grant an injunction restraining a person from further harassing another.

1,120 prosecutions and police cautions arising from the total number of referrals (Health and Social Care Information Centre 2013c). Although criminal prosecutions may not always be the most appropriate outcome, this does not mean that the police role is unnecessary or that prosecutions are never appropriate. The law should not distinguish between offences that take place between people who know each other and those who do not.

> **Exercise 7.7**
>
> **Scenario**
>
> An 80-year-old man who has severe dementia is living at home with his wife. She is unable to understand how his behaviour is a consequence of his illness. As a result, she is very impatient and short-tempered towards him to the extent that he is clearly unhappy and very distressed. Although carers are coming into the home to assist with his physical needs, they are insufficiently skilled to pick up the signs of emotional abuse. A friend of the family has told her doctor (who is also the doctor of the older man) that she is concerned about the situation. The doctor has contacted the CSSR and informed them of the friend's concerns – the friend wishes to remain anonymous.
>
> What action by the CSSR would be appropriate in this case?

In considering this situation, you should also take into account Chapter 2 (p. 27) and Chapter 5 (p. 96).

It is important for practitioners to recognize the criminal nature of many forms of abuse or neglect. In addition to raising the prospect of the perpetrator being prosecuted, it also sends the correct message to society that abuse is unacceptable. Many criminal offences also involve civil wrongs that may be actionable. Possible civil remedies will be discussed below (see p. 152).

A wide range of offences may arise out of cases of abuse, some of which are presented in Table 7.2.

Prosecution

Where the decision is made to prosecute, practitioners may have a role in collecting evidence that may be used in the criminal proceedings. At some stage, they may also be required to cross the line between investigative and therapeutic work. For the social work practitioner, therapeutic work involves providing assessment, support and guidance in the hope of ameliorating the situation and preventing further abuse. At all times, practitioners should be aware of the conflicts that may arise between their therapeutic and forensic roles.

'No Secrets' reminds us that:

> when complaints about alleged abuse suggest that a criminal offence may have been committed it is imperative that reference should be made to the police as a matter of urgency. Criminal investigation by the police takes priority over all other lines of enquiry. (Department of Health and Home Office 2000, para. 2.8).

The early involvement of the police will enable them to identify whether an offence may have been committed. 'No Secrets' identifies a number of key issues arising out of police involvement:

> The quality of the evidence needs to be higher than for civil proceedings or other forms of intervention – in criminal cases, the test is 'beyond all reasonable doubt'.
>
> Police involvement will help ensure that forensic evidence is not lost or contaminated.
>
> The police have considerable skills in investigating and interviewing. This will minimise the risk of unnecessary interviews and, probably more important, the risk of making an interview inadmissible in court because it breaches rules of evidence.
>
> Police investigations should proceed alongside those dealing with health and social care issues.
> (Department of Health and Home Office 2000, para. 6.7)

It is important to remember, however, that police involvement will not always lead to a prosecution.

Detailed guidance is available on interviewing and obtaining evidence (Ministry of Justice 2011). Following the police investigation, it will be for the Crown Prosecution Service (CPS) to take the decision whether to prosecute, having reviewed the evidence. It is important that the CPS be regarded as one of the agencies involved in the safeguarding process. There has been criticism that there is a reluctance to prosecute suspected cases of abuse, partly for reasons of misplaced concern over the welfare of vulnerable adults. Again, it must be emphasized that prosecution is not appropriate in all cases, and a difficult judgement has to be made. However, victims of abuse are entitled to the protection of the criminal law – it might, indeed, be argued that their need for protection is greater.

When reviewing the evidence and deciding whether to prosecute, the CPS adopts a two stage test, known as the 'Full Code Test':

Stage 1 The evidential test Is the evidence sufficient to provide a 'realistic prospect of conviction'? It is important that the expectations of the person are not raised unless there is a realistic chance that there will be a conviction. This test raises a number of issues. How is the admissibility and reliability of the evidence assessed? Will the witness 'stand up at trial?' Unjustified assumptions about the ability of the individual to present evidence must be challenged. For example, many older people will make good witnesses – they may not enjoy the process (witnesses rarely do) and it may cause them stress. However, that is not a reason for denying them access to the criminal justice system.

Stage 2 Is the prosecution needed in the public interest? Do the public interest factors against prosecution outweigh those in favour? Some guidance is given under the CPS Code for Crown Prosecutors.

Prosecution is more likely if:

- the defendant was in a position of trust;
- the victim was vulnerable, has been put in considerable fear, or suffered personal attack, damage or disturbance;
- there are grounds for believing that the offence is likely to be continued or repeated (e.g. a history of recurring conduct);
- the offence was motivated by discrimination against the victim's ethnic or national origin, gender, disability, age, religion or belief, political views, sexual orientation or gender identity, or the suspect demonstrated hostility towards the victim based on any of those characteristics; or
- a prosecution would have a significant positive impact on maintaining community confidence.

Prosecution is less likely where the possibility exists of it having a bad effect on the victim's physical or mental health, always bearing in mind the seriousness of the offence.

The CPS has published specific prosecution guidance and prosecution policy on crimes against older people. The policy document recognizes the importance of prosecutions for elder abuse. It states:

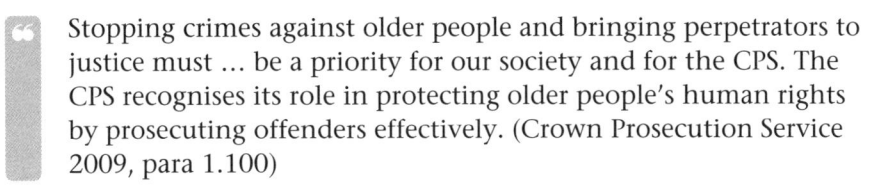

> Stopping crimes against older people and bringing perpetrators to justice must ... be a priority for our society and for the CPS. The CPS recognises its role in protecting older people's human rights by prosecuting offenders effectively. (Crown Prosecution Service 2009, para 1.100)

The guidance document states:

> Whatever the age of a victim or witness, their needs and case management issues should be assessed on an individual basis. Reliance should not be placed on pre-conceived or stereotypical

> notions and norms about older people in general. (Crown Prosecution Service undated)

Exercise 7.8
1. Why, in your opinion, is the criminal law so little used in relation to the protection of vulnerable adults?
2. To what extent, if any, do you agree that it should be used more frequently?

The criminal justice system

Following a decision to prosecute, how can the victim be supported through the process? The practitioners involved in the investigation (collection of evidence, interviewing or providing witness statements) must be careful not to compromise the case by being accused of 'coaching' the witness (i.e. telling them what to say in court). Voluntary groups such as Victim Support can often give support. Practical problems must be resolved (such as how the person is to get to the court, and whether the court is easily accessible). In addition, the person will probably never have given evidence before and will need to have information on what is going to happen. For most people, giving evidence in court is difficult and stressful. There had been special measures for some time to assist children in child abuse cases to give evidence during criminal proceedings (Pigot 1989). These were extended to adults by the Youth Justice and Criminal Evidence Act 1999. Special measures are available to eligible adults when presenting evidence at criminal trials, where their vulnerability may affect of the quality of their evidence. The special measures are not available to all adults and, most crucially, they are not available to the defendant.

Before the court grants permission to use special measures, the witness must fall within the criteria in the Act. A vulnerable adult may be eligible in the following circumstances:

1. *Vulnerable witnesses.* This is where the court decides that the quality of the evidence is likely to be diminished because:
   - the person has a mental disorder within the MHA 1983, or has some other significant impairment of intelligence and social functioning; or
   - the person has a physical disability, or is suffering from a physical disorder.
2. *Intimidated witnesses.* This is where the court decides that the quality of the evidence is likely to be diminished by reason of fear or distress – a number of factors are relevant, including:

- the nature of the alleged circumstances surrounding the alleged offence;
- the age of the witness;
- the social and cultural background of the witness; and
- any behaviour towards the witness by the accused, a member of their family, or any person likely to be accused or a witness.

The CPS Guidance on Special Measures states that:

> Victims of domestic violence, racially motivated crime and repeat victimisation, the families of homicide victims, witnesses who self-neglect/self-harm or who are elderly and/or frail might also be regarded as intimidated. (Crown Prosecution Service undated, Special Measures)

Practitioners may have to provide evidence, based on their professional knowledge of the person, to support an application for special measures. Special measures involve changing the dynamics of the open court proceedings, most notably by, in some cases, removing the need for the witness to be physically present. Arguably, this is unfair on the defendant as it denies them the right to 'face the accuser'. In addition, a central part of our criminal justice system is the use of oral evidence presented in open court. Ellison (2003: 10) argues that the 'principle of orality is the foundation of the adversarial trial' as it exposes inconsistency, inaccuracy and fabrication. She notes the unfairness to the defendant of assuming that the absent vulnerable witness would have been convincing if present in court (see also Ho 1999). However, the European Court of Human Rights has not recognized a right to have the witness physically present in court. In *Doorson v Netherlands*, the Court said:

> [P]rinciples of fair trial also require that in appropriate cases the interests of the defence are balanced against those of witnesses or victims called upon to testify. (*Doorson v Netherlands*, para. 70. See also Bates 1999.)

Special measures consist of:

- screening the witness from the accused (see *R v Smellie*)
- video-recorded evidence-in-chief
- evidence by live link
- evidence given in private
- removal of wigs and gowns
- allowing the witness to use communication aids
- video-recorded pre-trial cross-examination and re-examination (not in force)
- intermediaries – an approved intermediary to help a witness communicate with legal representatives and the court.

The judge must give the jury such warning as is necessary to ensure that the use of the special measures by the witness does not prejudice the accused (*R v Brown and Grant*). The use of some of these measures may make a prosecution more likely.

Civil law

Victims of abuse may, in addition to using the criminal justice system, use civil law remedies. Unlike criminal actions, the civil standard of proof is a balance of probabilities. Social workers will not be directly involved in such actions, but it may be useful to be aware of what justice-seeking options may be open to an individual.

Domestic abuse legislation

Many forms of abuse of vulnerable adults will fall within the legislation designed to address domestic violence to be found in the Family Law Act 1996. The main available actions are:

- *A non-molestation order*:
    This prohibits the abuser from molesting the person applying for the order, or any child. 'Molesting' includes the use or threat of violence and serious pestering or harassment. The court must consider all the circumstances surrounding the case, including the need to secure the health, safety and wellbeing of the applicant. An application may be made against a person with whom the applicant is 'associated', which includes:
    - spouse or civil partner (includes former spouses or civil partners);
    - cohabitants (including former cohabitants and same sex partners);
    - someone living or who has lived in the same household (other than as an employee, tenant, lodger, or border);
    - an immediate relative (e.g. sons or daughters and other close relatives – nephews or nieces, grandchildren, cousins);
    - people who have agreed to marry one another; and
    - people who have or have had an 'intimate relationship' with each other which was of 'significant duration'.

    A breach of a non-molestation order is a criminal offence.
- *An occupation order*:
    This is a more serious order than a non-molestation order. Whether one will be granted depends on the right to occupy the home and the relationship between the parties. One consequence of the order is that the other party is prohibited from entering the home, required to leave the home, or excluded from an area within

or surrounding the home. The court must include a power of arrest unless adequate safeguards to protect the person applying (and others) are in place. This means that a police officer can arrest the person if they have reasonable cause to suspect that the person is in breach of the order.

A breach of an occupation order is a criminal offence.

Actions in tort

A civil action can be brought against the wrongdoer, claiming damages or a court injunction preventing any repetition of the behaviour. Normally, torts arise out of negligent acts. However, other torts may be relevant –known as 'trespass to the person':

- *Assault and battery*. Assault involves putting a person in fear of an immediate battery. A battery is the use of physical force without any legal justification (e.g. not in self-defence).
- *False imprisonment*. This means depriving a person of their freedom of movement without lawful excuse. A person may be falsely imprisoned in their own home. For the tort to be committed, the person needs to be imprisoned It does not matter how long the person is imprisoned – it may be only for a relatively short period.

  If there is a lawful basis for the detention, it will not be false imprisonment. For example, a deprivation of liberty authorization provides a lawful basis for detention.
- *Negligence*. In the 1932 case of the snail in the ginger beer bottle (*Donoghue v Stevenson*), the judges recognized the existence of the tort of negligence. This tort is based on the idea that, in certain situations, we have a duty of care towards other people. Three things are required to establish negligence:
  - a duty of care
  - a breach of that duty
  - damage.

  There must be a relationship between the parties in which it is foreseeable that failure to take care will result in damage or injury.

Protection from Harassment Act 1997

As well as harassment being a criminal offence, a victim can take a private action against the perpetrator. If successful, the person can claim damages for anxiety or financial loss caused by the harassment, or an injunction restraining the person from continuing the harassment.

> **Exercise 7.9**
>
> Explain the essential difference between the criminal and the civil law procedures in relation to safeguarding.

Adult safeguarding boards

One of the means by which CSSRs exercise their responsibility to protect vulnerable adults is through an Adult Safeguarding Board. Although the appointment of an Adult Safeguarding Board is currently not a statutory duty, they have a critical role to play in terms of leadership and the management of safeguarding services across all partner agencies. Membership normally includes representatives, not only of the CSSR itself, but also of the NHS, the police, and other key service providers, including the voluntary and private sectors, where appropriate.

Boards should have mechanisms for ensuring that the views of those who have used (or may need to use) safeguarding services are taken into account. Apart from developing policies that should ensure cross-agency cooperation in safeguarding vulnerable adults, they should also have protocols for determining when an SCR should be set up since an Adult Safeguarding Board is the only body with authority to commission a serious case review.

Serious Case Reviews

Although SCRs are seen as providing a valuable learning experience when, regrettably, safeguarding or protection intervention have either not been tried or have failed, as in the case of Stephen Hoskins, they are not mandatory in the case of vulnerable adults, unlike the procedures relating to children (Flynn 2007). The review of 'No Secrets' identified concerns by respondents over the lack of clear guidance (Department of Health 2009b) and, in their study of SCRs, Manthorpe and Martineau (2010) noted that reports frequently did not specify what had made a particular case deserving of an SCR.

The Association of Directors of Social Services (ADSS) has, however, issued guidance (Association of Directors of Social Services 2010), which states that an SCR should be considered when:

> a vulnerable adult dies (including death by suicide) and abuse or neglect is known or suspected to be a factor in their death. In such circumstances, the Board should always conduct a review

> into the involvement of agencies and professionals associated with the vulnerable adult;
> a vulnerable adult has sustained a potentially life-threatening injury through abuse or neglect, serious sexual abuse, or sustained serious and permanent impairment of health or development through abuse or neglect, and the case gives rise to concerns about the way in which local professionals and services work together to safeguard vulnerable adults;
> serious abuse takes place in an institution, or when multiple abusers are involved, the same principles of review apply. Such reviews are likely to be more complex, on a larger scale and may require more time. (paras 4.1–4.3)

Functions of a Serious Case Review

There is no statutory guidance on the functions of an SCR, or on the procedures to be followed in holding one. The main guidance is, again, that which has been issued by the ADSS. It outlines the following functions:

- Establishing whether there are lessons to be learnt from the circumstances of the case about the way in which local professionals and agencies work together to safeguard vulnerable adults.
- Reviewing the effectiveness of procedures – multi-agency and those informing and improving local inter-agency practice.
- Improving practice by acting on learning (developing best practice).
- Preparing or commissioning an overview report that brings together and analyzes the findings of the various reports from agencies in order to make recommendations for future action.

The Winterbourne View SCR, published in 2012, highlighted serious and multiple deficiencies in the protection of learning-disabled patients who had suffered considerable abuse during their stay at Winterbourne View private hospital in Bristol (Flynn 2012). The Review revealed many weaknesses in the system that had been compounded by a lack of coordination between the various agencies involved which ought to have had the care and protection of such patients in mind.

> **case example**
>
> **7.2 Based on a Serious Case Review relating to A1: Worcestershire Safeguarding Adults Board, 2010**
>
> A, who suffered from depression, anxiety and behavioural problems, had been known to the local mental health services for over 10 years. Earlier in his life, he had also been diagnosed with paranoid schizophrenia. He rented a housing association bungalow but had lived with his 88-year-old mother for nearly a year before his death. His mother was admitted to

hospital in late December 2008. Following a multi-agency adult protection meeting, it was agreed with A's family that he should return to his own bungalow before his mother's discharge from hospital, because of concern over the mother's vulnerability and issues about John's behaviour and its impact on his mother. It was assumed that A had mental capacity but there was no evidence of a formal assessment having been carried out. Following his move to the bungalow, A. was visited by the Community Mental Health Team but he then missed a number of routine out-patient appointments. A letter was sent asking him to attend for a medical assessment but there was no follow-up and no communication between the agencies. Neighbours gradually became concerned about A and his body was found by the police a month after the date of the missed appointment.

The SCR concluded that, although there had been good practice by individual agencies on a number of occasions, the involvement was not multi-agency in its approach and there had been an absence of a holistic approach, compounded by such omissions as evidence of self-neglect not being fully considered, a lack of multi-agency communication – both informally and through formal assessment processes. Furthermore, there were inconsistencies and lack of recording that may have pointed professionals to an escalating problem. Also, there was no system for flagging cases of particular concern that could have alerted all agencies to the need for vigilance.

The Law Commission's report and the Scottish legislation

The Law Commission's report into adult social care included a chapter on safeguarding and protection. As part of its deliberations it considered whether it ought to include the use of compulsory powers in any proposed legislation. Conscious of the political implications of such radical proposals, it concluded that whether such powers should be included was a matter to be decided by the Westminster government and, within Wales, the Welsh government.

The Scottish legislation has already been mentioned. The ASP(S)A 2007 adopted the more radical approach (Mackay 2008). The legislation, and the work of the Scottish Law Commission that led up to the legislation, both show an awareness of the need for any powers of compulsion to be proportional and to recognize the competing rights of autonomy and protection. The following principles apply to decisions under the ASP(S)A 2007.

The general principle on intervention in an adult's affairs is that a person may intervene, or authorize an intervention, only if satisfied that the intervention:

- will provide benefit to the adult that could not reasonably be provided without intervening in the adult's affairs, and
- is of the range of options likely to fulfil the object of the intervention, that it be the least restrictive to the adult's freedom.

As with the statutory principles in the MCA 2005, these principles are helpful. For the practitioner, they mean that any decisions under the ASP(S)A 2007 can be tested against the statutory principles. The person directly affected by the intervention under the ASP(S)A 2007 has a basis on which to seek justification for any decision or, if necessary, a basis for a challenge.

Section 4 ASP(S)A 2007 imposes a duty on councils to make inquiries where an adult at risk may need protection under the legislation. The need for practitioners to report their suspicions is emphasized in 'No Secrets'. Under s.5(3) ASPA 2007 a clear legal duty to do so is imposed:

> Where a public body or office-holder ... knows or believes –
>
> (a) that a person is an adult at risk, and
> (b) that action needs to be taken (under this Part or otherwise) in order to protect that person from harm,
>
> the public body or office-holder must report the facts and circumstances of the case to the council for the area in which it considers the person to be.

This is controversial, but follows the mandatory reporting rules in many American states (Williams 2002; 2008). One advantage of this duty is that it relieves the practitioner of responsibility for making the decision – it is something over which they have no discretion.

The ASP(S)A 2007 contains the following powers:

- s.7 (1) – Visits. A council officer may enter any place to assist in making inquiries to decide whether it needs to do anything (under the ASP(S)A 2007 or otherwise) in order to protect an adult at risk from harm.
- s.11 – An assessment order from the Sheriff's court to assess whether the person is an adult at risk and, if so, whether it needs to do anything in order to protect the person from harm.
- s.20 – Banning order.
- s.15 – Removal order.

It is early days for the Scottish legislation, although early signs are encouraging (Mackay *et al.* 2011). Wales is considering legislation that might embrace the wider powers of the ASP(S)A 2007. Until England adopts similar legislation, practitioners will need to work within the 'No Secrets' guidance (or its successor) and the legislative framework that has been outlined.

Exercise 7.10

In light of the above, discuss whether you consider the Scottish approach to be the way forward.
(See Armstrong 2008; Maas-Lowit 2010.)

Conclusion

Adult safeguarding and protection is an area of law in need of reform. Section 42 Care Act 2014 imposes a duty on a CSSR to make enquiries in cases of suspected abuse or neglect. It goes no further. Whether this is far enough is debatable. The Scottish model is an interesting one, although it is also open to the accusation that it is too intrusive and anti-human rights. There is disagreement whether that is the case. New laws may help, although the real challenge is to tackle the causes behind the abuse of and neglect to adults at risk. It is also important that those who experience abuse and neglect have equal access to the protection of the law – in particular, the criminal law. A welfare response to abuse is important but it must be supported by the criminal law, whenever appropriate, so that abuse and neglect are not, in effect, decriminalized.

chapter 8 Seeking Redress

In this chapter, you will learn about:
- Informal mechanisms
- Local authority complaints procedures
- The local government ombudsman
- Judicial review
- Legal action
- Whistle-blowing
- Other avenues of complaint or redress

Remember to consult The Legal Toolbox on pp. xiii–xx. This will help you to understand processes and procedures referred to in this chapter.

Introduction

Although many people are satisfied with the services provided or facilitated by a CSSR, there will inevitably be cases where there is dissatisfaction with the way in which an individual feels they have been treated. Such dissatisfaction may lead to the person making a complaint, or taking legal action against the CSSR. Dissatisfaction may arise from any number of different circumstances. Examples include the following:

- a failure by a CSSR to assess a person for community care services;
- the conclusions made in an assessment;
- rudeness by practitioners or CSSR officers;
- a failure to take account of the service user's feelings;
- failure to provide appropriate services to meet service users' needs;
- a failure to involve the service user in decision-making;
- a failure by a CSSR to take account of the service user's wishes and desires;

- a breach of the service user's human rights;
- abusive or neglectful treatment of the service user;
- unacceptable delay in responding or providing services;
- breaches of confidentiality;
- a failure by the CSSR to adhere to its own policies, central guidance or the relevant legislation;
- negligence on the part of the CSSR;
- discrimination;
- disagreement over the application or interpretation of the law or guidance;
- fettering discretionary powers; or
- disagreement over assessments of capacity.

This is by no means an exhaustive list and many of the cases that have been discussed in the book provide examples where service users, or their carers, are dissatisfied with the service provided (or not provided) by the CSSR.

There is little, if any, central data on the number of complaints that are made against CSSRs. They are required to keep local data on the number of complaints they receive, the outcome of the complaints procedure, and whether the time limits for dealing with the complaint were met. Such information should be readily available from each CSSR.

A number of general points should be made about service users and others seeking redress:

- It is important to remember that service users have access to their files and other information on them held by the CSSR. The Data Protection Act 1998 (DPA 1998) gives what is known as a 'subject access right' to any information held on a person, whether it is written or in an electronic format. Only in exceptional circumstances can information be withheld. These include:
  - information that identifies other people, unless they consent to the disclosure – practitioners are usually not covered by this exception, unless disclosure of their identity would put them at risk;
  - where a disclosure would prejudice the carrying out of social work because of the serious harm to the physical or mental health of the person or anyone else that would be a likely result of disclosure; or
  - where disclosure would hinder the prevention or detection of crime, or the arrest or prosecution of offenders.
- As a general principle, complaints should be dealt with at as informal a level as possible. Very often, aggrieved users may simply require an explanation and an assurance that any necessary lessons are learnt. The use of mediation may help to achieve an amicable resolution of any complaint.

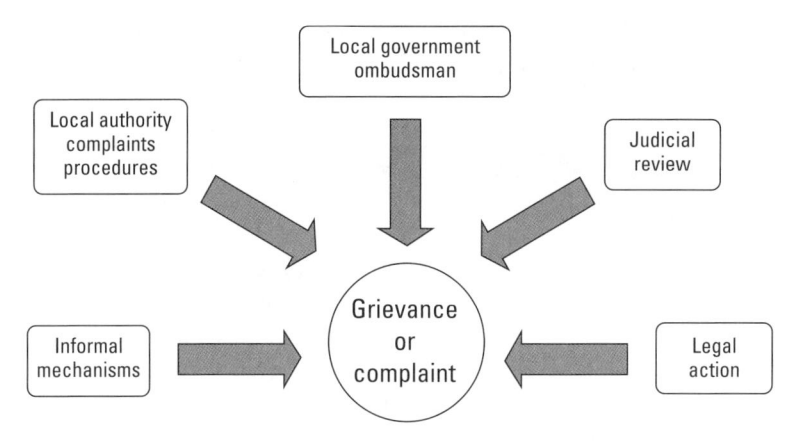

Figure 8.1 Procedures for seeking redress

- Complaints can be very distressing for practitioners, as their professionalism may be on the line. However, not all complaints are substantiated and some may be mischievous. As noted in Chapter 1, practitioners are required to make professional assessments and judgements; services users, carers and others may disagree with the assessment or judgement, but that does not mean that a practitioner acted incorrectly, or is some way negligent. The fact that people may disagree with a professional judgement does not make it wrong or unlawful.
- Good record keeping is critical in responding to complaints. Without being able to evidence decisions by good record keeping, responding to a complaint is difficult, and often impossible.

A number of routes are open to those who wish to complain about the service they received from a CSSR or a social care practitioner. Figure 8.1 identifies the principal means of seeking redress in relation to social care provision.

Informal mechanisms

As noted, informality is often the best means of resolving complaints or grievances. An explanation of the reason for a decision may satisfy the person and time spent doing this is not only a good investment in terms of resources, but also for those involved. Wherever possible, complaints can be avoided by effective communication between the CSSR or practitioner and the service user. Standard form letters written in 'officialese' do not constitute effective communication but, rather, aggravate the situation. People are entitled to reasons for decisions by a CSSR. Failure to provide reasons is a legitimate ground for complaint. Good practice suggests that people should be kept informed throughout their engagement with a CSSR and that they should not have to seek reasons actively once they have been informed of the decision.

Councils with Social Services Responsibilities complaints procedures

Complaints about social care are made under a joint health and social care complaints procedure (the Local Authority Social Services and National Health Service Complaints (England) Regulations 2009). This recognizes the close relationship between the two services, and the fact that complaints may often involve inter-agency working – or the lack of it. There is a duty on health bodies and CSSRs to cooperate in dealing with complaints that affect them both. Every CSSR is required to have a complaints procedure in place. The Regulations require that the complaints procedures in place ensure that:

1. Complaints are dealt with efficiently.
2. Complaints are properly investigated.
3. Complainants are treated with respect and courtesy.
4. Complainants receive, so far as is reasonably practical,
    a) assistance to enable them to understand the procedure; or
    b) advice on where they may obtain such assistance;
    c) complainants receive a timely and appropriate response;
    d) complainants are told the outcome of the investigation of their complaint; and
    e) action is taken if necessary in the light of the outcome of a complaint.

(The Local Authority Social Services and National Health Service Complaints (England) Regulations 2009, reg. 3)

An outline of the complaints process is found in Figure 8.2. Throughout this process a complainant can make use of any available advocacy or advice services. Although, there is a right to use an advocate or advisor, there is no duty on the CSSR to provide one unless it is a situation where an Independent Mental Capacity Advocate (IMCA) should be involved (see Chapter 2, p. 43).

> **Exercise 8.1**
>
> Look at the website of a CSSR and find their complaints policy for adult social care services.
>
> Can you find out how many complaints were made against that CSSR?

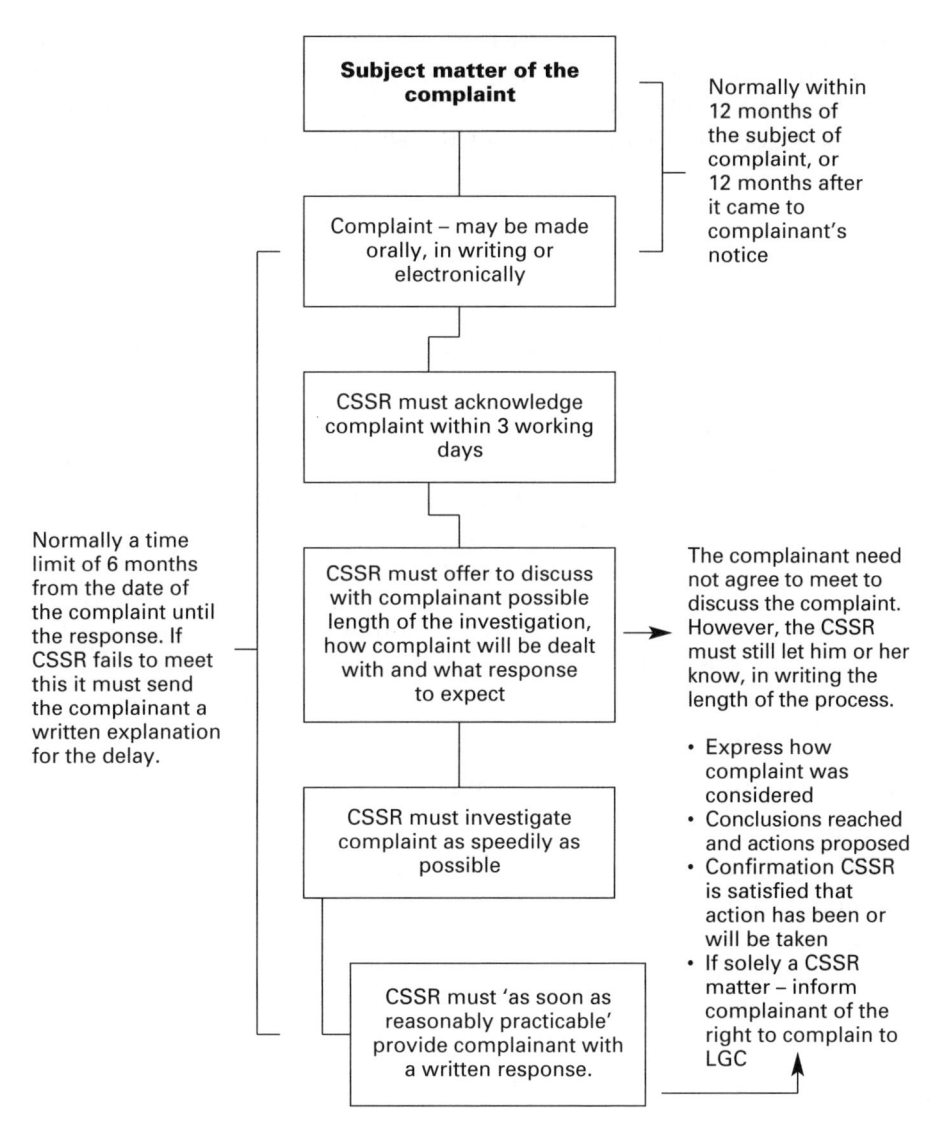

```
                    ┌─────────────────────┐
                    │ Subject matter of the│───┐  Normally within
                    │     complaint        │   │  12 months of
                    └─────────┬───────────┘   │  the subject of
                              │                │  complaint, or
                              │                │  12 months after
                    ┌─────────▼───────────┐   │  it came to
              ┌─────│ Complaint – may be  │───┘  complainant's
              │     │  made orally, in    │      notice
              │     │ writing or          │
              │     │ electronically      │
              │     └─────────┬───────────┘
              │               │
              │     ┌─────────▼───────────┐
              │     │ CSSR must acknowledge│
              │     │ complaint within 3   │
              │     │ working days         │
              │     └─────────┬───────────┘
Normally a time    │                          The complainant need
limit of 6 months  │     ┌─────────────────┐  not agree to meet to
from the date of   │     │ CSSR must offer │  discuss the complaint.
the complaint until│     │ to discuss with │  However, the CSSR
the response. If   │     │ complainant     │→ must still let him or her
CSSR fails to meet │     │ possible length │  know, in writing the
this it must send  │     │ of investigation,│ length of the process.
the complainant a  │     │ how complaint   │
written explanation│     │ will be dealt   │  • Express how
for the delay.     │     │ with and what   │    complaint was
                   │     │ response to     │    considered
                   │     │ expect          │  • Conclusions reached
                   │     └────────┬────────┘    and actions proposed
                   │              │            • Confirmation CSSR
                   │     ┌────────▼────────┐    is satisfied that
                   │     │ CSSR must       │    action has been or
                   │     │ investigate     │    will be taken
                   │     │ complaint as    │  • If solely a CSSR
                   │     │ speedily as     │    matter – inform
                   │     │ possible        │    complainant of the
                   │     └────────┬────────┘    right to complain to
                   │              │            LGC
                   │     ┌────────▼────────┐    ▲
                   │     │ CSSR must 'as   │    │
                   │     │ soon as reasonably   │
                   │     │ practicable'    │    │
                   │     │ provide complainant │
                   │     │ with a written  │    │
                   │     │ response.       │────┘
                   └─────└─────────────────┘
```

Figure 8.2 Outline of CSSR complaints procedures

The local government ombudsman

Where a complainant feels that their complaint has not been dealt with satisfactorily through a CSSR's complaints procedure, or that they have suffered an injustice at the hands of the CSSR, it may be possible for them to refer the case to the local government ombudsman (LGO). If the complaint involves both social care and health, the LGO can undertake a joint investigation with the Health Service ombudsman. This procedure is not confined to people whose care is funded by the CSSR. Since 2010, those who fund their care themselves can use the LGO. The process can include not only the service user, but also carers and any members of the complainant's family affected by the CSSR decision. Usually, complaints must be made within 12 months of the CSSR decision or action giving rise to the complaint. This may be extended if, for example, the person has been unwell.

The LGO has the power to investigate cases of possible 'maladministration or service failure'. 'Maladministration' is not defined in the legislation. Lord Denning, in one case, referred to the definition given in the Parliamentary debates leading up to the Local Government Act 1974:

> It will cover 'bias, neglect, inattention, delay, incompetence, inaptitude, perversity, turpitude, arbitrariness and so on'. It would be a long and interesting list, clearly open-ended, covering the manner in which a decision is reached or discretion is exercised: but excluding the merits of the decision itself or of the discretion itself. It follows that a 'discretionary decision, properly exercised, which the complaint dislikes but cannot fault the manner in which it was taken, is excluded'. (*R v Local Commissioner for Administration for the North and East Area of England ex parte Bradford Metropolitan City Council*)

The LGO website lists the types of situation that this might include.

- Delay
- Incorrect action or failure to take any action
- Failure to follow procedures or the law
- Failure to provide information
- Inadequate record-keeping
- Failure to investigate
- Failure to reply
- Misleading or inaccurate statements
- Inadequate liaison
- Inadequate consultation.

The LGO will not investigate a case on the basis that the complainant disagrees with the decision. Reference to the LGO must be based on procedural matters relating to the way in which their case was dealt with by the CSSR. So, for example, if the complaint is that the CSSR unreasonably delayed in responding, that will be something that the LGO will investigate. The cases presented in Boxes 8.1 and 8.2 were considered by the LGO and illustrate the point.

The LGO will only investigate cases where a sufficient injustice has been caused for which the CSSR is responsible. Cases where insufficient injustice has been caused will not be considered. Obviously, this is a

Box 8.1 *Kent County Council (11 009 473)*, 11 October 2012

Kent County Council delayed in investigating how an elderly man was seriously injured in an altercation with another resident of his care home. He died in hospital a few days later. The ombudsman found that:

> the Council's three failures to investigate the incident caused the man's daughter significant injustice. She had to wait for more than a year for an answer to whether her father's death could have been prevented. This has caused her significant distress.

Box 8.2 *Suffolk County Council (11 017 875 & 6 others)*, 11 October 2012

There were flaws in the way Suffolk County Council cancelled subscriptions to an audio book service for some blind and visually impaired adults. The LGO said 'They will rightly feel aggrieved that they have lost out on an opportunity to influence a decision affecting them and to have a say in what and how services are provided to them. They may have had opportunities to join in normal and important aspects of personal life, such as education and leisure activities, diminished.'

The local government ombudsman said that Suffolk County Council:

- did not properly consider the likely impact on disabled service users;
- did not consider the need to promote equality of opportunity and to take account of disabilities, even where that involves treating disabled people more favourably than others;
- failed to carry out individual consultation, or assess the impact on individual users before it decided to set, retrospectively, a 'minimum usage' of 20 books per user below which it would not fund a subscription;
- did not identify that it funded Talking Books under community care legislation;
- did not use the social care complaints procedure to respond to a complaint made by one complainant; and did not consider carrying out social care assessments for those whose subscriptions it stopped.

matter of judgement. The LGO gives the following example from housing law to illustrate the point:

> Two complainants approached the Ombudsman because there had been a month's delay in paying their benefit. One complainant had suffered slight hardship because, in paying her share of the rent that month, she had paid a total of £17 more than she needed to. The council had already apologised to her.

Her injustice was considered too slight to justify investigation. The other complainant had existing rent arrears of which the council had been made aware at the outset of her claim. She received a court summons because of the increased rent arrears. Her complaint was investigated. (See http://www.lgo.org.uk/guidance-on-jurisdiction/examples/s24a-general-discretion.)

Complainants will normally be required to exhaust the CSSR's complaints procedure before making a complaint to the LGO. In exceptional circumstances, a complaint may be referred to the LGO without the CSSR complaints procedure being exhausted; for example, where the subject matter of the complaint is urgent.

What can the LGO do if the CSSR is found to be at fault? The LGO can require the CSSR to do a number of things to try to redress the wrong; these include:

- apologize;
- make a payment in recognition of adverse effect;
- take action that should have been taken previously;
- reconsider a decision that was not taken properly; or
- improve procedures.

Of course, the LGO may find that the CSSR is not at fault.

> **Exercise 8.2**
>
> Visit the complaints outcomes for adult social care page of the LGO website. Read some of the cases in the archives.
>
> What simple lessons do they contain for CSSRs and for social care practitioners?

Judicial review

Judicial review is a means by which the courts can ensure that decisions of public authorities, such as CSSRs, are made lawfully and that they are not abusing or misusing their powers. It should be noted that it is only available against a public authority, and not a private body or individual. A judicial review action is taken in the High Court and is very expensive. As a result, it is not available to many social care users, unless they are supported by, for example, a voluntary organization. Before a judicial review hearing can take place, the High Court must give its permission for the case to be heard. Tight timescales apply here. The application must be made promptly and, in any case, within three months of the decision that is the subject of the complaint in accordance with s.31 Supreme Court of Judicature Act 1981.

On what grounds can a judicial review of a CSSR be sought? As with the LGO so, too, with judicial review; an application cannot be based on the merits of the CSSR's decision or action. Disagreement with a lawfully made decision is not amenable to judicial review. What is important is that the decision-making process is in some way flawed. Lord Diplock, in the case of *Council for Civil Service Unions v Minister for the Civil Service*, said that there were three grounds for judicial review: illegality, irrationality, and procedural impropriety.

Illegality. This means that the CSSR has misunderstood the law and applied it incorrectly. Illegality also covers acting *ultra vires* (outside the CSSR's powers). CSSR exercise statutory functions. They are created by statute and can only do those things that the legislation empowers them to do. It will also be illegal if the CSSR 'fetters its discretion' (see Chapter 1, p. 6).

Irrationality. This is known as 'Wednesbury unreasonable' – named after the case in which the courts developed this ground. In this case, a local authority sought to impose a condition on a cinema licence that no children aged under 15 years should be admitted. The House of Lords decided this was unreasonable (or irrational) as no 'reasonable authority could ever have come to it' (*Associated Provincial Picture Houses Limited v Wednesbury Corporation*). What is meant by 'irrationality' is that the decision is, as Lord Diplock said, 'so outrageous in its defiance of logic or of accepted moral standards that no sensible person who had applied his mind to the question to be decided could have arrived at it'. So, for example, no sensible person would decide not to provide services for somebody whose needs were assessed as being critical under the eligibility criteria (see Chapter 4, p. 72).

Procedural impropriety. Under this ground, the judicial review is based on the claim that the CSSR has not followed the procedures laid down by the law; for example, a failure to consult a person when this is required by the statute (*Smith v North Eastern Derbyshire Primary Care Trust*).

Various remedies are available in judicial review proceedings:

- an order that declares the decision null and void (known as *certiorari*);
- an order preventing the CSSR from making a decision that, if made, would be declared null and void (known as *prohibition*);
- an order compelling the CSSR to act;
- a declaration of the legal position of the parties;
- an injunction preventing the CSSR from acting in an unlawful way;
- damages.

One action that the court will not take in a successful application for judicial review is to impose a new decision. Instead, the CSSR will be required to decide the matter in accordance with the correct rules and procedures identified by the court.

> **Exercise 8.3**
>
> Do you consider that the inability of the court to consider the merits of the case in judicial review hearing to be a strength or a weakness?

Legal action

As well as using the above means of redress, a complainant may wish to take civil action against the CSSR, or against a social care practitioner. Such action may be based on, for example, negligence, assault, or breach of confidentiality. Such actions require the complainant to use the civil courts to seek justice. Typically, a successful civil action leads to the award of damages (a monetary sum to compensate the person for any loss they may have incurred), or an injunction (an order of the court restraining somebody from doing something).

As noted, CSSRs are created by legislation. It is possible to bring a private action against a CSSR for what is known as a 'breach of statutory duty'. Usually, a CSSR will be accountable under public law: that is, the law that deals with the working of central and local government. Judicial review is a good example of a public law remedy. However, in very exceptional cases, an aggrieved person may use the private law procedure of breach of statutory duty. This is difficult to prove and will be available only rarely (*X* (*Minors*) *v Bedfordshire County Council*).

Although CSSRs have a duty to provide care services under a number of statutes, these duties are usually set out as general duties (sometimes referred to as 'target' duties), rather than as specific duties owed to particular individuals. It is rare, therefore, for the courts to be persuaded that an individual has a right to bring an action for breach of a statutory duty. However, in the case of *R v Ealing District Health Authority ex parte Fox*, it was held that the duty to provide after-care services under s.117 Mental Health Act (MHA 1983) (see Chapter 4, p. 78), could be regarded as a specific duty owed to the individual concerned. Similarly, in *R v Gloucestershire ex parte Barry* (see Chapter 4, p. 70), it was confirmed that individuals defined as 'disabled' under the National Assistance Act 1948 could also acquire an individual right to services.

Whistle-blowing

A social care practitioner may have identified serious shortcomings in the way in which their employing body performs its functions, as in a case of suspected abuse or neglect, in the inappropriate use of untrained staff, financial irregularities, or illegality. Exposing such behaviour may be difficult, especially if the perpetrators of the wrong are in a senior position – which may effectively cut off hope of any internal resolution. In such situation, the practitioner requires some protection if they are going to expose such behaviour to an external body or person.

A degree of protection is given to employees who are whistle-blowers. The Employment Rights Act 1996 (ERA 1996) and the Public Interest Disclosure Act 1998 provide protection for what are known as a 'qualifying disclosure'. These are defined as disclosures by an employee where:

- a criminal offence has been committed, is being committed or is likely to be committed;
- a person has failed, is failing, or is likely to fail, to comply with any legal obligation to which they are subject;
- a miscarriage of justice has occurred, is occurring or is likely to occur;
- the health or safety of any individual has been, is being or is likely to be endangered;
- the environment has been, is being or is likely to be damaged; or
- information tending to show any matter falling within any one of the above has been, or is likely to be deliberately concealed.
(s.43(b) ERA 1996)

As the name 'qualifying disclosure' suggests, only disclosures falling within the categories listed here will provide the employee with protection. These categories overlap, so a protected disclosure may involve one or more of them.

In order to be a qualifying disclosure, it must be made in good faith and not maliciously. An ulterior motive in making the disclosure will also remove the protection; for example, where the disclosure is made as part of the employee's efforts to get a pay rise or promotion. The employee must also show that they reasonably believed that the contents of the disclosure were substantially true. Whether there was a reasonable belief must be assessed on the basis of the facts as understood by the employee, and not what is discovered to be the truth (*Darnton v University of Surrey*). One word of caution must be sounded. If the disclosure amounted to a criminal offence, then it would not be protected. The most obvious and usual example of this is if disclosure amounted to a breach of the Official Secrets Act 1989; it is highly unlikely that a social care practitioner will encounter this.

It is important that the person or authority that is responsible for the alleged wrongdoing is made aware of the concerns of the employee. A disclosure to the employer is a qualifying disclosure. This will enable the employer to investigate and, if necessary, put things right. However, the person or body responsible for the alleged wrongdoing may not actually employ the person wishing to disclose. For example, an agency social worker may be working in a care home. A disclosure to those responsible for the care home would be protected.

It may be necessary to consider disclosing any concerns an employee may have to an external body. The legislation does not allow disclosure to anyone, no matter how serious the matter may be. For the disclosure to be a qualifying one – and thus entitled to protection – it must be made to a body prescribed by the Secretary of State. The list is found in the Schedule to the Public Interest Disclosure (Prescribed Persons) Order 1999. Table 8.1 presents some of the prescribed bodies that may be relevant for social care practitioners.

What protection does the legislation provide for a person who makes a qualifying disclosure? An employee dismissed because of making a protected disclosure will be treated as being unfairly dismissed. In addition, employees have a right not to be subjected to any 'detriment' by their employers because they made a protected disclosure.

The above is an overview of the protection given by the law. Anyone considering making what they believe to be a qualified disclosure is advised to seek advice from, for example, a trade union, professional body, or other advice provider to ensure that they follow the requirements of the law.

The charity Public Concern at Work set up a whistle-blowing commission to examine the effectiveness of existing arrangements for workplace whistle-blowing. Its report has recently been published. The report noted:

> Evidence suggests that workers fail to speak up because of fear of reprisal and/or a concern that they will not be listened to and that nothing will be done. Too often, those who speak up are ignored or their concerns do not come to the attention of management. (Public Concern at Work 2013, para. 27).

The report also found that less than half of UK employees are aware of a whistle-blowing policy in their workplace (Public Concern at Work, para. 31). One of the many recommendations made in the report is that a code of practice on whistle-blowing arrangements should be issued. The code would be taken into account by a court or tribunal whenever it is relevant to do so (Public Concern at Work, p. 26). The report provides a useful account of the existing law and its shortcomings.

Table 8.1 Prescribed bodies that may be relevant for social care practitioners

Prescribed body	Matters that may be disclosed
Audit Commission for England and Wales and auditors appointed by the Commission to audit the accounts of local government and health service, bodies.	The proper conduct of public business, value for money, fraud and corruption in local government and health service bodies.
Charity Commissioners for England and Wales	The proper administration of charities and of funds given or held for charitable purposes.
Children's Commissioner	Matters relating to the views and interests of children.
Matters relating to the views and Health and Safety Executive.	Matters that may affect the health or safety of any individual at work; matters, which may affect the health and safety of any member of the public, arising out of or in connection with the activities of persons at work.
Regulator of Social Housing	The registration and operation of private registered providers of social housing, including their administration of public and private funds, and management of their housing stock.
Information Commissioner	Compliance with the requirements of legislation relating to data protection and to freedom of information.
Care Quality Commission	The registration and provision of a regulated activity as defined in s.8 Health and Social Care Act 2008 and the carrying out of any reviews and investigations under Part 1 of that Act, or any other activities in relation to which the Care Quality Commission exercises its functions.

Other avenues of complaint or redress

In addition, anyone may report any suspected criminal behaviour to the police. Although there is no general duty to report a crime, the law does require it in cases such as suspected acts of terrorism. However, for a social care practitioner who suspects or observes abuse of a child or vulnerable adult, there is a duty to report that concern under the protection and safeguarding procedures of the CSSR (see Chapter 7) or similar body: that is part of their professional and employee duty (see Chapter 1).

Every CSSR must appoint a senior person to act as a Monitoring Officer under s.5 Local Government and Housing Act 1989. The Monitoring Officer has a duty to report any proposals or decisions of the authority that are illegal or that might amount to maladministration. The Monitoring Officer must prepare a report and present it to the elected members of the authority who have responsibility for the subject matter; for example, the social services. The report must be considered within 21 days. During that time, no action can be taken that is based on the proposal or decision in question. Social practitioners can report their concerns to the Monitoring Officer.

Conclusion

It is an important principle that individuals are able to hold CSSRs to account when they are thought to have acted improperly in carrying out their functions. This chapter has outlined the various ways in which CSSRs can be challenged, either informally or through the use of formal internal and external procedures. CSSRs should be prepared to recognize the inequality in power that inherently exists between them and service users. Advocacy, advice and support should play a key role in the redress of grievances and the resolution of complaints.

appendix 1 Cases

A Local Authority v A [2010] EWHC 978 (Fam)
A Local Authority v DL, RL and ML [2010] EWHC 2675 (Fam)
A Local Authority v H [2012] [2012] EWHC 49 (COP)
Airedale NHS Trust v Bland [1993] 1 All ER 821
Ashindene v United Kingdom, 93 (1985) 7 EHRR
Associated Provincial Picture Houses, Limited v Wednesbury Corporation [1947] EWCA Civ 1
B v An NHS Hospital Trust [2002] EWHC 429 (Fam)
Carty (by his Litigation Friend) v Croydon London Borough [2005] EWCA Civ 19
CC v KK and STCC (2012) EWHC 2136
Clunis v Camden and Islington Health Authority [1997] EWCA Civ 2918
Council for Civil Service Unions v Minister for the Civil Service [1984] 3 All ER 935
Darnton v University of Surrey [2002] UKEAT 882
Debique v Ministry of Defence [2009] UKEAT 0048
DL v A Local Authority (2012) EWCA Civ 253
Donoghue v Stevenson [1932] UKHL 100
Doorson v Netherlands [1966] 22 EHRR 330
G v E [2010] EWHC 621 (Fam)
Gillick v West Norfolk and Wisbech Health Authority and another [1986] 1 AC 112
GJ v The Foundation Trust [2009] EWHC 2972 (Fam).
HE v A Hospital NHS Trust [2013] UKSC 67
HE v A Hospital NHS Trust [2003] EWHC 1017 (Fam),
HL v UK [2004] ECHR 471
Instan [1893] 1QB 450
JT v UK [2000] FLR 909
London Underground Ltd v Edwards [1995] ICR 574
Morgan v Phillips [2006] All ER (D) 189 (Mar)
Park v Park [1953] 2 All ER 1411
Pearce and another v United Bristol Healthcare NHS Trust [1998] EWCA Civ 865

R (H) v MHRT North and East London Region (2001) EWCA Civ 415
R (Hertfordshire CC) v LB Hammersmith and Fulham (2011) EWCA Civ 77
R (K) v Camden and Islington Health Authority (2001) EWCA Civ 240
R (Modaresi) v Secretary of State [2011] EWHC 417 (Admin.)
R (on the application of B) v Camden London Borough Council and others [2005] EWHC 1366 (Admin)
R (on the application of D and another) v Manchester City Council [2012] EWHC 17 (Admin)
R (on the application of Heather) v Leonard Cheshire Foundation [2002] EWCA Civ 366
R (on the application of McDonald) v Royal Borough of Kensington and Chelsea (2011) [2011] UKSC 33
R v Avon County Council ex parte M [1994] 2 FLR 1006.
R v Barnet LBC ex parte Shah [1983] 2 AC 309
R v Bournewood Community and Health NHS Trust ex parte L [1998] UKHL 24
R v Bristol City Council ex parte Penfold (1997–98) 1 CCLR 315
R v Brown and Grant [2004] EWCA Crim 1620.
R v Ealing District Health Authority ex parte Fox [1993] 1 WLR 373
R v Gloucestershire County Council and another ex parte Barry [1997] 2 All ER 1
R v Harrow London Borough Council ex parte Cobham [2002] UKHL34
R v Hereford and Worcester CC ex parte Chandler and ex parte Bevan (1992) unreported
R (Hertfordshire CC) v LB Hammersmith & Fulham (2011) EWCA Civ_77
R v Kensington and Chelsea Royal London Borough Council ex parte Kujtim [1999] EWCA Civ 1804
R v Khan and Khan [1998] Crim LR 830, CA
R v Local Commissioner for Administration for the North and East Area of England ex parte Bradford Metropolitan City Council [1979] 2 All ER 881
R v London Borough of Islington ex parte Rixon [1997] ELR 66,
R v Manchester City Council ex parte Stennett and Two Other Actions [2002] UKHL 34
R v Mersey Care NHS Trust (2003), *The Times*, 25 July.
R v North Yorkshire CC ex parte Hargreaves (1995) 26 BMLR 121
R v Smellie (1919) 14 Cr App Rep 128
R v Stone [1977] QDB 354
Re (O) v West London MH NHS Trust (2005) EWHC 604 (Admin)
Re A(Children) (AP) [2013] UKSC 60
Re AK (Adult Patient) (Medical Treatment: Consent) [2001] 1 FLR 129
Re C (Adult, refusal of treatment) [1994] 1 All ER 819
Re F (2009) EWHC B30 (Fam)
Re F (adult: court's jurisdiction) (2000) EWCA Civ 192
Re F (Mental Health Act guardianship) [2000] 1 FLR 192

Re F (Mental Patient: Sterilisation) [1990] 2 AC [1990] 2 AC 1
Re JT (Adult: Refusal of Medical Treatment) [1998] 1FLR 48
Re M; ITW v Z (2009) EWHC 2525 (Fam).
Re MB (Caesarian Section) (1997) EWCA Civ 1361
Re MM (an adult) [2007] EWHC 2003 (Fam)
Re P [2009] EWHC 163 (Ch)
Re T [1992] EWCA Civ 18
Re Y (adult patient) (transplant: bone marrow) [1997] 35 BMLR 111
S v London Borough of Newham (2003) (unreported)
Scamell v Farmer [2008] EWHC 1100
Shepherd (1862) 9 Cox CC 123
Sidaway v Bethlem Royal Hospital Governors and others [1985] UKHL 1
Smith v North Eastern Derbyshire Primary Care Trust [2006] EWHC 1338
St George's Healthcare NHS Trust v S (No.1) [1998] 3 All ER 673
St Helens BC v PE [2006] EWHC 3460
TTM v Hackney LBC and East London NHS Foundation Trust [2010] EWHC1349
Winterwerp v Netherlands 33 (1979) 2 EHRR 38C1349
X (Minors) v Bedfordshire County Council [1995] 2 AC 633
YL v Birmingham City Council [2007] UKHL 27

appendix 2
Legislation and Statutory Instruments

Legislation

Adult Support and Protection (Scotland) Act 2007
Care Standards Act 2000
Carers (Equal Opportunity) Act 2004
Carers (Recognition of Services) Act 1995
Carers and Disabled Children Act 2000
Children Act 1989
Children Act 2004
Children and Young Persons Act 1933
Chronically Sick and Disabled Persons Act 1970
Community Care (Delayed Discharges etc.) Act 2003
Community Care (Direct Payments) Act 1996
Data Protection Act 1998
Disability Discrimination Act 1995
Disabled Persons (Services and Consultation and Representation) Act 1986
Domestic Violence, Crime and Victims Act 2004
Employment Rights Act 1996
Equality Act 2010
Family Law Act 1996
Freedom of Information Act 2000
Health and Social Care Act 2001
Health and Social Care Act 2008
Health and Social Services and Social Security Adjudications Act 1983
Health Services and Public Health Act 1968
Human Rights Act 1998
Local Authority Social Services Act 1970
Local Government Act 1972
Local Government Act 1974
Local Government Act 2000
Local Government and Housing Act 1989

Medicines Act 1968
Mental Capacity Act 2005
Mental Health Act 1983
Mental Health Act 2007
National Assistance (Amendment) Act 1951
National Assistance Act 1948
National Health Service Act 2006
National Health Service and Community Care Act 1990
Official Secrets Act 1989
Protection from Harassment Act 1997
Public Interest Disclosure Act 1998
Race Relations Act 1976
Registered Homes Act 1984
Sex Discrimination Act 1975
Sexual Offences Act 2003
Supreme Court of Judicature Act 1981
Youth Justice and Criminal Evidence Act 1999

Statutory instruments

Carers and Disabled Children (Vouchers) (England) Regulations 2003 SI 2003 No. 1216
Community Care (Delayed Discharges etc.) Act (Qualifying Services) (England) Regulations 2003 SI 2003 No.196
Health and Social Care Act 2008 (Regulated Activities) Regulations 2010 SI 2010 No. 781
Local Authority Social Services and National Health Service Complaints (England) Regulations 2009 SI 2009 No. 309
Mental Health (Conflicts of Interest) (England) Regulations 2008) (SI 2008 1205)
Public Interest Disclosure (Prescribed Persons) Order 1999 (SI 2003 No. 1993)

Bibliography

'Action on Elder Abuse'. Available at http://www.elderabuse.org.uk/Mainpages/Abuse/abuse.html (accessed 21 November 2013).

Age UK (2010) *Local Authority Assessment for Community Care Services* (London: Age Concern): 8.

Age UK (2013) 'Government to announce care costs cap today', 11 February. Available at http://www.ageuk.org.uk/latest-news/archive/government-announces-care-costs-cap/.

Aldridge, J. and Becker, S. (1993) 'Children as carers', *Archives of Disease in Childhood*, 69(4): 459.

Alzheimer's Society (2011) *Getting Personal? Making Personal Budgets Work for People with Dementia* (London: Alzheimer's Society).

Armstrong, J. (2008), 'The Scottish legislation: the way forward' in A. Mantell and T. Scragg (eds) *Safeguarding Adults in Social Work* (Exeter: Learning Matters): 60–71.

Association of Directors of Social Services and Association of Directors of Children's Services (2009) *Working Together to Support Young Carers*.

Association of Directors of Social Services (2010) *Vulnerable Adult Serious Case Review. Guidance: Developing a Local Protocol* (London: ADSS).

Audit Commission (2012) *Reducing the Cost of Assessments and Reviews* (London: Audit Commission).

Austen, S. and Jeffrey, D. (2007) *Deafness and Challenging Behaviour* (Chichester: Wiley).

Banks, S. (2012) *Ethics and Values in Social Work* (Basingstoke: Palgrave Macmillan).

Barnardo's (2006) *Hidden Lives: Unidentified Young Carers in the UK* (Ilford: Barnardo's).

Bates, P. (1999) 'New legislation: the Youth Justice and Criminal Evidence Act – the evidence of children and vulnerable adults', *Child and Family Law Quarterly*, 11(8): 289–303.

Baxter, S. and Carr, H. (2007) 'Walking the tightrope: the balance between duty of care, human rights and capacity', *Housing, Care and Support*, 10(3): 6–11.

BBC (2010) '"Hidden" young carers across UK', 16 November.

BBC (2012) 'Regulator criticised after woman assaulted in care home', 23 April Available at http://www.bbc.co.uk/news/health-17777113.

Bindman, J., Reid, Y., Szmukler, G., Tiller, J., Thornicroft, G. and Leese, M. (2005) 'Perceived coercion at admission to psychiatric hospital and engagement with follow-up', *Social Psychiatry and Psychiatric Epidemiology,* 40(2):160–6.

Brammer, A. (1994) 'The Registered Homes Act 1984: safeguarding the elderly?', *Journal of Social Welfare & Family Law,* 16(4): 423–37.

Braye, S., Lebacq, M., Mann, F. and Midwinter, E. (2003) 'Learning social work law: an enquiry-based approach to developing knowledge and skills', *Social Work Education,* 22(5): 479–92.

Braye, S. and Preston-Shoot, M. (2009) *Practising Social Work Law* (Basingstoke: Palgrave Macmillan).

British Medical Association and the Law Society (2010) *Assessment of Mental Capacity: A Practical Guide for Doctors and Lawyers,* 3rd edn (London: Law Society).

Bryan, K. (2010) 'Policies for reducing delayed discharge from hospital', *British Medical Bulletin,* 95(1): 33–46.

Buckner, L. and Yeandle, S. (2007) 'Valuing carers – calculating the value of unpaid care' (Carers UK and University of Leeds).

BUPA (2011) *Who Cares? Funding Adult Social Care over the Next Decade* (London: BUPA).

Campbell, J. (2010) 'Deciding to detain: the use of compulsory mental health law by UK social workers', *British Journal of Social Work,* 40(8), December: 2398–413.

Care Quality Commission (2010a) *Essential Standards of Quality and Safety* (London: CQC).

Care Quality Commission (2010b) *The Operation of the Deprivation of Liberty Safeguards in England* (London: CQC).

Care Quality Commission (2012) *tate of Care Report 2011/12: "Quality and Safety of Health and Social Care* (London: CQC).

Carers UK (2007) *Real Change, Not Short Change: Time to Deliver for Carers* (London: Carers UK).

Carers UK (2009) *'Policy Briefing'*(London: Carers UK).

Carerstrust (undated) 'Key facts about carers'. Available at www.carers.org.

Clarke, A., Williams, J., Wydall, S. and Boaler, R. (2012) 'An evaluation of the access to Justice Pilot Project for victims of elder abuse', *Welsh Government Social Research*: 1–73.

Clements, L. and Bangs, J. (2012) 'Young carers and the Draft Support Bill' (unpublished). Available at www.lukeclements.co.uk.

Clements, L. and Thompson, P. (2011) *Community Care and the Law,* 5th edn (London: Legal Action Group).

Clover, B. (2013) 'Exclusive: delayed hospital discharge to blame for A & E pressures', *Health Service Journal,* 3 October.

Cole, P.L. (2012) '"You want me to do what?", Ethical practice within interdisciplinary collaborations', *Journal of Social Work Values and Ethics,*9(10): 1–26.

Commission for Social Care Inspection Report (2008) *Safeguarding Adults: A Study of the Effectiveness of Arrangements to Safeguard Adults from Abuse* (London: CSCI).

Community Care (2005) 'How to work in multi-disciplinary teams', *Community Care,* 27 October.

Cooklin, A. (2010) 'Living upside down: being a young carer of a parent with mental illness', *Advances in Psychiatric Treatment*, 16, 141–6.

Corney, R. and Bowen, A. (1980) 'Referrals to social work: a comparative study of a local authority intake team with a general practice attachment scheme', *British Journal of General Practice*, 30(212): 139–47.

Crown Prosecution Service (2009) *Crimes Against Older People – CPS Prosecution Policy* (London: CPS).

Crown Prosecution Service (undated) *Prosecuting Crimes Against Older People – Legal Guidance* (London: CPS).

Crown Prosecution Service (undated) 'Special Measures'. Available at http://www.cps.gov.uk/legal/s_to_u/special_measures/ (accessed 5 May 2013).

Davies, S. (2011) 'Outsourcing, public sector reform and the changed character of the state-voluntary sector relationship', *International Journal of Public Sector Management*, 24(7): 641–9.

Department of Constitutional Affairs (2005) '*Mental Capacity Act 2005. Code of Practice* (London: Stationery Office).

Department of Health (1989) *Caring for People: Community Care in the Next Decade and Beyond*', Cm.849 (London: HMSO).

Department of Health (1993) Approvals and directions for arrangements from 1 April 1993 made under schedule 8 to the National Health Service Act 1977 and sections 21 and 29 of the National Assistance Act 1948, LAC(93)10.

Department of Health (1995) 'Carers (Recognition and Services) Act 1995', LAC (96)7.

Department of Health (1998) *Modernising Social Services: Promoting Independence, Improving Protection, Raising Standards*, Cm 4819 (London: HMSO).

Department of Health (2001a) *Older People National Service Framework* (London: Department of Health).

Department of Health (2001b) 'Fairer Charging Policies for Home Care and other Non-Residential Services', LAC 32.

Department of Health (2002) *The Single Assessment Process. Guidance for Local Implementation* (London: Department of Health).

Department of Health (2003) 'The Community Care (Delayed Discharges etc.) Act 2003: Guidance for Implementation', LAC (203) 21 (London: Department of Health).

Department of Health (2004a) 'The Community Care Assessment Directions 2004', LAC (2004) 24.

Department of Health (2004b) 'Guidance on National Assistance Act 1948 (Choice of Accommodation) Directions 1992 and National Assistance (Residential Accommodation) (Additional Payments and Assessment of Resources) (Amendment) (England) Regulations 2001', LAC (2004) 20.

Department of Health (2007) *Putting People First: A Shared Vision and Commitment to the Transformation of Adult Social Care* (London: Department of Health).

Department of Health (2008a) 'Refocusing the care programme approach: policy and positive practice guidance', COI 2008.

Department of Health (2008b) *Code of Practice: Mental Health Act 1983* (London: Department of Health). (A separate Code is published for use in Wales.)

Department of Health (2009a) *Community Care, Services for Carers and Children's Services (Direct Payments Guidance)* (London: Department of Health).

Department of Health (2009b) *Safeguarding Adults: Report on the Review of 'No Secrets"* (London: Department of Health).

Department of Health (2010a) *Prioritising need in the context of Putting People First: a whole system approach to eligibility for social care. Guidance on eligibility criteria for adult social care* (London: Department of Health).

Department of Health (2010b) *Valuing People Now: The Delivery Plan 2010–2011. "Making it Happen for Everyone'* (London: Department of Health).

Department of Health (2010c) *Personalisation through Person-centred Planning* (London: Department of Health).

Department of Health (2011) *Ordinary Residence: Guidance on the Identification of the Ordinary Residence of People in Need of Community Care Services. England* (London: Department of Health).

Department of Health (2012a) *Caring for our future: reforming care and support*, Cm 8378 (London: HMSO).

Department of Health (2012b) *National Framework for NHS Continuing Healthcare and NHS-funded Nursing Care* (London: Department of Health).

Department of Health (2012c) *Attitudes to Mental Illness – 2011 Survey Repor'* (London: Department of Health)

Department of Health and Home Office (2000) *No Secrets: guidance on developing and implementing multi-agency policies and procedures to protect vulnerable adults from abuse* (London: Department of Health and Home Office).

Dilnot, A., Warner, N. and Williams, J. (2011) *Fairer Care Funding* (London: Commission on Funding of Care and Support).

Drakeford, M. (2006) 'Ownership, regulation and the public interest: the case of residential care for older people', *Critical Social Policy*, 26(4): 922–3.

Dyer, C. (2011) 'Care Quality Commission cuts inspections to meet deadlines for registration', *British Medical Journal*, 343:d7873.

Ellison, L. (2003) *The Adversarial Process and the Vulnerable Witness* (Oxford: Oxford University Press).

Equal Opportunities Commission (2011) *Sex Stereotyping: From School to Work* (EOC).

Fisein, E., Holland, A., Clare, I. and Gunn, M. (2009) 'A comparison of mental health legislation from diverse Commonwealth jurisdictions', *International Journal of Law and Psychiatry*, May, 32(3): 147–55.

Flynn, M. (2007) *The Murder of Steven Hoskin: a serious case review. Executive Summary'* (Cornwall Adult Protection Committee, Cornwall County Council).

Flynn, M. (2012) *Winterbourne View Hospital – a serious case review* (South Gloucestershire Council).

Foster, J. (2005) 'Where are we going? The social work contribution to mental health services', *Social Perspectives Network for Modern Mental Health*, May.

Glendenning, F. (1997) 'What is Elder Abuse and Neglect?', in P. Decalmer and F. Glendenning (eds), *The Mistreatment of Elderly People* (London: Sage).

Godden, S., McCoy, D. and Pollock, A. (2009) 'Policy on the rebound: trends and causes of delayed discharges in the NHS', *Journal of the Royal Society of Medicine*, 102(1): 22.

Golightley, M. (2011) *Social Work and Mental Health*, (4th edn (London: Sage).

Grant, E. (1992) 'Guardianship orders: a review of their use under the Mental Health Act 1983', *Medicine, Science and the Law*, October, 32(4): 319–24.

Griffiths, R. (1988) *Community Care: An Agenda for Action* (London: HMSO).
Hansard (2012) HL Deb 9 May 2012, vol 737, col 1.
Health & Care Professions Council (2012a) *Standards of Proficiency. Social Workers in England* (London: HCPC).
Health & Care Professions Council (2012b) *Mapping of the HPC's Standards of Proficiency for Social Workers in England against the Professional Capabilities Framework – June 2012* (London: HCPC).
Health and Social Care Information Centre (2013a) *Community Care Statistics 2011–12 Social Services Activity Report'* (London: HSCIC).
Health and Social Care Information Centre (2013b) *Inpatients Formally Detained in Hospitals under the Mental Health Act 1983 and Patients Subject to Supervised Community Treatment, England 2012–2013, Annual Figures* (London: HSCIC).
Health and Social Care Information Centre (2013c) *Abuse of Vulnerable Adults in England: provisional data for the reporting period 1 April 2012 to 31 March 2013* (London: HSCIC).
Henderson, C. (2012) 'The health and social care divide in the United Kingdom', *LSE Companion to Health Policy*, 233.
Hepple, B. (2010) 'New Single Equality Act in Britain', *Equal Rights Review*, 5: 11–24.
Herring, J. (2011) *Family Law*, 5th edn (Harlow: Longman Law Series).
Ho, H. (1999) 'A theory of hearsay', *Oxford Journal of Legal Studies*, 19(3): 403–20.
Hunt, L. (2008) '"CTOs should not be a substitute for services" Mental Health Foundation warns over compulsory treatment orders', *Community Care*, 3 November, 11: 49.
House of Commons Health Committee (2011) 'Ninth Report Annual Accountability Hearing with the Care Quality Commission', 14 September, HC 1430.
Hunter, M. (2009) 'Lack of protection for whistleblowers', *Community Care*, 26 May.
Ife, J. (2001) *Human Rights and Social Work* (Cambridge: Cambridge University Press): 28.
Jenkins, S. and Wingate, C. (1994) 'Who cares for young carers?', *British Medical Journal*, 308 6931: 733–4.
John, R. (2007) 'Who decides now? Protecting and empowering vulnerable adults who lose capacity to make decisions for themselves', *British Journal of Social Work*, 37: 557–64.
Joint Committee on Human Rights (2008) 'A life like any other? Human rights of adults with learning disabilities', HL Paper 40–1, HC 73–1 (London: Stationery Office).
Joseph Rowntree Foundation (2005) *The Voluntary Sector Delivering Public Services: Transfer or Transformation?* (York: Joseph Rowntree Foundation).
Joseph Rowntree Foundation (2009) *Identifying a Fairer System for Funding Adult Social Care* (York: Joseph Rowntree Foundation).
Law Commission (2011) *Adult Social Care* (Law Com No 326) (London: Stationery Office).
Lawlor, C. Johnson, S. Coe, L. and Howard, M. (2012) 'Ethnic variations in pathways to acute care and compulsory detention for women experiencing a mental health crisis', *International Journal of Social Psychiatry*, 58(1): 3–15.

Lawton-Smith, S., Dawson, J. and Burns, T. (2008) 'Community treatment orders are not a good thing', *British Journal of Psychiatry*, 193: 96–100.

Local Government Ombudsman (2012) Available at http://www.lgo.org.uk/guide-for-advisers/maladministration-service-failure/ (accessed 15 November 2012).

Lymbery, M. and Postle, K. (2007) *Social Work: A Companion to Learning* (London: Sage Publications).

Maas-Lowit, M. (2010) 'Risk, support and protection: learning matters' in Hothersall S. and Bolger, J. (eds), *Social Policy for Social Work, Social Care and the Caring Profession: Scottish Perspective*, (Aldershot: Ashgate): 109–24.

MacDonald, A. (2010) 'The impact of the 2005 Mental Capacity Act on social workers' decision making and approaches to the assessment of risk', *British Journal of Social Work*, 40:1229–46.

Mackay, C., McLaughlan, C., Rossi, S., McNicholl, J., Notman, M. and Fraser, D. (2011) 'Exploring how practitioners support and protect adults at risk of harm in the light of the Adult Support and Protection (Scotland) Act 2007' (Stirling: University of Stirling).

Mackay, K. (2008) 'The Scottish adult support and protection legal framework', *Journal of Adult Protection*, 10(4): 25–36.

Mantell, A. and Scragg, T. (2008) *Safeguarding Adults in Social Work* (Exeter: Learning Matters).

Manthorpe, J. and Martineau, S. (2011) 'Serious case reviews in adult safeguarding in England: an analysis of a sample of reports', *British Journal of Scoial Work*, 41 (2): 224–41..

Manthorpe, J., Rapaport, J. and Stanley, N. (2009) 'Expertise and experience: people with experiences of using services and carers' views of the Mental Capacity Act 2005', *British Journal of Social Work*, 39: 884–900.

McKenzie, K. and Bhui, K. (2007) 'Institutional racism in mental health care', British Medical Journal, 31 March, 334(7595): 649–50.

Melanie Henwood Associates (2010) *Journeys without Maps: The Decisions and Destinations of People who Self-fund – a qualitative study* (London: Social Care Institute for Excellence).

Ministry of Justice (2008) *Deprivation of Liberty Safeguards – Code of Practice to Supplement the Main Mental Capacity Act 2005 Code of Practice* (London: Stationery Office).

Ministry of Justice (2011) *Achieving Best Evidence in Criminal Proceedings: guidance on interviewing victims and witnesses, and guidance on using special measures* (London: Ministry of Justice).

National Assembly of Wales (2002) *Creating a Unified and Fair System for Assessing and Managing Care* (Cardiff: NAW): para. 5.16.

National Carers Forum (2013) *Personnel Statistics Report* (Coventry: National Carers Forum).

Newbigging, K. with Lowe, J. (2005) *Direct Payments and Mental Health: New Directions* (York: Joseph Rowntree Foundation in association with Pavilion Publishing and Research into Practice).

NHS Confederation (Mental Health Network) (2011) 'Key facts and trends in mental health', Fact sheet (London: NHS Confederation). Available at http://www.nhsconfed.org/Publications/Factsheets/Pages/Key-facts-mental-health.aspx (accessed 15 November 2012).

O'Keeffe, M., Hills, A., Doyle, M., McCreadie, C., Scholes, S., Constantine, R., Tinker, A., Manthrope, J., Biggs, S. and Erens, B. (2007) *UK Study of Abuse and Neglect of Older People: Prevalence Survey Report* (London: Department of Health).

Oxford English Dictionary, Online version 2011.

Palmer, S. (2007) 'Public, private and the Human Rights Act 1998: an ideological divide', *Cambridge Law Journal*, 66(3): 559.

Payne, M. (2009) *Social Care Practice in Context* (Basingstoke: Palgrave Macmillan): 89.

Pigot, T. (1989) *The Report of the Advisory Group on Video Evidence* (London: Home Office).

Public Concern at Work (2013) *Report on the Effectiveness of Existing Arrangements for Workplace Whistleblowing in the UK* (London: Public Concern at Work).

Public Services Ombudsman for Wales (2009) 'Complaint No. 1999/20600720 against Carmarthenshire CC', 16 September 2009.

Pugh, R. and Williams, D. (2006) 'Language policy and provision in social services organizations', *British Journal of Social Work*, 36(7): 1227–44.

Ray, M. and Pugh, R. (2008) 'Mental health and social work', Research briefing 26, July (London: SCIE).

Roberts, G. and Preston-Shoot, M. (2000) 'Law and social work', in M. Davies (ed.), *The Blackwell Encyclopaedia of Social Work* (Oxford: Blackwell).

Schwehr, B. (1997) 'A study in fairness in the field of community care law (I)', *Journal of Social Welfare and Family Law*, 19(2): 159–72.

Scottish Law Commission (1997) 'Report on Vulnerable Adults', Scot Law Com No. 158 (Edinburgh: Stationery Office).

Scourfield, R. (2007) 'Are there reasons to be worried about the 'caretelization' of residential care?', *Critical Social Policy*, 27(2): 155–80.

Social Care Institute for Excellence (2011) *People who Pay for Care: Quantitative and QualityAanalysis of Self-funders in the Social Market* (London: SCIE).

Social Services Inspectorate (2004) *Treated as People: An Overview of Mental Health Services from a Social Care Perspective 2002–2004* (London: SSI).

Styrborn, K. (1995) 'Early discharge planning for elderly patients in acute hospitals: an intervention study', *Scandinavian Journal of Social Medicine*, 23(4): 273–85.

Swinkels, A. and Mitchell, T. (2009) 'Delayed transfer from hospital to community settings: the older person's perspective', *Health and Social Care in the Community*, 17(1): 45.

Watts, J.P., Grant, W., Traynor, J. and Harris, S. (1990) 'Use of guardianship under the Mental Health Act', *Medicine, Science and the Law*, October, 30(4): 31316.

Williams, A. (2008) 'YL v Birmingham City Council: contracting out and "functions of a public nature"', *European Human Rights Law Review*, 4: 524–31.

Williams, J. (2002) 'Public law protection of vulnerable adults', *Journal of Social Work*, 2(3): 293–316.

Williams, J. (2008) 'State Responsibility and the Abuse of Vulnerable Older People: Is There a Case for a Public Law to Protect Vulnerable Older People from Abuse?', in J. Bridgeman, H. Keating and C. Lind (eds), *Responsibility, Law and Family* (Aldershot: Ashgate): 81–105.

Williams, J. (2011) 'Care home design and human rights', *Elder Law Journal*, 1(4): 395–402.

Williams, J., Wydall, S. and Clarke, A. (2013) 'Protecting older victims of abuse who lack capacity: the role of the independent mental capacity advocate', *Elder Law Journal*: 167–74.

Index

accountability   1, 19, 25, 89, 144, 145
Adult Safeguarding Boards   134, 154
advocate   43, 93, 162
arrest   153, 160
Audit Commission   54, 171
autonomy   9–10, 20, 26, 62, 76, 140, 156

Care Act 2014   62, 77, 95, 110, 141, 142, 158
Care Quality Commission (CQC)   88–9, 124, 171, 179
carers   1, 5, 8, 11, 17, 20, 21, 22, 23, 38, 49, 52, 54, 56
children   4, 16, 20, 58, 76, 77, 83, 86, 102, 106–10, 135, 143, 150, 154, 167, 171
civil law   113, 134, 152, 154
clinical commissioning groups   78, 104
codes   25, 27, 29, 30, 31, 36, 45, 49, 94, 112, 116, 117, 121–3, 128, 130, 132
community care
   assessment   6, 11, 16, 18, 21, 23, 35, 53–68, 72, 73, 75, 76, 77, 81, 83, 85, 86, 91, 94, 96, 99, 101–4, 106, 110–12, 118, 123–5, 133–4, 142, 144, 147, 156, 157, 159, 160–1
   definition of community care services   5, 6, 45, 55–7, 61–5, 69, 71–3, 75–85, 89, 94, 98, 103–5, 113, 130, 136, 159
   delivery of community care   69, 80–6
   discharge from hospital   53, 62, 64, 99, 104, 156

domiciliary care   4, 11, 55, 63, 69, 87, 89–93
duty to assess   53, 55, 57, 59, 62, 94, 130
eligibility criteria   60, 69–72, 75–6, 86, 94, 100, 110, 167
needs and wants   59
paying for care   91–3
person-centred planning   69, 84–5
referrals   20, 53–4, 57, 68
refusal of assessment   62
registration and regulation   86–91
residential care   2, 4, 11–12, 14, 24, 40, 43, 46, 55, 61–3, 69, 82, 84, 86–7, 90–3, 95
self-funders   12, 57, 69, 90, 93
single assessment process for older people   65, 66
top-up payments   94, 105
commissioning   25, 66–8
complaints   83, 89, 145, 148, 159–66, 172
conflict of interest   46, 125, 129
continuing health care   63–4
Council with Social Services Responsibilities   6–8, 11–12, 15, 19, 25, 32, 35, 43, 53, 56, 57, 60–5, 68–72, 78–7, 90–5, 100, 102–6, 108, 116, 119–21, 126, 129, 130, 141–2, 145, 147, 154, 159–64, 166–8, 172
delegation   19, 87
dignity   9–11, 13–14, 17, 20, 25, 62, 76, 89
direct payments   2, 69, 82
Director of Adult Social Services   16

187

disability 4, 10, 13, 14, 15, 21, 29, 30, 42, 53, 68, 70, 73, 75, 76, 78, 84, 87, 93, 98, 100, 109, 116, 118, 135, 138, 149, 150
disabled 18, 61, 64, 67, 70, 71, 80, 83, 91, 96, 99, 100, 101, 102, 105, 109, 155, 165, 168
discrimination 13–16, 21, 72, 89, 149, 160

European Convention of Human Rights 7–8, 11–13, 33, 47–8, 88–90, 97, 113–14, 117, 121, 128, 133, 135
European Court of Human Rights 8, 39, 48, 49, 80, 114, 122, 124, 151

fair hearing (right to) 9
family life (right to) 8, 9, 12, 28, 33, 88, 97, 129

guidance 1, 5, 6, 28, 29, 49, 52, 57–60, 65–8, 72–3, 80, 83, 88, 92, 94, 99, 101, 110, 122, 135, 143, 145, 147–9, 151, 154, 157, 160, 166

human rights 1, 2, 5, 7–10, 13, 28, 31, 39, 43, 59, 68, 87, 88, 96, 97, 113, 114, 122, 124, 135, 137, 140, 149, 152, 158, 160

inherent jurisdiction 32–3

judicial review 12, 16, 25, 70, 159, 161, 166, 167, 168

learning disability 4, 10, 14, 29, 42, 53, 68, 75, 93, 100, 112, 118, 119, 145
legal action 88, 159, 161, 168
local authority complaints procedures 162–4

mental capacity
advance decision 44–5, 127
assessing capacity 28
best interests 9, 18, 20, 28, 29, 31, 33, 37–41, 43, 47, 48, 62, 122, 140
Bournewood case 27, 47, 114

burden of proof 11, 30
Court of Protection 27, 33, 39, 46, 49, 50, 83, 123, 127, 146
definition of capacity 31–7
deprivation of liberty 8, 9, 27, 48, 49, 50, 88, 113, 123, 129, 142, 153
Deprivation of Liberty Safeguards 8, 27, 48, 49, 50, 88
Deputy of the Court of Protection 41, 46–7, 83, 127, 146
fluctuating capacity 27, 34, 37, 38
Independent Mental Capacity Advocate 43, 162
Lasting Power of Attorney 41, 45–6
life-sustaining treatment 40, 47
mental capacity 8, 27–31, 33, 35, 36, 43, 58, 83, 114, 116, 140, 146, 156
Mental Capacity Code of Practice 30, 31, 36, 39, 41, 44, 45, 46, 47
statutory principles 18, 29, 38–9, 157
unable to decide 34, 37
unwise decisions 31
mental health
Approved Mental Health Professional 16, 19, 113, 116, 119–21, 125–6, 128–9, 131
appropriate medical treatment 112, 120, 124, 127
Community Treatment Order 130–1
formal admission 124–7
guardianship 67, 78, 118, 128–30, 132, 146
hospital managers 132
informal admission 123–4
leave of absence 131–2
medical treatment 127–8
mental disorder 83, 113, 118, 128–30, 132, 136, 146
Mental Health Review Tribunals 112, 132
nearest relative 112, 121, 122, 125–6, 129, 132
place of safety 112, 118, 128, 141
s.117 care after discharge 5, 77–9, 91, 113, 130, 132, 168

188 *Index*

treatability   112, 119–20
warrant to enter   128

negligence   18, 25, 153, 160, 168
nursing care   2–3, 87

older people   4, 13, 53, 62, 65, 66, 76, 78, 82, 93, 135, 149, 150
ombudsman   93, 145, 159, 161, 163, 165
ordinary residence   64, 80, 130

partnership and coordination   26–7
police   24, 118, 128, 144, 145, 147, 148, 153, 154, 156, 171
power of removal (s.47 National Assistance Act 1948)   141
powers and duties   1, 6, 100
private life (right to)   8, 12, 28, 88, 97, 129, 135, 137
professional judgement   17, 20, 35, 73, 161

record keeping   22, 117, 161, 164
redress   1, 8, 144, 159–63, 168, 171–2
refusal (by patient or service user)   28, 29, 31, 39, 44, 45
registration of social care   55, 69, 86–9, 171
registration of social workers   1, 19
religion (right to)   9, 13, 89, 116, 149

safeguarding
abuse   6, 9, 20, 33, 51, 62, 74, 89–91, 106–7, 115, 119, 122, 134–55, 158, 169, 171
Adult Safeguarding Boards   154
civil law   134, 152–4

criminal justice system   84, 134, 149–52
criminal law   144, 145, 148, 150, 158
Crown Prosecution Service   148–51
harassment   14, 15, 134, 146, 152–3
Law Commission   136–7, 139, 140, 142, 156–7
neglect   9, 20, 62, 74, 90, 91, 106–7, 134–7, 140, 142–3, 146–7, 151, 154–8, 164, 169
non-molestation order   152
'No Secrets'   6, 24, 134, 135, 137, 143–5, 148, 154, 157
occupation order   152–3
Scottish legislation   156–7
Serious Case Reviews   154–7, 160
vulnerable adult   1, 6, 20, 24, 28, 107–8, 134–5, 137, 140, 143, 145, 150, 152, 154–5
Scottish Law Commission   136, 156
service user   17, 20–4, 27, 58–60, 66, 73, 75, 83, 97, 100–1, 105, 130, 159–61, 164
social work practice   1, 3, 5, 7–9, 17–19, 21–6, 135
social worker   20, 21–6, 46, 121, 140, 141, 170

undue influence   33

Wales   65, 156–7
Wednesbury unreasonable   71, 167
whistle-blowing   19, 145, 159, 169, 170

young carers   96, 108–10